$HOPPING on the INTERNET and BEYOND!

Jaclyn
Easton

CORIOLIS GROUP BOOKS

Publisher	Keith Weiskamp
Editor	Ron Pronk
Proofreader	Jenni Aloi
Interior Design	Michelle Stroup and Bradley O. Grannis
Cover Design	Gary Smith
Layout Production	Michelle Stroup
Publicist	Shannon Bounds
Indexer	Jenni Aloi

Distributed to the book trade by IDG Books Worldwide, Inc.

Library of Congress Cataloging-in-Publication Data

Easton, Jaclyn 1961-
    Shopping on the Internet / Jaclyn Easton
        p. cm.
    Includes Index
    ISBN 1-883577-33-0 : $19.99

Printed in the United States of America

10 9 8 7 6 5 4 3 2 1

This book is lovingly dedicated to

My father, Jac Holzman
    For passing along his incomparable
    technology and business DNA.

My mother, Nina Lamb
    For telling me I should be in
    broadcasting ever since I can remember.

Advance Praise for Jaclyn Easton's *Shopping on the Internet and Beyond!*

If you ever buy anything about the Internet, buy this book! Jaclyn Easton has managed to turn online shopping into an adventure—and a hoot. Her sharp, funny book will make you laugh as you save money.
 Vic Sussman, Senior Editor/Cyberspace, *U.S. News and World Report*

Jaclyn Easton's *Shopping on the Internet and Beyond!* turns online shopping into a finely tuned art form. It's an excellent guide for consumers and a good starting point for those who seek to understand the emerging world of cyber-shopping.
 Lawrence J. Magid, Syndicated Columnist

I hate shopping! But *Shopping on the Internet and Beyond!* inspired me to head into cyberspace with my credit card in hand.
 Robert Seidman, Editor of *In, Around and Online*

Only Jaclyn could have found this stuff. It's terrific!
 Marc Schiller, Vice President, House of Blues New Media

Jaclyn Easton is the queen of the online world...her tips will entertain you. This book is a great read!
 Jim Griffin, Director of Information Technology, Geffen Records

Power shoppers and bargain hunters, get ready for the ultimate shop-a-thon!
 Patrick Vincent, author of *Free $tuff from the Internet* and
 Free $tuff from the World Wide Web.

Jaclyn Easton has discovered so many bargains and astounding shops online—this book is a great source for all shopping and gift-giving.
 Luanne O'Loughlin, author of *Free $tuff from America Online* and
 Free $tuff from CompuServe.

Shopping on the Internet and Beyond! made me salivate like a Pavlov dog. Shopaholics should stay away from this book! It's a great resource for anyone who intends to shop online.
 D.M. Silverberg, President, L.A. Online

Contents

Automobiles & Motorcycles 29

Beauty Products 43

Books............................. 51

Business & Office *67*

Catalogs & Department Stores 81

Destinations in Travel *155*

Education *171*

Flowers, Plants, & Gardening *183*

Special Occasions *325*

Sports *331*

Regional Usenet
Private Party Ads *349*

Index *353*

Introduction

Get Ready to Have Some Fun

It's no exaggeration when I say that the modem is the best thing to happen to shopping since the paper catalog—and now *you* are a part of this revolution.

Shopping via the Internet and the major online services is quick, convenient, and a big money saver. Add to these benefits the environmental savings (no more needless catalogs) and the forthcoming option of video and sound to provide better and more exciting product descriptions and you'll agree: Shopping online is the next best thing to being there.

But this is only the beginning of a major transformation in the way people do business. And this is the first book that celebrates this remarkable new way to shop for both everyday items and the hard to find—from name brands to out-of-the-way shops. It's as easy to buy chocolate from Godiva as it is to order from the Chocolate Factory in Trumbauersville, Pennsylvania. And shopping via your computer is fun too—you'll discover companies and services you never knew existed.

In fact, there are thousands upon thousands of places to shop online. But with this book, I didn't try to provide a comprehensive directory of online shoppping sites. Some sites frankly aren't that good or perhaps their merchandse, prices, or their services aren't quite up to par. That's why I've elected to profile and "honorably mention" what I deem to be the *best* shopping sites in "cyberspace."

Shopping on the Internet Provides Big Savings

Bargains abound online, especially on the Internet's World Wide Web. It's extremely inexpensive to put up an electronic storefront (averaging $50 to $150 per month) for a typical, medium-size site. Compare that to the thousands of dollars retailers must spend for mall space, and you'll begin to understand how much money these companies save in overhead along—savings passed on to us in the form of unbeatable prices.

For example, a diamond engagement rings that sells for $3,000 at your neighborhood mall jewelers can be bought online for $1,000—not from some fly-bynight wholesaler, but from one of the top jewelers in the country. You'll find bargains in every shopping category, from famous name sports gear to designer perfume. You can even order non-perishable groceries sent to you anywhere in the world—all thanks to the Internet.

An unscientific, personal survey shows that prices online for everyday items run about 25 percent less than what you would pay at a "physical" retail store. Factor in your "Shopping on the Internet and Beyond!" Exclusive Deal coupons, and the savings soar!

The Selection Online Is Excellent

Because it's relatively cheap to put a "store" online, niche businesses are everywhere. You like hats? You'll find them in the pages that follow, from the Jughead-like Palookaville to an official Ogden Raptors minor league baseball cap. How about genuine Hawaiian jewelry or online medical advice or handmade Native American quilts or Amish Cheeses or beer-making kits or.... You get the idea. You can even buy genuine dinosaur relics via your online connection.

Shopping by Modem Is Convenient

Need it in a jiffy? Hate hanging on 800-lines on hold, then having to recite your order information for 10 minutes to a clerk who seems to be new at the job? *When you buy online using Shopping on the Internet and Beyond!* you get to the store you want, place your order, and you're done.

How This Book Saves You Big Bucks

There are a lot of ways to save money by shopping online. But one of the better ways to save is *only* available when you have this book. Here's why.

Shopping on The Internet and Beyond! Exclusive Deals

There are over $3,000 in "Exclusive Deal" coupons on the pages that follow. Hundreds of them. They average savings per deal is about $5 to 10. So, after only a few purchases, this book pays for itself. And if you shop a lot, you could save enough to pay for a trip for two to Hawaii (well, almost).

And if you're in the market for a genuine Camarasaurus skeleton, circa 155 million B.C. and selling for a mere $2.5 million, boy are you going to save a bundle. In the *Inventive Notions* chapter you'll find a super-special, 10-percent-off Exclusive Deal that can save you as much $250,000.

Money Saved in Online Charges

With this book, you get right to where you want to be, so you save tons of dough in online charges. No needless mouse clicks or spending hours following links or a series of menus.

For example, there are over 100 places online to buy flowers. Which do you choose? Offline, simply flip to the *Flowers, Plants, and and Garden* chapter to find exactly what you're looking for. Then, fire up your modem, go right to the site of your choice, and place your order.

The Best Bargains

So online shopping provides convenience, great values, and great selection. For me, that's an unbeatable combination. Want to upgrade your monitor? Send email to a few of the computer product companies profiled and ask for their best price for the item. No more poring over stacks of magazines. In just a short time, you'll know who has the best deal and save yourself big bucks.

How to Redeem the Exclusive Deal Coupons

As I've already mentioned, on virtually every page of this book you'll notice Exclusive Deal coupons that entitle you, as a *Shopping on the Internet and Beyond!* book buyer, to money-saving specials with many of the online retailers profiled.

Redeeming an Exclusive Deal is simple. If you order online using an electronic order form, put the words "shopping book" in parentheses after your name or, in the order form's Comments Field, type "Shopping on the Internet and Beyond!" and the deal as stated in the coupon. Or do both.

Keep in mind that some electronic forms automatically calculate your order, but it won't show your net discount amount because the form is not sophisticated enough to handle that. Be assured that these are bona fide special offers that will be honored, and that your Exclusive Deal will be applied when the company fulfills your order.

If you are purchasing via email, fax, or through an 800-number, simply mention the Exclusive Deal when placing your order.

I personally arranged for these incentives with the heads of the companies profiled. If you have any problems, please email me at *easton@easton.com* and I will look into it. But first, be sure to get your free update right away by emailing *shop@easton.com*. This document will let you know if a company has changed their special deal, which in many cases includes an even better incentive than the one they originally submitted for the book.

How to Get Free Updates to This Book

It's just too easy. All you do is send an email letter to: *shop@easton.com*. You can put literally anything you want in the subject/topic and body of your letter—even leave it blank if you want.

If you subscribe to America Online, CompuServe, or Prodigy, these services won't let you send a blank piece of email. You must put something in both the topic and letter body, so if you're stuck, just type "Thanks Jaclyn!"

The nanosecond my e-mail system gets your letter, it will automatically send you the update. Sometimes the Internet gets a tad sluggish, but in a perfect world you should get your free update in a matter of minutes. If it doesn't come right away, give the response as much as a full day. It will go out immediately after we get your request; it's just that sometimes the major online services' "electronic postal carriers" get overloaded.

It's a Small World After All

Over 70 percent of the retailers listed will ship internationally, so if you're reading this in Paris, Melbourne, or even Greenland, you have the same shopping options as someone online in North America. And if you have relatives in far away places, you can shop for them online and have your purchases shipped directly.

What About Credit Card Security Considerations?

Credit-card issues on the Internet are resolving themselves through "encryption technology"— a way of coding information so it cannot be tampered with or cyber-heisted.

But even so, some online experts advise against putting your credit card number on the Internet. Even while we are in this interim step, I take the side of "Don't Worry. Shop Happy." Here's why.

I don't believe credit-card fraud between online retailers and individual customers occurs. In fact, I have challenged all of my radio show listeners and other online-devotees with a cash reward, for the identity of *one* person who has experienced credit-card fraud on the Net. No one has stepped forward.

And let's take a quick look at the facts. As a consumer, you generally are not liable for much if any fraudulent credit charges. The fuel flaming the Internet debate over security issues comes from—guess who?—the credit card companies themselves, because *they* are the ones who pay.

Second, I don't believe that giving a credit card number over the Net is any different than handing it to a waiter who disappears for a tangible amount of time with your actual card. How do we know one of the staffers in the back isn't running to a phone—Spiegel catalog in one hand, your Visa in the other—with big dreams of a new dinette set?

While I believe there is no risk, I also respect that you may not share my view. If that's the case, I suggest any of the following precautions.

- Browse online, but place your order via the company's 800-number, if they offer one.
- Fax your credit card number separately, if the company offers a fax option.
- Email your credit card number in parts, in two separate emails. Online thieves randomly intercept email, so the chance that they would be lucky enough to get *both* pieces of your email is so staggering that if this happens to you, buy a lottery ticket—you've beaten astronomical odds.

If you are ordering via a major online service such as America Online, CompuServe, or Prodigy, these system are inherently secure since they're privately run and controlled, so you run zero risk of fraud.

Subscribe to America Online, Compuserve and Prodigy. How Do I Get to the World Wide Web from Here?

Good question. Regardless of the service you use, the answer's easy: On America Online, use the keyword *web*. On CompuServe, go *netlauncher*. On Prodigy, jump *web*.

All of the services have a tutorial that explains the basics of using the Web. And it truly is easy. Keep in mind that America Online, CompuServe, and Prodigy have to make it effortless for you or you won't bother trying new features. The more features you use, the more money they make. It's in their best financial interests to make it easy to keep your online meter running. If you've been putting it off, put it back on and try the Web today.

Went to a Site and It's Not There! Now What?

First, remain calm. Next, double-check that you typed in the Web site address *exactly* as it's listed. Some areas on the Internet are case sensitive. If a capital letter is used in the address, by all means type that letter as a capital. Also make sure you didn't type period instead of a slash or vice versa, or that you didn't omit or add a character. These are all common mistakes. (I know—I've made them too.)

If you still get some cryptic message, then double-check your free electronic update (*shop@easton.com*). Businesses online move around just like businesses in your town, but doing so online is much easier, so it happens more frequently. If a site has moved, you should be able to find the new address in the free *Shopping on the Internet and Beyond!* update.

Let's assume that, as far as I've been told, a site you can't locate should be there. The best next step is to go to the "top of the mall."

Most of the shopping sites are grouped together in a mall-type fashion. The address I give will get you straight to the actual store instead of metaphorically escorting you in the front door, up a few escalators, and past 20 other shops.

To get to the top of the mall, type the first part of the address from "http://" through the first "/".

Here's is a sample full address:

http://www.dol.com/astrogram/daystar.html

To get to the "top," type:

http://www.dol.com/

What you will see is usually an ad for the company that provides the electronic mall service. Look for a link titled "businesses" or "customer pages," and it should get you to a listing of the shops in their mall.

Sometimes you can do everything right and still not get into a Web site. Instead, you might get a cryptic error message. Often it means the computer system you are "calling" on the other end is busy because a lot of people are on the system at once. Try again in a few minutes and you should be able to get on.

If you get a message that specifically includes the phrase "not found" it's usually means there is a problem with the address. If you've typed it exactly as it is in the book, with the capitalized letters in caps, the next step is to go to the top of mall as I previously described.

Other factors come into play as well. Computers come offline for maintence. When that happens, you'll often get an error message. Sometimes chunks of the Internet go down temporarily. For instance, if a portion of Sprintlink fails (which happens from time to time), it can affect hundreds and hundreds of retail sites because it's like losing phone service completely.

When all else fails, you can always use the fallback strategy of emailing the retailer. Email addresses are the most stable way to reach someone on the Internet. If you have a question or are having problems getting on a site, send the company a quick electronic note.

Most importantly, if a site in this book moves or goes offline, it will be included in the book updates available for free via email. Always double-check your updates.

The Book I Was Born to Write

Rumor has it that I emerged from the womb with a modem in one hand and a Visa card in the other. Probably not true, but one fact is certain—this book combines two of my favorite activities: being online and shopping.

Shopping online is really thrilling. This method of selling has flourished to the point that plenty of great stuff is available. *Finding* it is the tough part. There's no central directory. No referral service. Just a lot of pointing and clicking.

If you don't know exactly where to go, it's just like being dropped in the middle of Europe with no guide or maps. If you wander around long enough, you will find fabulous museums, cathedrals, and other notable sights, but you will spend a lot of time getting there and you will have no idea if these are the best cathedrals or museums.

Oh The Sites I've Seen...

I spent over eight months researching and writing this book and, in the process, visited over 5,000 shopping sites on the Internet, World Wide Web, America Online, CompuServe, and Prodigy.

I set out with only one objective: find the *best* shopping sites online. Period. I had no pre-set number in mind, but I did have a mandate: The merchandise or services being offered had to be of high quality and the company had to have good prices.

Of the 5,000 electronic storefronts I visited, about 1,000 (approximately 20 percent) made the cut. Out of that 1,000, I choose the cyber-retailers I thought were the most outstanding— these are the ones that are fully profiled in each chapter. The balance of my picks can be found in the back half of each chapter in the *Honorable Mentions* section.

I interviewed virtually all of the profiled retailers. I spoke with them at length about their companies, their products, and their plans for the future. This is why you'll often get much more information about a business and their merchandise in this book than you might find on their site.

And yes, after 8 months and 5,000 locations, my right hand *is* permanently cupped in the shape of a mouse. Thanks for asking.

Acknowledgments

To the fine folks at the Coriolis Group:

> Shannon Bounds: This book literally would never have come to be if it were not for this 20-something wonder woman. Shannon, a thousand thank-yous for your relentless "can do" attitude, enthusiasm, and friendship.

> Keith Weiskamp: For saying "Yes," for being patient, and for treating a first-time author as though she had the track record of Danielle Steele.

> Ron Pronk: The editor by which all should be compared. Someday I expect to find a gold statue of you in the Editors Hall of Fame. Thank you for making what I wrote read so well, and for writing all the hilarious photo captions.

> Jeff and Carol Dunteman: For helping create a publishing house that is a sheer joy to work with.

> Tom Mayer: For allowing me to be a partner in the marketing process and for adding infinite ingenuity to my preliminary ideas.

> Brad Grannis: For designing such a nifty cover. Few authors are so lucky.

> Michelle Stroup: For breaking the Olympic record for page layout and for making sure the pages looked so good.

My Editors at the *Los Angeles Times*: Daily Calendar Editor Oscar Garza; Deputy Calendar Editor, Sherry Stern, and Executive Calendar Editor John P. Lindsay, who realized long before the curve that online computing is as much about entertainment as it is about information.

My computer gurus (alphabetically speaking) Vince Emery, Jim Griffin, Larry Magid, George Peck, Robert Seidman, Gina Smith, Josh Quittner, and Vic Sussman.

Michael Castelvecchi for all the reasons he knows but would be eternally embarrassed if I listed them.

My radio sidekick, the remarkable Roger Reitzel, for making "Log On U.S.A." so much fun and for bearing with me while I wrote "the book."

My stepfather, Kirk Lamb, for his love and neutrality.

Carrie Carlisi for 26 years (and counting) of a magnificent friendship.

Jack Chipman for instilling life lessons that I reference daily.

Susan Goldberg and Michael Switzer for their infinite enthusiasm and for periodically prying me away from my keyboard, ignoring my cries of "deadlines, deadlines!"

My brothers, Marin Holzman and Adam Holzman, my sister-in-law Jane Getter, and my amazing nephew Russell Getter Holzman.

Extra, extra special thanks to Carrol Allen, Heather Austin, Tracey Cooper, Sheldon Getzug, M.D., Sandy Gibson, Graphic Communications, Irving Klasky, M.D., Dirk Harms-Merbitz, Lori Kleinman, Dennis Loveday, Steve Marmel, Ben Platt, Steven Poster, Susan Prince, Judith Rosenthal, Marc Schiller, David Silverberg, Michelle Slatalla, Gina Silvester and Evelyn Sumida.

And last but certainly not least I'd like to tip my hat to the hundreds of online retailers I interviewed who are patiently pioneering the shopping-by-modem frontier. I am in awe of your spirit, your respect for the medium, and the heart with which you approach your online presence.

Animals

Every exotic pet owner should have at least one red eyed tree frog.

Exotic Pets Online

Okay, it's 4:00 AM, you can't sleep, and you just realized your life will have no meaning unless you get a Ball Python snake. What do you do?

Well AnimalMania is your answer. One of the largest specialty pet stores in Florida, they can fulfill any pet wish—and since you order online, you can do it at any hour.

Established in 1985, AnimalMania carries a full stock of exotic reptiles, amphibians and birds. If you don't see what you want, ask them. They are happy to accomodate unique requests.

If you live in Southeast Florida, AnimalMania will deliver the new family member right to your door. If you live outside this area, they offer same-day shipping to the airport nearest you. Just place

your order and an AnimalMania representative will contact you with the flight number and arrival time. They also guarantee that your new pet will arrive in good health.

Company
AnimalMania (Fort Lauderdale, FL)

Where
World Wide Web

Web Address
http://animals.com/animals

Email
help@animals.com

Instant Information
Send email to: info@animals.com

Price
From $10 (scorpions) to $350 (albino pythons).

Shipping Fees (in the U.S.)
Free shipping on orders over $40.

Dog treats galore.

Dog & Cat Treat of the Month Club

Have you noticed that your neighbor's dog or cat religiously follows its owner out to the mailbox everyday? If this is the case, this pet owner probably gifted his beloved Rover of Fluffy with a subscription to the Dog or Cat Treat of the Month Club.

It works like this: Every month a box will arrive addressed to your pet. Dogs receive a gift box called Poochie Presents while cats get Feline Feasts. Inside are handmade treats void of any preservatives and decorated based on the season, holiday, or special occasion (such as your pet's birthday).

To personalize your gift, you can even request that a card in your name be included.

So who do you think will get more enjoyment out of this monthly ritual: you or your pet?

Shopping on the Internet and Beyond

Exclusive Deal

Unique Concepts
Dog & Cat Treat of the Month Club

Seventh month free on a
six month order.

Exclusive deal for readers of this book only!
You must mention this offer when you place your order.

Company
Unique Concepts (Chicago, IL)

Where
World Wide Web

Web Address
http://branch.com:1080/treats/treats.html

Prices
$5.95 per month (dogs), $4.95 per month (cats).

Shipping Fees (in the U.S.)
$2.95 per month.

Private Party Animal Ads

I don't know quite what I was expecting to find when I visited the America Online classifieds for pets, animals, and related items. I figured there would be the token puppy and kitty giveaways and perhaps a firesale on old bird cages and used kennel carriers. But this is really a mecca for the most unusual pet items as well.

Let's start with the listing for African pygmy hedgehogs available in albino, snowflake, and white—all with a vet health certificate (email *cdg22@aol.com*). There's a man searching for a musk oxen (email *finula@aol.com*) and a company offering to paint a portrait of your favorite feline or canine (email *celticart@aol.com*).

Private Party Animal Ads (continued)

Speaking of dogs, I also stumbled on Hound Hammocks (*mbrien@aol.com*). I'm still trying to picture how the heck a hound gets in and out of this most unusual bed.

Highly specific items were also available, such as eye products for dogs and cats, for everything from unsightly tear stains to protecting eyes during shampooing or dipping (email *knlvet@aol.com*)

This classifieds collection is not only amusing but a terrific resource as well.

Where
America Online

Shortcut:
Keyword *classifieds* then select *general merchandise boards* then select *pets, animals, and related items.*

Try eating off your dog—dog's plate, that is.

Gifts for Dog Lovers

ImageMaker wins the award for having the most dog-related merchandise ever assembled. While this company carries the standard dog decals, re-frigerator magnets, and "breed of your choice"

notepads, you will also find doggie honey pots, wine corks, tooth pick holders, and lotion bottles. And that's just skimming the surface.

All items are hand-crafted with artwork from Monique Akar. For the past 15 years, Akar has been crafting pen and ink drawings of over 156 dog breeds. According to company literature, Akar "is known worldwide for her ability to capture each breed perfectly, from the texture of their coats to their unique facial expressions."

I just want to know which breed looks best on their customized napkin holders.

Company
ImageMaker's Gifts for Dog Lovers
(Flagstaff, AZ)

Where
World Wide Web

Web Address
http://www.onramp.net/imagemaker

Email
townsend@onramp.net

Prices
Various but reasonable.

Shipping Fees (in the U.S.)
$5.00 per order

Alpaca lunch and meet you in an hour.

Alpacas 'R' US

I know. I know. What the heck is an Alpaca?

Alpacas are members of the camelid family that originated in South America. They look similar to llamas but are half the size (about three feet high.) Unlike llamas, who are cute but aggressive, alpacas are very sweet and sociable animals who tend to bond with their caretakers. Add to the mix their intelligence, curiosity, and cleanliness and you have the perfect mate...I mean pet.

Alpacas are prized for their luxurious coat, which is sheared once a year and yields enough fiber for four to six sweaters. In fact, after mohair, alpaca is the second strongest fiber available. It is also lightweight, incredibly soft, and several times warmer than wool. Weavers gravitate to the animals for their diversity of color as well. There are 22 basic colors, including golden fawn, mocha, coffee bean, and rose grey.

AlpacaNet is a onestop for all that is alpacan—from sweaters to hats and jewerly. If you are interested in purchasing an Alpaca or want to become a breeder, one visit to AlpacaNet will get you to the right people.

If you are simply curious about this animal, referred to as "The World's Finest Livestock Investment," you can find gobs of information, including a brief history of the mammal and tips for your first purchase.

Company
AlpacaNet (West Linn, OR)

Where
World Wide Web

Web Address
`http://www.webcom.com/~odyssey1/alpaca/`
`alpaca.html`

Email
`charnoff@alpaca.com`

Prices
$1,000 for a neutured male of "pet quality." Up to $60,000 for a top-notch breeding male

Remember!

For free periodic updates of this book and additional discount offers, send email to *shop@easton.com*. See *Introduction* for more details.

Hey Annie! Let them cool down first!

Gourmet Dog Biscuits

If you want to be absolutely certain that your favorite canine is getting the freshest, most wholesome dog biscuits available, fire-off email to Annie's Dog Biscuits.

Annie, by the way, is not the chef. She's a Chinese Shar-Pei who has the delightful dog duty of taste-testing each batch of baked biscuits whipped up by her owner, Michele.

Given the quality of ingredients, however, Annie could be a human and probably get just as much enjoyment from these treats.

The peanut butter biscuits are made with homemade peanut butter, the beef and chicken with only grade A meat. In fact, Michele even bakes with canola oil instead of animal fat for health-conscious pet owners.

You might even be inclined to try these natural doggie treats yourself, like the disc jockey who ate one live on the air. Even though he stopped after his first, he did order a batch for his dog.

Annie's Dog Biscuits are shipped anywhere in the U.S. If you live in the Phoenix, Arizona area you can get your gourmet doggie biscuits delivered right to your door, piping hot from the oven. Now there's a tail-waggin' proposition.

Company
Gourmet Dog Biscuits (Phoenix, AZ)

Where
Email

Email
biscuitgal@aol.com

Prices
$4.95 per pound (40 to 45 biscuits).

Shipping Fees (in the U.S.)
$3.25

The Oxyfresh product line even looks clean.

Pet Hygiene

If your dog is smelling much too much like a dog, it may be Oxyfresh time for Fido or Fifi.

Pet Hygiene (continued)

The Oxyfresh pet line is composed of a pet deodorizer, shampoo, gel, and also antioxidant treats to better tame free radicals that can be the cause of unpleasant odors in the first place.

Their deodorizer is scientifically blended to vanquish even the most unpleasant scents at the source. You can use it on the offending animal to eliminate bad breath or on items that have come in contact with the creature, like carpets and clothing. And since Oxyfresh products include chlorophyll, there is no perfume coverup.

The Oxyfresh line was originally created for humans, so there is plenty for us two-leggers to choose from as well. So while you pick up something to make your pet less redolent, consider selecting something for *your* coat too.

Shopping on the Internet and Beyond

Exclusive Deal

Oxyfresh
Pet Hygiene Products

Pick any $7 item for free
on orders of $35 or more.

Exclusive deal for readers of this book only!
You must mention this offer when you place your order.

Company
Oxyfresh (Salt Lake City, UT)

Where
World Wide Web

Web Address
http://www.oxyfresh.com/Oxyfresh/

Reminder! This address is case sensitive. Make sure you enter it *exactly* as shown.

Email
oxyfresh@oxyfresh.com

Prices
From $7.00 to $45.00.

Shipping Fees (in the U.S.)
6% of your total order.

Horses Online

Equinet is a horse-lovers haven, packed with every conceivable equestian-related product, from livestock to vitamins. In fact, the only item I couldn't find for sale was Mr. Ed himself.

The cornerstones of Equinet are their free two-month classified ads for individuals (companies pay a small, reasonable fee). All categories focus on horses and include horse property, services, software, trailers, stallions, tack, veterinary products, book publications, and the latest horse news. This site attracts worldwide traffic, which is reflected by the breadth of offerings.

The service is run by a vet and is clearly a great resource for any equestrian fan.

Company
Equinet (Portland, OR)

Where
World Wide Web

Web Address
http://horses.product.com

Email
help@horses.product.com

Instant Information
Send email to: info@horses.product.com

Remember!

Access the Web from any major online service. On AOL, keyword *web*. On CompuServe, go *netlauncher*. On Prodigy, jump *web*.

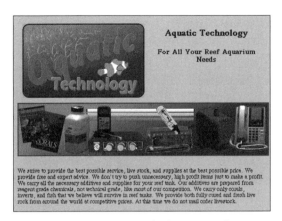

Aquatic Technology's inviting home page.

Aquarium Supplies

When Aquatic Technology invites you to go to their site "for all your reef aquarium needs," they aren't kidding. Perhaps their best selling feature, though, is that they provide service with a conscience.

For instance, they offer free expert advice and claim to sell the best products available without pushing high-profit inventory. In addition, their policy is to carry only corals, inverts, and fish that will surive in the reef tank environment. Though they don't currently offer livestock by mail order, all other inventory is "in stock and ready to ship."

Given the authenticity of the tanks you can create with their products, you just might find you'll never resort to a mask and snorkel again.

Company
Aquatic Technology (Olmsted Falls, OH)

Where
World Wide Web

Web Address
`http://www.actwin.com/AquaticTech/index.html`

Reminder! This address is case sensitive. Make sure you enter it *exactly* as shown.

Email
`aquatic-technology@actwin.com`

Prices
Will meet or beat any competitors' mail order catalog prices. Supply them with the magazine name, month, and page number.

Shipping Fees (in the U.S.)
Actual UPS charges with no handling fees.

A happenin' night on the Lizard Lounge Log.

Reptile and Terrarium Accessories

Reptile Relaxation Rock Formations. Lizard Lounge Logs. Aquarium Castles. These are sample items available from The Clayhouse, which manufactures and designs an exclusive

Reptiles, etc (continued)

line of stoneware accessories for your terrarium or aquarium.

I'm particularly fascinated by the Lizard Lounge Log and wish they made one for humans. Alas, their largest model is only 12 inches long. But it does provide a hollow hiding place for your reptile, to give him a feeling of extra security. There are four entrances/exits to increase mobility and add to the realistic and natural feel.

You've heard of castles in the air. Well, the Clayhouse is putting them underwater with three styles to choose from. Small Castle comes in a lavendar-silk porcelain buoy with a purple glazed top. The Camelot Castle is an original with three spires and 12 open windows and doors—and guaranteed not to change the water temperature. The Mythical Masterpiece is a storybook castle that is "gothic and majestic in form and appearance."

All of these provide perfect ways to spoil your favorite guppy.

Shopping on the Internet and Beyond

Exclusive Deal

The Clayhouse
Reptile and Terrarium Accessories

10 percent off your first order.

Exclusive deal for readers of this book only!
You must mention this offer when you place your order.

Company
The Clayhouse (San Carlos, CA)

Where
World Wide Web

Web Address
`http://www.pdrc.com/clayhouse`

Email
`clayhouse@pdrc.com`

Prices
From $10 to $40.

Remember!

For periodic updates of this book and additional discounts, send email to *shop@easton.com*. See *Introduction* for more details.

Is this art? Absolut-ly. And by the way, there are only two glasses in this photo. If you see more than that, better cut yourself off.

Absolut Advertising

Apparently, the Absolut Vodka campaign is one astounding artistic achievement—so much so, that the company is now selling a 3-disk set that contains 200 photographs, paintings, and fashion designs from their noteworthy advertisements.

They refer to the package as a "totally unique 3-D computer program." It *is* unique—but you need a 386-or-better DOS-based computer (complete with sound card) to appreciate the "virtual environment created by this new 3-D technology."

Your tour begins with the first-ever Absolut ad, "Absolut Perfection." Next, you can meander to the Russian wing to enjoy the "Absolut Glasnost" campaign, featuring the works of 26 talented artists. From there, you can continue to tour the Absolut museum for hours.

If you are not ready to commit to the 3-disk set, you can download up to six free samples from the program.

If you do purchase the disks, know that you are supporting the fight against AIDS because all net proceeds are donated to the American Foundation for AIDS Research (AmFAR).

Now that's Absolut altruism.

Company
Absolut (New York, NY)

Where
CompuServe

Shortcut
Go *abs*

Price
$29.95

Six free samples, available for downloading.

Hot Tip!

Be sure to check out CompuServe's Consumers' Forum, which is chock full of fabulous freebie info and great shopping resources. Go *conforum*.

Home, home on the Exchange.

Art Cellar Exchange

The Art Cellar Exchange bills itself as "a full service art consultancy designed for buying and selling fine art on the secondary market." They are not brokers or dealers. Instead, they charge a flat 10 percent commission on all sales.

These are no lightweight artists either. You can choose from Chagall, Dali, Erte, Haring, Hockney, Neiman, Nagel—you name it. And if you can't find someone in particular, they will find the artist's work for you.

In addition to a great selection, the Exchange's prices are quite amazing. Keith Haring's *Growing Suite* serigraph with a suggested retail price of $70,000 had an asking price of $13,500. A LeRoy Neiman with a retail price of $9,000 was going for a mere $1,900.

Even if you prefer to spend a few hundred dollars instead of a few thousand, there are pieces available to you—and considering the great buys, many of these probably make great investments.

While most of the art is at least 50 percent off, gallery owner Pierrette Van Cleve adds that "all the prices are still highly negotiable."

Van Cleve and the Art Cellar Exchange guarantee the successful transfer between buyers and sellers. The expert staff handles all packaging, shipping, insurance, and financial transactions. In 10 years in business, they say no one has ever been burned.

Considering the great deals you'll find here, you might find yourself springing for a Norman Rockwell *and* an Andy Warhol.

Shopping on the Internet and Beyond

 Exclusive Deal

Art Cellar Exchange

Buyers get $25 off shipping costs.
Sellers get $15 off a photo classified.

Exclusive deal for readers of this book only!
You must mention this offer when you place your order.

Company
Art Cellar Exchange
(San Diego, CA)

Where
World Wide Web

Web Address
`http://www.artcellarex.com/ace/`

Email
`ace@artcellarex.com`

Prices
Asking prices start in the low hundreds and climb to several thousand. All prices are negotiable.

Shipping Fees
Vary according to order.

Remember!

If you have full Internet access, you also have access to the World Wide Web. All you need is a Web browser, such as Mosaic or Netscape.

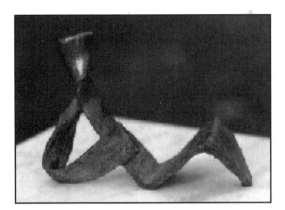

Go ahead, just try to tie this one on.

Necktie Art

Nicholas Daddazio is up to his neck in fine art—literally—as the creator of an ongoing series of bronze necktie sculptures.

According to the artist, bronze necktie sculptures "represent a new art form based on the ubiquitous necktie as the theme for solid art." Some of the sculptures are abstracts while others are representational. Sizes range from giant for indoor or outdoor placement, to smaller-scale pieces, free-standing or mounted on bases.

A visit to his Web site will reveal photos of Daddazio's imaginative themes, such as Reclining Tie, Tie Saxophonist, and Tie Ballerina, all of which fall into his abstractions category.

Daddazio's work is really impressive. Yes, it may be about neckties, but even people with the most conventional tastes should agree that this art is just plain fun to look at.

In addition to his Internet presence, Daddazio's work is exhibited at shows and galleries on the East Coast. Furthermore, he was recently commissioned to be the official designer of the Necktie Assocation of America's annual award. Can you think of anyone more qualified?

Shopping on the Internet and Beyond

Exclusive Deal

Daddazio—The Bronze Necktie

With your first order, $100 courtesy discount on a piece selling for $2,000 or more.

Exclusive deal for readers of this book only! You must mention this offer when you place your order.

Company
Daddazio—The Bronze Necktie
(New York, NY)

Where
World Wide Web

Web Address
http://www.gems.com/showcase/daddazio/

Prices
Non-commissoned works start at $900 and go to $5,000 and up.

Shipping Fees
Destination-dependent, but reasonable.

Accessible Art

If you're looking for an online gallery that offers works by prestigious artists—priced for just about any budget, then you might want to point and click yourself to Access Art.

This virtual gallery has a lot to offer. To cut right to your topic of interest, they categorize the art into four groups: fantasy, glamour, landscape, and pin-up.

"Fantasy" features art-world luminaries such as Ted Kimer. Kimer's work fits into just about any budding collector's budget. For as little as $20,

Accessible Art (continued)

you can get an open-edition print, or if you're ready to spend the big dough—$2,500, to be exact—you can nab an original.

The glamour and pin-up sections feature Alberto Vargas (probably best known for his busty pin-ups, one of which was featured on a Car's album cover) and the artist Olivia, one of Access Art's biggest sellers.

There are loads of works to inspect (and the gallery is constantly updating this list), and you can view them by artist or by title.

Shopping on the Internet and Beyond

Exclusive Deal

Access Art

$20 off your first order
of $100 or more.

Exclusive deal for readers of this book only!
You must mention this offer when you place your order.

Company
Access Art (St. Peterburg, FL)

Where
World Wide Web

Web Address
http://www.mgainc.com/

Email
info@mgainc.com

Prices
From $15 for mass prints to $4,000 for originals.

Shipping Fees (in the U.S.)
Varies. Next day shipping available.

A sample of the underwater world of Loretta DeMars.

Sea Art

Loretta DeMars is an underwater photographer who combines the latest technology with the unparalled beauty of the undersea world.

Using a specialized Kodak digitizing photo CD system, DeMars has captured some stunning underwater landscapes and is selling them on a CD-ROM.

Each of the twelve available images is stored in one of five different resolutions so they can be viewed on a low-resolution monitor or—using the highest resolution—printed out as 8×10 enlargements.

Most art/design software packages (Corel, Pagemaker, Photoshop, and others) can import the images. And there are no copyright hassles either; DeMars simply asks that, if you modify or reuse her photos, say they are "based on the original work by Loretta DeMars."

So what's actually on the disk? Well, these Cousteau-esque photos depict sea-level treasures like the red soft coral of Truk, Micronesia, French Angelfish in the Cayman Brac, and Schooling Grunts from Little Cayman. Schooling Grunts? What a great name for a rock band!

Sea Art (continued)

Company
DeMars Photo Gallery—Underwater Photographic Images (Phoenix, AZ)

Where
World Wide Web

Web Address
http://cybermart.com/demars/

Email
ldemars@demars.com

Price
$59

Shipping Fees (in the U.S.)
$3

Conscience Art

This site, sponsored by Fellisimo of New York, markets posters, T-shirts, and other artwork by renowned artist Robert Rauschenberg. The proceeds go to humanitarian groups.

When I checked, Felissimo was offering a T-shirt with the unique design shown at right, with proceeds going to assist the victims of the Kobe, Japan, earthquake. The art products that you'll find when you visit this site might be different.

Think of it as great art for great causes.

Proceeds from this T-shirt benefit victims of the Kobe earthquake.

Company
Felissimo

Where
World Wide Web

Web Address
http://www.earthpledge.org

Email
/hoffman@earthpledge.org

Conscience Art (continued)

Prices
Vary, based on current offering.

Shipping Fees (in the U.S.)
$5

On CompuServe, Go mma for Van Gogh and much more.

Metropolitan Museum of Art

For some people, the best part of visiting a museum is making the trip to the gift shop afterward. Well, if you're a CompuServe member (or know someone who is), you can skip the Rembrandts and Picassos—and just start shopping.

Exclusivity is the hallmark of the Metropolitan Museum of Art store, both online and offline. Most of the products they offer are made especially for them, including their reproductions and publications, the proceeds of which support the Museum.

You can purchase jewelry, textiles, stationery, gift books, posters, prints, and items for kids in this CompuServe area. There's even a sale section with some terrific deals, which are par-

ticularly enticing to Museum members who already get 10 percent off.

Unless you're a member, you won't get their paper catalog, but on CompuServe, it's free for the asking. You can also sign up for the free electronic mailing list, which will inform you of special deals via email.

While many items listed have images attached for viewing the product, you can also fax or mail a request for a photo of any item online. Send your query to the museum's email address.

Company
Metropolitan Museum of Art (New York, NY)

Where
CompuServe

Shortcut
Go *mma*

Email (via the Internet)
70007,1263

Email (via CompuServe)
70007.1263@compuserve.com

Shipping Fees (in the U.S.)
From $3.50 to $9.75, based on order total. Shipping to Canada and other foreign areas available at reasonable rates. Rush delivery available.

 Free catalog upon request.

International orders are accepted.

Remember!

For periodic updates of this book and additional discounts, send email to *shop@easton.com*. See *Introduction* for more details.

Arnold Thompson's "Flight of the Bird."

Haitian, Southwestern, Amazonian Art, and Beyond

The Electric Gallery specializes in native art of places as diverse as Haiti, the Southwest, and the Amazon.

Each grouping has its own wing loaded with images for your perusal. If you're a Windows user, you can download the entire catalog for free, or purchase it on disk for a reasonable handling charge.

The catalog is quite a trove. It contains all the paintings in the gallery and presents some background on the artists. All of the information is searchable and any image can be used as a screen saver.

The Haitian art group contains all original paintings, many of which are from museums, galleries, and private collections. According to the gallery, "Despite the trauma suffered by the island country, Haiti remains a wellspring of creativity."

If you have an affinity for Southwestern art, be sure to check out the contemporary Southwestern images of Native American people and landscapes rendered by famous Southwestern painters Lawrence Lee and Mary Wyant.

However, if you're intrigued by work from the Usko-Ayar Amazon School of Painting, the Amazon Project wing should be your destination. The artists are all from 8 to 24 years old and their work depicts the myths and traditions of the Peruvian Amazon jungle.

The Electric Gallery recently added a new wing devoted to jazz and blues images. Here, you'll find several innovative works that portray such jazz immortals as Charlie Parker and Miles Davis.

Company
Electric Gallery (Falls Church, VA)

Where
World Wide Web

Web Address
http://www.egallery.com/egallery/homepage.html

Email
rwpb11@pipeline.com

Haitian Art and Beyond (continued)

Prices
Unframed, ranging from $175 to $6,000.

Shipping Fees (in the U.S.)
Approximately $40.

 Download a catalog packed with fine art images (great for use as desktop wallpaper or for use with your screen saver).

This site isn't just a hoot—it's a great cultural experience.

Authentic Eskimo Art

The Isaacs/Inuit Gallery of Toronto on the Uniquely Canadian Web site offers art from the Inuit Eskimos of Arctic Canada. From this cyber-gallery, you can view and buy authentic Inuit sculptures, drawings, and more.

Most importantly, many items are certified by the Candian government as original and hand-made by the Inuit. Why go to these lengths? Apparently, there has been a bounty of poorly crafted, imitation sculptures that are dinging the sales and cache of the genuine articles.

When you see these works you will understand why people would (unfortunately) make knock-offs of their sculptures. This very detailed art often functions as a metaphor for the extreme environmental harshness the Inuit endure.

There are photos of all the items available, along with a reference section detailing the brief history of this native art. Here you will learn about the different types of regional Inuit sculptures, as well as a fascinating genesis of the people's drawings and prints.

Company
Uniquely Canadian (Toronto, Canada)

Where
World Wide Web

Web Address
`http://www.novator.com/UC-Catalog/ UC-Internet.html`

Reminder! This Web address is case sensitive. Make sure you enter the address *exactly* as shown.

Email
`msf@novator.com`

Prices
Quoted in Candian dollars but automatically converted to American on credit-card sales.

Shipping Fees (in the U.S.)
Vary according to size and weight of the item.

Stainless Steel World Map

It used to be that when I thought of stainless steel (which wasn't very often), images of soap pads and saucepans came to mind. Not anymore.

In 1905, the San Diego Sheet Metal Works company began supplying stainless steel products to wholesalers and other commercial enterprises.

In 1995, on the eve of their 90th anniversary, the company branched out and started selling special maps, which had previously hung in their offices as decorations.

The world map is a solid florentine matte finish stainless steel cut 1/4" to 1/2" thick. It is approximately 4'6" by 2'9", weighs 28 pounds, and is mounted on a super-quality, high-density wood. The precision laser-cutting and hand assembly results in extraordinary detail. The rivers are cut straight through, and if you were to backlight the map, the light would glow through beautifully.

Keep in mind that while this world map is extremely accurate, it is not to scale and therefore functions as an artist's representation.

To date, most of these stainless-steel maps have been purchased by offices, with only a smattering of residential orders.

By the way, if you're a homebody, a North-America-only version is available.

Company
San Diego Sheet Metal Works
(San Diego, CA)

Where
World Wide Web

Web Address
http://www.2.connectnet.com:80/catalog/art/
smw1.html

Email
lmhoxsey@cts.com

Price
$2,100

Shipping Fees (in the U.S.)
Based on location.

For More...

For more great art shopping opportunities, see the next page.

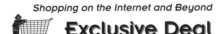

Shopping on the Internet and Beyond

Exclusive Deal

San Diego Sheet Metal Works

5 percent off your first order.

Exclusive deal for readers of this book only!
You must mention this offer when you place your order.

Honorable Mentions
in the category of
Art

Antiques and Auctions

Private party ads for supplies on CompuServe.

CompuServe
Go *classifieds* then select *tv/misc/hobbies/collecting/cooking*

Collecting and Antiques

Private party ads for supplies on America Online.

America Online
Keyword *classifieds* then select *general merchandise boards*

Fine Art

View collections of Norman Rockwell, African Art, Sports Memorabilia and Official Harley Davidson Art on Prodigy.

Company
CyberView Gallery

Prodigy
Jump *classifieds* then select *Browse Ads*

Fine Art and Trading Cards

Private party ads for supplies on CompuServe.

CompuServe
Go *classifieds* then select *tv/misc/hobbies/collecting/cooking*

Graphic Design and Art Supplies

Private party ads for supplies on America Online.

America Online
Keyword *classifieds* then select *general merchandise boards*

Hot Tip!

Internet Usenet groups are available from all the online services. On America Online, keyword *usenet*. On CompuServe, go *usenet*. On Prodigy, jump *usenet*.

Automobiles & Motorcycles

BHMA's goodies aren't just for the folks at 90210.

Top Quality Auto Accessories

The big sales push at the Beverly Hills Motoring Accessories (BHMA) Web site is on car covers, although BHMA carries hundreds of other car-related accessories—all of which are listed in their 56-page catalog (free for the asking).

To the company's credit, I never realized how much thought goes into a high-end car cover. BHMA's stats are impressive. They sell more car covers than all other car-cover companies combined. They have collected over "28,000 precision master patterns" to provide "an exact fit." They boast "where your car curves, our cover curves, where your car dips, our covers dip." They certainly have thought of eveything. Even the fabric is pre-shrunk, so you'll have no surprises after the first rainfall.

If you really want to treat yourself, you can have BHMA customize your car cover with your intials, license number, automobile logo, or message which also can help deter would-be car-cover thieves. Makes sense to me. I'd like to emboss mine with "Property of a Trigger-Happy Vilgilante."

Company
Beverly Hills Motoring Accessories (Beverly Hills, CA)

Where
World Wide Web

Web Address
`http://www.shopping2000.com/shopping2000/bev-hills/`

Prices
$20 for simple accessories to $10,000 for a top-notch car stereo.

Shipping Fees (in the U.S.)
Actual fees. No handling charges.

International orders are accepted.

Remember!
For periodic updatres of this book and additional discounts, send email to *shop@easton.com*. See *Introduction* for more details.

Born to be a wild Spirit.

Custom Motorcyles and Quality Parts

American Motor Works (AMW) "specializes in precision, high-performance American Big Twin engines, stroker kits, and other billeted accessories." They also custom build motorcycles. If you are on a waiting list for a Harley-Davidson—which apparently can be up to four years—and want a completely custom machine, then the AMW "Spirit" might just satiate your desire for a premium-quality, American-made bike.

The Spirit features a Big Twin fuel-injected engine; a Tri-Iso Mount chrome moly frame; inverted fork front suspension; a CNC machined T-6 aluminum wing arm; and White Brothers adjustable, nitrogen gas-charged shocks. Also, all the sheet metal and fenders are hand-crafted, not stamped. Price? As of this writing, about $19,500, but AMW anticpates a price increase.

America Motor works prides itself on building *your* bike the way *you* want it and promises delivery within 90 days, (actual delivery time will depend on your design specs).

If you already own a motorcycle and want to upgrade its parts, AMW will supply you with just about anything you need in the way of premium-quality components. Any part found on their Spirit motorcyle is also available for sale separately. In fact, if you wanted, you could build your own Spirit. But according to the company's president, you would spend a whole lot more if you did build the bike yourself (although you might have a whole lot more fun doing so).

Company
American Motor Works (Palm Bay, FL)

Where
World Wide Web

Web Address
http://iu.net/amw

Email
amw@iu.net

Shipping Fees (in the U.S.)
Actual costs for parts. $300 for motorcycles anywhere in the U.S.

International orders are accepted.

Road and Track Magazine Merchandise

If you're a *Road and Track* enthusiast, shift into fifth and head over to the Road and Track merchandise store on America Online.

Road and Track Magazine (continued)

They basically have five offerings: Road and Track caps in white, black, magenta, or royal blue; library cases (to store back issues); exotic car calendars, and signed and unsigned copies of Peter Egan's "Side Glances," an anthology of 105 of his columns from the past 10 years.

Apparently there is more to this merchandise than meets the eye. The R and T calendar, for example, is a "limited edition work of art that sells out its production run every year," so early orders are encouraged.

Company
Road and Track

Where
America Online

Shortcut
Keyword *road*

Prices
From $12 to $70.

Shipping Fees (in the U.S.)
Varies from $4 to $10—item dependent.

My Miata dream machine.

Auto Information Service

AutoNet is probably the best deal in cyberspace for new car information and pricing. I know of many services that charge up to $30 for the same information. The only downside here is that AutoNet is currently offered only on CompuServe. If you are planning to buy a new car and are not a CompuServe membership, pick up a membership kit or find a friend who has an account. You'll save hundreds if not thousands of dollars.

AutoNet is simple. First you choose a car by make and model. If you're undecided about what to purchase, AutoNet will offer suggestions based on your buying criteria—such as price range, features, fuel economy, and size.

If you already know what you want, you can directly read and print reams of data on your car choice, including details on standard and optional equipment lists and dealer invoice prices.

For no particular reason (ahem), I choose to run a report on a Mazda Miata. Pricing-wise I discovered that the sticker is $1,732 higher than the dealer invoice, that there is a large markup on floormats (70 percent) but that the rest of the options run in the 13 to 20 percent markup range—just the right ammo I need when battling the dealer, which I hope will be soon.

Now, once you figure out the price you want to pay based on your newfound "real price" information, AutoNet can even calculate your monthly payments.

By the way, AutoNet also spews out fun facts in their reports. You get a brief history of the car's future design plans and a profile of the average buyer. Did you know that Miata sales are evenly split between men and women?

Company
AutoNet (Acton, MA)

Where
CompuServe

Auto Information Service (continued)

Shortcut
Go *autonet*

Prices
90 cents for each pricing report or $1.20 for two (as a side-by-side comparison). Full data sheets, which include pricing and a photo, cost $1.50.

Do you stick these on your car or your computer?

Internet-Themed Bumper Stickers

The point of CyberStickers is to "identify yourself as an Internet surfer...on your bumper, on your wall, or slapped on your favorite computer."

As of this writing, there are six stickers to choose from. The color ones read "Virtual Reality Is a Crutch," "I (heart) Cyberspace," and "When Computers Are Outlawed, Only Outlaws Will Have Computers."

The black and white collection contains "I E-mail therefore I Am," "My Other Home is the Internet," and "Honk if You Are an Internaut," which I imagine is a teriffic way to poll your traffic buddies.

Quantity discounts are available, and these folks are open to any suggestions about additional slogans to add to their product line.

Company
CyberStickers (Loveland, CO)

Where
World Wide Web

Web Address
http://plaza.xor.com/cyberstickers/

Email
kharmon@krh.com

Price
$5.00 each.

Shipping Fees (in the U.S.)
25 cents.

Used Car Pricing Service

When the Automobile Information Center (AIC) came online, the idea was to offer convenient, accurate, used car pricing. While this objective remains the cornerstone of AIC's business, they do offer other direct-to-dealer purchasing options for new car buyers as well.

The information available on used cars is really handy and is appropriately called "Used Car Valuation Reports." These reports list the used vehicle base value and a list of options, followed by three columns of information: what you would pay a wholesale dealer, private party, and retail dealer.

Used Car Pricing Service (continued)

Their example of a 1988 Chevmobile Sunshine (can anyone picture this car?) shows a base value ranging from $7,960 if bought from a wholesaler, $9,160 if bought from a private party, and $9,960 if purchased from a dealer. When you look at these numbers, you can also see that the dealer paid $7,960 from the wholesaler, thus helping you determine your bargaining power if you prefer to buy from a retail lot.

The Automobile Information Center also offers a Buyer's Guide that tells how to check out a used car, how to get the best deal from a dealer, and how to safely buy from private parties.

All reports are delivered electroncially via CompuServe.

Company
Automobile Information Center
(Seattle, WA)

Where
CompuServe

Shortcut
Go *ai*

Email (via the Internet)
70007.1502@compuserve.com

Email (via CompuServe)
70007,1502

Prices (in the U.S.)
$5.95 for used car valuation reports. $14.95 for a list of over 50 buying services.

International orders are accepted.

Help! I'm gonna get run over on the Information Highway!

Internet License Plate Frames

As if personalized license plates alone were not enough to make a "rolling statement" to the world, along comes a way to advertise your email address to fellow drivers—Internet license plate frames.

It makes perfect sense too—especially if you're "single and looking" and prefer to socialize with other onliners. Email is completely safe because it helps you make new friends without forcing you to give out any tangible personal information.

The manufacturer also offers a free electronic mailing list of participants in an email chat forum where people can swap Internet license plate frame stories. Here, frame folklore abounds of people who have met that "special one" and those who have made valuable business contacts. Hey, that would make these frames a tax deduction!

License Plate Frames (continued)

Company
DHM Information Management, Inc.
(Redondo Beach, CA)

Where
World Wide Web

Web Address
http://www.power.net

Instant Information
info@power.net/lpf.html

Prices (in the U.S.)
$16.00 per frame.

Shipping Fee (in the U.S.)
$3.50

International orders are accepted.

Car Pricing Club and International Car Dealer

AutoQuot-R offers a little bit of everything when it comes to car pricing, but their best features are the Goldkey Club and their national car-buying service, which will even ship cars overseas.

For U.S. residents, the 30-year-old company offers the Goldkey Club, which, for $39 per year, gives you annual benefits that include seven free new car reports, five used car reports, free leasing quote services, 24-hour towing, nationwide repairs at 40 percent off, and an extended warranty service "at cost."

As if that wasn't enough, the plan also includes discount movie tickets, dental plan savings, fac-tory outlet shopping, discount floral services, and magazine subscriptions at wholesale prices. No joke.

If you live outside the U.S., AutoQuot-R can help you purchase a car and then get it to wherever you are. They have experience in shipping to Europe and the Orient, from Malta to Malaysia. All transacations are in U.S. dollars, but the staff speaks English, French, Spanish, and Italian.

Just think: You could be the first person in China to tour the perimeter of the Great Wall in a brand spanking new Trans-Am—T-roof and all.

Company
AutoQuot-R (Fort Lauderdale, Florida)

Where
CompuServe

Shortcut
Go *aq*

Email (via the Internet)
70007.1241@compuserve.com

Email (via CompuServe)
70007,1241

Prices (in the U.S.)
$39 per year for the Goldkey Club. Varies on other services.

International orders are accepted.

Hot Tip!

If you're interested in private party auto-related classifieds, they're available on the Internet. Check out the Usenet group at *rec.autos.marketplace.*

Would you believe the car in this photo is only a few inches tall?

Car Miniatures, Books, and Videos

No matter what kind of car you own, EWA & Miniature Cars USA has something for every car enthusiast—whether it's a book about cars, a video, a magazine, or an auto miniature.

Check out these statistics: "EWA stocks over 2,800 different car books, 550 different videos about cars, 9,000 different miniature car models (fully built or kits), and fulfill subscriptions for 26 British car magazines including *Autosport, Classic & Sportscar, Jaguar World, Racecar Engineering*, and many others."

You can download this voluminous catalog directly from their site or request a copy to be sent to you by email.

All the auto heavyweights shop here, including Mario Andretti, as well as some celebrities noted for their heavy foot on the gas pedal, such as David Letterman. Considering the 90,000 item inventory, there's bound to be something here for you too.

Shopping on the Internet and Beyond

Exclusive Deal

EWA & Miniature Cars USA

10% off your first order of $50 or more (excluding magazine subscriptions).

Exclusive deal for readers of this book only! You must mention this offer when you place your order.

Company
EWA & Miniature Cars USA
(Berkeley Heights, NJ)

Where
World Wide Web

Web Address
`http://shops.net/shops/EWACARS/`

Reminder! This Web address is case sensitive. Make sure you enter it *exactly* as shown.

Email
`ewa@ewacars.com`

Prices
From $5 to $999

Shipping Fees (in the U.S.)
$6.95 for order up to $300, free for orders over $300.

International orders are accepted.

Hot Tip!

To look at private party ads from individual online-service subscribers, use these shortcuts:

America Online: Keyword *classifieds*
CompuServe: Go *classifieds*
Prodigy: Jump *classifieds*

Lamborghini isn't just tough to spell, it's tough to buy, too.

Really, Really Expensive Cars

Rolls Royce of Beverly Hills is *the* site for creating your own version of *Lifestyles of the Rich and Famous*. Not only is this spot entertaining, it's educational as well. Even living in the heart of the "expensive car capital of the world," I was stumped by some models in this virtual showroom.

The Rolls Royces and Bentleys I easily recognized, as well as the Lotus Esprit S4. But the "All New Flying Spur" (a car named after Roy Rogers?) and the Bugatti EB110 were new to me, but now incorporated into my Beverly Hills vernacular.

This site lists features but not prices (probably a heart-attack precaution), which in a way makes sense if you agree with the adage "if you have to ask how much, you can't afford it."

Although the company lists contact information, there is no way to order these *crème de la crème* vehicles online. Don't despair, though. If you happen to be the Sultan of Brunei, Bill Gates, or multi-billionaire equivalent, the company assures me that a phone call and platinum American Express card are acceptable.

Company
Rolls Royce of Beverly Hills
(Beverly Hills, California)

Where
World Wide Web

Web Address
http://www.clark.net/pub/networx/autopage/
dealers/de001.html

Email
garyw@earthlink.net

Prices
Don't ask. But if you must: $149,000 (Rolls Royce Silver Dawn) to $328,000 (Rolls Royce Silver Spur Touring Limosine).

AUTOMOBILE ONLINE SHOWROOMS AND BROCHURES

Many manufacturers and suppliers provide online showrooms where you can review information about vehicles.

Car Maker	Prodigy	CompuServe	Notes
Cadillac	Jump *cadillac*	Go *cmc*	Available on Prodigy: Online Showroom, Explanations of features (Northstar System), Leasing info, "Ownership Privileges" and a free catalog.
			CompuServe has the same offerings as above, plus you can download GIFs of Cadillacs from the Graphics Showcase section.
Chrysler, Plymouth	Jump *chrysler*		Gives pricing along with specs and free brochures, model features, and photos online.
Ford	Jump *ford*	Go *fmc*	Descriptions and prices on cars and trucks, estimated monthly finance charges and lease payments along with a credit application. You can also "shop the world of Ford accessory items, clothing, software, and videos ("Monster Trucks in Action").
Honda	Jump *honda*		Info on all models, free brochures, info on nearest dealers, highlights of current product line.
Lincoln	Jump *lincoln*	Go *lm*	Showcase, "coming soon," credit options, "talk to Ford," Thunderbird apparel, T-Bird collectibles, and other items T-Bird items.
Luxury Car Promotions	Jump *luxury promotions*		Split into two categories: over $30,000 and under $30,000. Mix of domestic and foreign makers including Mazda, Honda, Cadillac, and Lincoln.
Mazda	Jump *mazda*	Go *lm*	Entire product line, free brochures, "what's new at Mazda," monthly payment calculator to determine damage before you visit a showroom.

Car Maker	Prodigy	CompuServe	Notes
Mercury	Jump Mercury	*Go LM*	Entire line is featured, along with related info, including a dealer locator.
Nissan		Go *nissan*	Virtual Showroom, Information Central (photo library, articles, Nissan Multimedia— downloaded program for those considering an Altima purchase, allows for option and pricing scenarios and a tutorial that demonstrates the difference between leasing and buying), dealer locator and brochure requests.
Oldsmobile	Jump *gm oldsmobile*		Free brochures upon request via snail mail on all Oldsmobile models.
Plymouth Voyager	Jump *voyager*		Can print specifications immediately, free brochures on all models.
Pontiac	Jump *pontiac*	Go *pon*	Opportunity to order free catalogs on most models via snail mail, online photos, Pontiac "News," Dealer locator, leasing options. On CompuServe you'll find downloadable GIFs in the "Graphic Showcase."
Saturn	Jump *saturn*		Saturn Owners Forum (free), Saturn Live Chat, Entire Product Line, and option for free snail-mail brochures.
Toyota	Jump *toyota*		Toyota Today(news), Toyota Talk, Caring for Your ToyotaOwner Services, The Toyota Line, Sneak Preview, and the Toyota Store.

For More...

For more great auto related shopping, see the next page.

Honorable Mentions

in the category of

Automobiles & Motorcycles

Anti-Theft Devices

Auto theft protection without bells and whistles.

Company
Techlock

Web Address
http://www.erinet.com/kenny/techlock.html

Automotive Supplies

Private party ads for auto supplies on Prodigy.

Prodigy
Jump classifieds then select *browse ads*

Automotive Supplies

Private party ads for supplies on CompuServe. Includes ads for late-model and classic cars.

CompuServe
Go classifieds then select *cars/boats/planes/rvs/ cycles*

Auto Advice

Personal advice regarding all aspects of your new car buying needs, such as buying, financing, leasing, trade-ins, and warranties.

Company
Professional Auto Buyers Network

Web Address
http://www.icw.com/auto/auto.html

Car Covers

An arctic nylon pack-cloth, coated with polyurethane film naturally shields all ice, snow, and water. Fits all cars, vans, and trucks.

Company
American Canvas Products

Web Address
http://www.tulsa.com/tom/acpi/acpi.htm

Car Racks

Removable car top and rear mount carriers.

Company
Thule Car Rack Systems

Web Address
http://www.allshop.com/thule

Classic Car Prices

The first international electronic database monitoring classic car prices throughout the world.

Company
Classic Car Connection

Web Address
http://www.primenet.com/~dadalus/
classic.html

Dealer Incentives

Free listing of dealer incentives, organized by car make and model.

Company
Cyberspace Automative Performance

Web Address
http://www.cyberauto.com//catalogs/
auto_info/sales/incentives.html

Exports

Antique/classic cars for yourself or for resale. Shipping to any country. Trucks—4x4 and commercial vehicles.

Company
Jacob Goldman's Car Export Service

Web Address
http://www.netpart.com/jacob/

Floor Mats

Floor mats that are custom cut to original patterns and are made of heavy 24 ounce automotive carpet, and backed with nonslip nib backing.

Company
Car Mats R Us

Web Address
http://www.ip.net/shops/Car_Mats_R_Us/

How-to Repair

How-to videos including titles related to automobiles, motorcycles, and sports cars.

Company
InfoVid Outlet

Web Address
http://branch.com:1080/infovid/c304.html

How-to Repair

How-to books on automotive repair/maintenance.

Company
S.S. Publishing

Where
http://www.amug.org/~a165/

Leasing

GE capital Auto Lease (GECAL) is the largest independent auto leasing company in the U.S.

Where
GE capital Auto Lease

Web Address
http://www.ge.com/cogi-bin/gecal/exec.tcl

Motorcycles and Motorcycle Accessories

Private party ads for motorcycle supplies on CompuServe.

CompuServe
Go classifieds then select *cars/boats/planes/rvs/cycles*

National Classifieds

Free service to bring together buyers and sellers of used cars for all states.

Company
Webfoot's Used Car Lot

Web Address
http://www/webfoot.com/lots/
international.car.lot.html

Parts and Supplies

Distributors of high-quality automotive parts and supplies.

Company
Westex Automotive Corporation

Web Address
http://human.com/mkt/westex/index.html

Pricing Network

New and used prices for cars, trucks, and vans.

Company
Car Price Network

Web Address
http://www.w2.com.car1.html

Pricing Service

New car pricing.

Company
Edmund's Automobile Buyer's Guides

Web Address
gopher://gopher.enews.com:2100/11/
showroom/edmunds

Trucks, RVs, and Vans

Private party ads for truck, RV, and van supplies on CompuServe.

How to Access
Go *classifieds* then select *cars/boats/planes/rvs/cycles*

Beauty Products

Get a whiff of the Web, courtesy of the Fragrance Source.

Discount Designer Fragrances

The Fragrance Source has a threefold mission: sell fragrances only (for both men and women), offer a huge selection of over 600 items, and discount products from 15 to 45 percent.

The company has over 45 women's brands in stock. You can choose from the mass market-oriented lines (Jean Nate, Guess, and Exclamation) to the highly prized (Tiffany, White Diamonds, and Opium). Within each brand, you'll find virtually all the scent-related products.

For example, in the Lauren product line, you can buy the perfume spray, cologne, natural spray cologne, "all over body powder," "all over body lotion," and body cream. Each line also includes a "Specially Featured Item," which offers the highest discount for that particular scent. The

Lauren section offers 15 percent off the natural spray cologne. In the Bennetton line, the spray toilette was featured at 35 percent off. In the Shalimar line, Eau de Toilette spray was featured at 40 percent off the regular retail price.

Men save, too: with more than 15 leading brands to choose from. Grey Flannel's cologne is their "Specially Featured Item," at a 30 percent savings. The other Grey Flannel aftershaves, balms, and lotions are also discounted as much as 30 percent.

With these great prices and a more than substantial selection, the Fragrance Source makes great scents. (Sorry, I had to say it.)

Company
Fragrance Source (Fairfield, NJ)

Where
World Wide Web

Web Address
`http://branch.com/fragrance/menu.html`

Prices
From $10 to $200.

Shipping Fees (in the U.S.)
$5 (ground), $10 (two day), $15 (next day).

International orders are accepted.

Tonight—a little dance, a little romance, and a dab of Ellegance.

Custom, Natural Makeup

If you buy makeup and want to save money, create custom color blends, and use a product made with only natural ingredients, Ellegance has developed a line you will love. And there's no risk, either, because they offer trial sizes on most of their line, *including* custom blends.

Trying to eke out the last few molecules of a favorite makeup item because it's no longer available? Need a specific color to match a particular outfit? Ellegance's custom blend services, offered at *no extra charge,* can solve just about any makeup woe.

Simply tender a sample of your "matchee" and the company will create a "matcher." If you want to be sure of the result before you commit to a full-size product purchase, Ellegance will sell you a trial portion of the custom color for only $2. If you tend to stick to standard colors, trial sizes are available for only 99 cents each.

Ellegance is a complete makeup line and includes lip and eye pencils, lipsticks, mascaras, foundation, and talc-free and dye-free pressed powders.

Another innovative aspect of the Ellegance line is their packaging. They offer a "Colour Refill Pouch" that saves landfill space and dollars (the refills are 15 percent less than the originally packaged item).

Company
Ellegance (Bailey, CO)

Where
World Wide Web

Web Address
http://www.dash.com/netro/sho/ema/naturell/naturell.html

Email
makeup@dash.com

Prices
$5.00 to $30.
99 cent trials sizes also available.

Shipping Fees (in the U.S.)
$4.00

International orders are accepted.

In journalism, we say "always verify your source." On the Web, Verify *is your source—for lip color.*

Perfect Lip Cover

The Verify Web page is a dual-opportunity outlet: You can be a basic customer and purchase their lipsticks for personal use, or you can buy the product line to establish your own wholesale distributorship.

You can choose from five full-size lipsticks or five, six-shade travel kits (single-use sizes that can also function as tester kits for promotional purposes.) In their quest for the perfect lips, Verify suggests you blend colors together and use their "special formula sealer," which the company claims will keep your lipstick on all day, under normal circumstances (sorry, no guarantees if you consume a greasy burger.) The sealer, along with a lip cleanser and lip conditioner, is included free with each order.

"Long wearing, kiss-proof," and available in over 30 shades, the Verify product line is a good source for "mistake-free lip shade selections."

Shopping on the Internet and Beyond

Exclusive Deal

Verify, Ltd.

20 percent off your first order.

Exclusive deal for readers of this book only!
You must mention this offer when you place your order.

Company
Verify, Ltd. (North Bergen, NJ)

Where
World Wide Web

Web Address
`http://branch.com/verify/verify.html`

Email
`cosmetic@ios.com`

Prices
$20

Shipping Fees (in the U.S.)
Included in the price.

International orders are accepted.

Alpha Hydroxy Skin Care System

Alpha hydroxy acid skin care products are everywhere, but they're also very expensive. Department stores, for example, charge as much as $70 for 1.7 ounces of a famous-name beauty peel.

Well, David Akerberg is out to change that with his product line, which he considers far superior to other commercial products, although his products cost significantly less. Akerberg sells a *total* regime of five products designed to work together.

Alpha Hydroxy Skin Care (continued)

This "synergist system is a complete five-step process (using all five fruit acids) that slows down the aging of your skin." There is a wash, a peel, a special moisturizer, a mild grain scrub, and another moisturizer with sunscreen. The products are apparently so effective that you only need to use a green pea's worth *three* times a week.

"By sloughing off dead skin cells, the system precipitates the skin to replenish itself naturally. It also utilizes a unique moisturizer that buffers the acid and causes the skin to retain an abundance of moisture."

Akerberg backs his Skin Renewal System with the guarantee that "you will see a remarkable improvement in your complexion" or your money back. Orders are accepted in English, Spanish, German, and Portuguese.

If you think you're not quite old enough to need facial peel products, consider Akerberg's motto: "Start young and keep what you have."

Shopping on the Internet and Beyond

Exclusive Deal

**David Akerberg's
Skin Renewal System**

30 percent off the Alpha Hydroxy
Skin Kit ($34.50 value).

Exclusive deal for readers of this book only!
You must mention this offer when you place your order.

Company
David Akerberg's Skin Renewal System
(Knoxville, TN)

Where
World Wide Web

Web Address
http://www.usit.net/skinrenu

Email
davida@usit.net

Prices
Good values. Varies depending on kits.

Shipping Fees (in the U.S.)
Actual charges. No handling fees.

International orders are accepted.

Hemp Seed Oil Skin Care Products

While the hemp plant (also known as cannabis sativa) and its by-products are illegal in the United States, the government does allow for the importation of hempseed and hemp oil.

For body-care-conscious folks, this is a boon since hemp oil contains the largest concentration of essential fatty acids available from any vegetable source. Fatty acids cannot be manufactured by the body and are essential for good cardiovascular and nervous system functioning. In fact, hemp oil is so rich in health benefits, it could be considered the vegetable counterpart to (the dreaded) cod liver oil.

Unlike cod liver oil, though, the properties of hemp seed oil are as well absorbed by the skin as they are internally, so they're the perfect basis for total body care.

The Herbal Delights Hemp Essential product line includes lip balms, healing salves, lotions, moisturizing cream, massage oil, massage butter, seed meal soap, and hemp-fabric facial mitts. According to the company, the hemp seed oil makes up at least 50 percent of the oil portion of these vegetable-source products.

Hemp Seed Skin Care (continued)

Most of the items are available unscented or, if you prefer, you can smell like a sandalwood/jasmine blend, natural cocoa, mango, or lemon.

Company
Herbal Delights (Cazadero, CA)

Where
World Wide Web

Web Address
http://www.spiderweb.com/hempess/

Email: hemp@spiderweb.com

Prices
From $3 to $20 for a gift set.

Shipping Fees (in the U.S.)
Actual charges. No handling fees.

International orders are accepted.

Image Consulting and Beauty Treatments

Executive Image is a multi-faceted site with activities for men and women. Either gender is welcome to take an "image quiz" and to peruse the company's list of "skin strategies for men" and "aromatherapy products for women."

Stay calm, look calm, feel calm, and smell calm with Herbal Serenity.

Since image *is* everything, all the products and services are a small part of a bigger whole. In other words, the company wants to help you to optimize your appearance by using well-suited colors choices and top-quality skin care products.

Online, you can order Executive Image's men's skin care and women's body treatments, which are made with "calming herbal extracts to help condition your skin and relax your mind."

The women's body line, called Herbal Serenity, includes splashes, oils, gelees, soaps, and scrubs. The men's online catalog offers more cosmetic-oriented products, including toning cleansers, eye gels, and alpha hydroxy regenerating creams.

If you want to work on more than your skin, Executive Image does offer one-on-one consultations for those you fearing your current fashion choices are making you look far too much like Pat from Saturday Night Live.

Remember!

For periodic updates of this book, send email to *shop@easton.com*. See *Introduction* for more details.

Image Consulting, Beauty (continued)

Shopping on the Internet and Beyond

Exclusive Deal

Executive Image

10 percent off an order of $70 or more.

Exclusive deal for readers of this book only!
You must mention this offer when you place your order.

Company
Executive Image (San Diego, CA)

Where
World Wide Web

Web Address
http://www.cts.com/~aardvark/kat01.html

Email
aardvark@cts.com

Prices
$12.50 to $30.00.

Shipping Fees (in the U.S)
$3 flat.

International orders are accepted.

For More...

For more great beauty shopping opportunities,
see the next page.

Honorable Mentions

in the category of

Beauty Products

Beauty Supplies

Get fog-free mirrors and towelettes.

Company
Visi-Tech

Web Address
http://www.tiac.net/users/visitech/home.html

Body Contouring

Contour your body with this complete system.

Company
Skinny Dip Body Shop

Web Address
http://www.iagi.net/hub/A-Skinny-Dip-Body-Shop/

Cosmetics

Find information on Mary Kay Cosmetics.

Company
Mary Kay Cosmetics

Web Address
http://cyberzine.org/html/Cosmetics/cosmetics2.html

Clothing, Cosmetics, and Jewelry

Private party ads for supplies on America Online.

America Online
Keyword *classifieds* then select *general merchandise boards*

Facials

Download a facial muscle enhancement exercise manual for men and women.

Company
CCMI

Web Address
http://www.cs.colorado.edu/homes/mcbryan/public_html/bb/216/6.html

Hair Care

Find information on camouflaging thin hair.

Company
Derm Match, Inc.

Web Address
http://www.iagi.net/hub/dm.html

Hair Care

Find information on Helsinki hair care products that "regrow" hair.

Company
Neways

Web Address
http://www.ip.net:80/shops/A-Helsinki-
Hair-Care-Shop

Personal Care Products

Find information on personal care products for African Americans.

Company
Black Heritage Products

Web Address
http://www.melanet.com/melanet/bhp/

Books

Judaic and Psychotherapy Books

Jason Aronson booksellers could literally be renamed "Judaic and Psychotherapy Books R Us," because those are the only two subjects they cover.

The Judaic books range from the scholarly (*Arguments for the Sake of Heaven: Emerging Trends in Traditional Judaism*) to the highly specific (*The Cantor's Manual of Jewish Law*). You'll also find books on Jewish spirituality, an encyclopedia of Jewish symbols, and a collection of great Jewish speeches.

The topic list for the psychology books is broken down into 23 categories. Couples therapy, crime, narcissism, and borderline conditions highlight the breadth of choices.

This site also includes special interviews with some of the authors.

Company
Jason Aronson Publishers
(Northvale, NJ)

Where
World Wide Web

Web Address
http://www.flightpath.com/Clients/Aronson/

Reminder! This address is case sensitive. Make sure you enter it *exactly* as shown.

Email
orders@aronson.com or aronson@haven.ios.com

Prices
Average price is $30.

Shipping Fees (in the U.S.)
$2.95 for the first book and 75 cents for each additional book.

International orders are accepted.

Audio Books

In the past few years, audio books have become an acceptable alternative to print material. With this acceptance has come a surge in popularity, reflected in the Books On Tape company's extensive growth. The company began in 1975 with four titles. Today, their catalog is a thick 300 pages, and offers the largest selection of *unabridged* audio books available, with an inventory exceeding 3,000.

Books On Tape contain every word of the original text, are professionally read, and are rented rather than bought (although they are happy to sell them for an average price of $64).

The book lengths are traditionally from 8 to 15 hours long. The rental period for each book is 30 days from the time you receive it. The cost averages $14.50 (with some $9.95 specials), plus shipping and sales tax (if any). The company also offers a selection of $9.95 bargain rentals.

Audio Books (continued)

Books On Tape has really perfected the book-rental mail-order process. When you receive your tapes, you also get a pre-printed, pre-paid return mailer that you simply drop in any mailbox when you are done.

Books On Tape are really terrific for anyone who spends a lot of time commuting. I have found that they make house cleaning and exercising much less tedious. If the concept appeals to you, Books On Tape offers introductory incentives for first-time renters, which makes it easy to test the service.

Company
Books On Tape (New York, NY)

Where
CompuServe

Shortcut
Go *bot*

Email (via CompuServe)
70007,1243

Email (via the Internet)
70007.1243@compuserve.com

Prices
From $9.95 to $14.50 for rentals. Purchases average $64.

Shipping Fees
Actual costs. No handling fees.

Hot Tip!

New and used books are sold on the Internet by readers. To see what's available, check out *rec.arts.book.marketplace*.

Skeptic magazine—because some inquiring minds really want to know.

Skeptics Society Books and Tapes

Dedicated to the cerebral exercise of critical thinking, the basis of the Skeptics Society is one simple question: How well does a particular claim hold up under scientific scrutiny? The cognitive investigation centers on assertions made by "scientists, pseudoscientists, and pseudohistorians on a wide variety of theories, which include (but are not limited to) evolution, cults, religion, Holocaust revisionism, extreme Afrocentrism, conspiracy theories, cryonics, immortality, witch crazes, mass hysteria and urban myths"—basically, any topic ever featured on *Geraldo*.

This member-supported organization offers a selection of books, audiocassettes, and videotapes that explore these issues—and then some. The book selection includes titles like *The Mask of Nostradamus*, by James "The Amazing" Randi, and *True Stories of False Memories*, by E. Goldstein.

Skeptics Society Books (continued)

The Skeptics Society also sponsors a lecture series at Cal Tech in Los Angeles and sells video and audio of these presentations through their Internet presence.

The choices from the lecture series are quite intriguing. A sampling: *Evolution and Creationism: How to Debate a Creationist; Sex, Brains and Hands: Sex Differences in Cognitive Abilities & Handedness;* and *The Devil Made Me Do It: The Decline of Personal Responsibility.*

If you prefer to read these lectures, consider a subscription to the quarterly magazine *Skeptic,* which includes transcripts of the speeches. Ordering information for the magazine is available at the society's Web site or via email.

Shopping on the Internet and Beyond

Exclusive Deal

Skeptics Books and Tapes

$10 off a one-year subscription to *Skeptic* Magazine, and a free copy of their special issue on "Pseudomedicine and Alternative Healthcare."

Exclusive deal for readers of this book only! You must mention this offer when you place your order.

Company
Skeptics Books and Tapes (Alta Dena, CA)

Where
World Wide Web

Web Address
http://www.skeptic.com/

Email
info@skeptic.com

Prices
From $9.95 to $23.95.

Shipping Fees (in the U.S.)

$3.00 for first book/tape, $1 for each additional.

International orders are accepted.

 Single sample issue of *Skeptic* Magazine.

Practice makes perfect worlds.

Books on "Random Acts of Kindness"

It's almost ironic that Conari Press' first release, *Coming Apart*—a book about ending relationships—would later become best known for publishing the "Random Acts of Kindness" series—books about bringing people together through casual, yet generous, interactions.

Remember!

Access the Web from any major online service. On AOL, keyword *web*. On CompuServe, go *netlauncher*. On Prodigy, jump *web*.

"Random Acts of Kindness" (continued)

What's the philosophy behind "Random Acts of Kindness?" "Imagine what would happen if there were an outbreak of kindness in the world, if everybody did one thing on a daily basis." It is the book's goal to "inspire you to start with the small, the particular, the individual—to bring delight and goodness to yourself and others."

There are four "Random" offerings: The first publication, its sequel *More Random Acts of Kindness,* a primer for kids, and a screen saver.

Online you will also find a free *Teachers Guide to Random Acts of Kindness,* which you can print, plus some good-deed suggestions you can do on the official "Random Acts of Kindness Day," celebrated in February.

Though best known for their "Kindness" publications, Conari also carries "non-Random" writings geared toward self-improvement and self-realization. The award-winning *I Swore I'd Never Do That!—Recognizing Family Patterns and Making Wise Parenting Choices,* and *Slowing Down in a Speeded Up World* are good examples.

Shopping on the Internet and Beyond

Exclusive Deal

Conari Books

15 percent off your first order.

Exclusive deal for readers of this book only! You must mention this offer when you place your order.

Company
Conari Books (Emeryville, CA)

Where
World Wide Web

Reminder! Most Web addresses are case sensitive. Make sure you enter the address *exactly* as shown.

Web Address
`http://conari.com/Books/Conari`

Email
`conaripub@aol.com`

Prices
From $8.95 to $21.95.

Shipping Fees (in the U.S.)
Actual cost. No handling charges. International orders are accepted.

Shop 'til your modem connection drops—at Coriolis Group Books.

World's Greatest Computer Books

Warning: The following is a shameless plug for one of the best computer book publishers anywhere. Compare the company name following this topic with the one on the spine of this book, and you'll see what I mean by "shameless."

Greatest Computer Books (continued)

Coriolis has a reputation for producing the most reader- and user-friendly computer books available. A visit to their Web site will introduce you to selections in four categories: Internet and Web, Game and Multimedia, Programming, and Special Interest. The cornerstone of their product line is their online computing titles. These books are overflowing with information you won't find anywhere else.

My favorite selections are in the "Free $tuff" series, the best-selling guides "to getting hundreds of valuable goodies" from various online resources. They publish a *Free $tuff from the Internet* along with "Free $tuff" titles for America Online, CompuServe, and the World Wide Web.

If you are a Webnaut or want to learn more about the Web, be sure to check out the Coriolis Web category as well. Here you'll find books to help you navigate the Web, as well as a step-by-step guide for building your own sites using their top-rated "Web Surfing & Publishing Kit."

You also have the option of reading a sample chapter online before you buy. Ordering online is quick and easy, and, because you are buying directly from the publisher, you'll be saving big bucks, too.

Shopping on the Internet and Beyond

Exclusive Deal

The Coriolis Group

An additional 10 percent off your first order. (Type the word "Rhonda" in the "Comments" field.)

Exclusive deal for readers of this book only! You must mention this offer when you place your order.

Company
The Coriolis Group (Scottsdale, AZ)

Where
World Wide Web

Web Address
`http://www.coriolis.com/coriolis/bookstor/ bookstor.htm`

Email
`orders@coriolis.com`

Prices
From $12.99 to $39.99. All orders made through the Web are discounted 20 percent off the bookstore price (plus an additional 10 percent off with the coupon).

Shipping Fees
$3 per book in the U.S. $5 per book outside the U.S.

International orders are accepted.

Online Bookstore on America Online

If you're an America Online subscriber with a specific book in mind, I recommend the Online Bookstore run by Read USA.

There are no pictures or groovy graphics, but there is a good range of general interest and computer books at discounts of 10 to 20 percent off, depending on the genre. However, if you're an AOL member, you'll receive an extra 5 percent off, bringing your total discount to 15 to 25 percent off.

In addition to its search feature, the electronic storefront offers a browse area where you click on a series of sub-categories to find an area that interests you.

Online Bookstore (continued)

If a title grabs you, simply highlight and select, and you will be given a brief description of the book, its publication date, page length, and price.

Company
Read USA (Center Moriches, NY)

Where
America Online

Email (via America Online)
Read USA

Email (via the Internet)
readusa@aol.com

Prices
Discounts on all books.

Shipping Fees (in the U.S.)
$3.95 for orders totaling $10 or less. $4.95 on orders of $10.01 or more.

"Look Before You Buy" Books

Dial-A-Book is a real browser's paradise. The company sells electronic books and traditional paper publications, but lets you preview either type before you buy.

The downloadable books are all computer titles as of this writing—13 in all—from Ziff-Davis Press and Albion Books. You can preview the first chapter in ASCII format (straight text that can be loaded into any word processor), and if you choose to buy, then download in Adobe Acrobat format. When you use Dial-A-Book's software to read the downloaded book, you'll get all the graphics and proper formatting. In addition to the ecological advantages of this distribution, you'll also save money because these electronic editions are sold at 20 percent off the list price.

Downloading books is so easy maybe these folks should think about renaming their operation "Modem-A-Book."

If you are more of a paper person, you can peruse the first chapter and table of contents online before buying the bound version. The choices here include several versions of The Bible (42 editions in 11 languages, to be exact), plus award-winning children's books, and the U.S Chess Federation's recommended Batsford chess books.

Company
Dial-A-Book (New York, NY)

Where
World Wide Web

Web Address
http://dab.psi.net/dialabook/

Email
srg@dialabook.com

Prices
Electronic titles are 20 percent off list price.

Some final words of wisdom from Gene Roddenberry, courtesy of University Press Books.

University Press Books

The University Press Books/Berkeley bookstore is perhaps the only bookstore in the world devoted exclusively to books published by university presses.

Founded in 1974, the retail store carries more than 20,000 books from more than 100 presses. The store also has an association with Donald L. Foley books, which is an "out-of-print book service specializing in university press publications."

To make choosing easy, efficient, and satisfying for the discriminating reader, the store features only books they feel are of "significant literary and social importance."

If you are intrigued by a title while perusing their suggestions, you are given the option of clicking on it to get a complete write-up, as well as a graphic of the book title, thus taking the mystery out of which books best fit your tastes and preferences.

Company
University Press Books/Berkeley (Berkeley, CA)

Where
World Wide Web

Web Address
http://www.fractals.com/upb/html/upb_intro.html

Email
upb@fractals.fractals.com

International orders are accepted.

Small Computer Book Club

The concept behind The Small Computer Book Club is to deliver computer-related titles on a membership basis.

When you join, you'll select up to three titles for $3.00. Some premium books count as two selections, but you are allowed to choose up to $120 worth of books, with an obligation to buy one more book some time during the following 12 months.

The club promises savings of up to 50 percent, and automatically enrolls you in the Bonus Book Plan, which is a "frequent buyer" type program. You will receive paper mailings 15 times a year.

Hot Tip!

Consumer Reports magazine is available from all three major online services.

Shortcut
Keyword *consumer* (America Online), Go *consumer* (CompuServe), Jump *consumer reports* (Prodigy).

Small Computer Books (continued)

The Small Computer Book Club vows that you will never receive an "economy edition," or any other merchandise of inferior printing. Moreover, the books they offer are similar to what you will find lining the Internet shelves of your favorite bookstores, and include many recent titles. In fact, they include publication dates in their descriptions, which I found quite handy.

Be forewarned that the online catalog offers no pictures and only brief title descriptions. If there's a specific topic you'd like to read more about, and are not looking for many beginner-level titles, the Club may prove to be a great resource.

Company
Small Computer Book Club (New York, NY)

Where
CompuServe

Shortcut
Go *bk*

Email (via CompuServe)
70007,1550

Email (via the Internet)
70007.1550@compuserve.com

International orders are accepted.

Technical Books Galore

Powell's Technical Bookstore is practically a Portland, Oregon landmark. Given the enormous collection they offer, they are bound to achieve a similar presence online.

Powell's is an independent bookseller that carries "new, used, hard-to-find, and antiquarian titles in the field of architecture, chemistry, computing, communications, construction, environmental sciences, engineering, electronics, mathematics, medical sciences, and physics." With the help of a graphical map, you can browse the stacks of the store, read book reviews of prospective purchases, and even search "Books In Print" *and* "Books Out of Print" CD-ROMs.

Their database is also scheduled to offer a real nifty service, which will enable you to submit a search that remains active for as long as six months. If any new or used titles arrive that match the search, they will automatically notify you by email.

If you live anywhere near the Portland area, their Web site offers travel directions from every point of entry.

Company
Powell's Technical Books
(Portland, OR)

Where
World Wide Web

Web Address
http://www.technical.powells.portland.or.us/

Email
admin@technical.powells.portland.or.us

Prices
Quantity discounts on some titles, for single orders of $500 or more, or for a non-profit/educational institution.

International orders are accepted.

Get a genuine taste of the Southwest—with these tempting recipe books.

Cookbooks From New Mexico's Best Chefs

Ask a food-related question to anyone who has recently traveled through New Mexico, and they're sure to rave about the culinary meccas of Santa Fe and Taos. As a tribute to the outstanding Southwestern cuisine of these fine restaurants, a series of cookbooks is now available via the World Wide Web.

You have a choice of three titles: *Santa Fe Recipes, Santa Fe Lite & Spicy Recipes*, and *Taos Recipes. Santa Fe Recipes* is a collection of 299 recipes from 30 local restaurants, with such tempting dishes as Benedict Mexican with Con Queso Sauce, Mexican Drunken Shrimp, and Avocado Gazpacho Soup.

If the Sante Fe concept sounds good but you prefer leaner fare, the *Santa Fe Lite & Spicy Recipes* cookbook will appeal to you. It features 350 *light* recipes from the chefs of 40 regional restaurants. Although lean on calories, this cook-

book is fat on fare, and is packed with innovative dishes like Drunken Blue Fried Trout.

If Bad Hombre Eggs and Pinon & Chili Pesto Fettucini sound tantalizing, then the *Taos Recipes* cookbook would be a good choice, with 170 recipes from 16 restaurants.

"The sketches and photographs included in these books share with you the historic flavor distingushing this area of the Southwest. Just travel as far as your kitchen to create your own Southwestern gourmet feast."

Shopping on the Internet and Beyond

Exclusive Deal

Southwestern Exposure

Free domestic shipping on your first order.

Exclusive deal for readers of this book only! You must mention this offer when you place your order.

Company
Southwestern Exposure (Glorieta, NM)

Where
World Wide Web

Web Address
http://www.rt66.com/swest/cookbook.html

Email
swe@roadrunner.com

Prices
From $12.95 to $15.95.

Shipping (in the U.S.)
$3 for the first book. $1 for each additional title.

International orders are accepted.

Specialty Book Clubs

Newbridge is the Grandaddy book club of all book clubs—actually it is more of an umbrella club, offering many themes under one banner.

The categories focus on technology and science, with a smattering of home and business selections. The choices are: The PC Users' Book Club, the Library of Computer and Information Sciences, The Mac Professional's Book Club, The Astronomy Book Club, The Executive Program, The Reader's Subscription, The Garden Book Club, the Architects and Designers Book Service, the Behavioral Science Book Club Service, The Natural Science Book Club, and the Nurses' Book Society.

Newbridge is offering a traditional book club arrangement. You get several titles at a low introductory fee and to get their discount on other books, you must buy a certain number of additional titles in the next 12 months. The follow-up is done by snail mail. About every three weeks you'll get a reply card and a newsletter describing the available choices.

For anyone with an interest in or has a business related to any of the topics, these clubs look like a great deal, especially considering how few of these titles are carried in even the biggest bookstore chains.

Company
Newbridge (New York, NY)

Where
CompuServe

Shortcut
Go *nb*

Email (via CompuServe)
70007,1550

Email (via the Internet)
70007.1550@compuserve.com

Books for Professionals

Niche is the key word for Warren, Gorham & Lamont publishers, who produce authoritative books with high-level information, analysis, and guidance. Topics include legal, tax, human resources, and accounting, keeping you up to date on "changes in law, technology, trends, and techniques...resources you'll turn to again and again to solve the challenges you face every day."

Such information does not come cheaply. Their book *Technology Management* sells for $120, which still seems like a bargain when compared to their *End-User Computing Management Text* that goes for $511.20—which isn't unusual for highly researched texts. These books are not intended for the average consumer, of course.

The Auerbach Publications division caters specifically to information systems people in business industry and government, with books designed to help "manage computer technology effectively." Despite the not-so-little monetary investment, all the WG&L and Auerbach books are practically risk-free, backed by a 30-day review period.

Company
Warren, Gorham & Lamont & Auerbach (New York, NY)

Where
CompuServe

Shortcut
Go *wgl*

Email (via CompuServe)
71154,1163

Email (via the Internet)
71154.1163@compuserve.com

Prices

From approximately $100 to as much as $500 or more.

International orders are accepted.

Reach out and touch the future at the Science Fiction Shop.

Science Fiction Book Shop

The Science Fiction Shop describes itself as "an international mail-order outlet for virtually all science fiction, fantasy, and supernatural horror paperbacks and hardcovers, audiocassettes, and graphic novels...carrying most small press and specialty publishers and magazines."

The store has been in business for more than 20 years and carries over 6,000 titles—which accounts for most everything in the sci-fi category.

Their longevity is reflected in their inventory, with stock that goes back for years. Enthusiasts will appreciate this when searching high and low for volume 2 in a 4-part series.

As an added bonus, the staff is extremely knowledgeable, partly because they have a special affinity for the subject, many being Science Fiction writers themselves.

Company

Science Fiction Shop (New York, NY)

Where

World Wide Web

Web Address

`http://www.tagsys.com/Ads/SciFiShop`

Reminder! This Web address is case sensitive. Type in the address *exactly* as shown.

Prices

$3.99 and up.

Shipping Fees

These vary, but are very reasonable.

International orders are accepted.

Discount Books

intertain.com is just like a chain bookstore, except that it's online. They carry more than 38,000 adult fiction titles, more than 121,000 non-fiction adult selections, and over 43,000 kids books, which adds up to more than 200,000 texts—making this one of the biggest bookstores on the Internet.

In addition to having a phenomenal selection, intertain.com sells all books at a 10 to 15 percent discount, and that includes bestsellers. If you are a frequent purchaser, intertain.com allows you to establish a personal information profile that significantly hastens the ordering process. The service functions much like a book database. Although there are no graphics that show the book covers, intertain.com offers you search capabilities that are a snap to use.

Discount Books (continued)

All you do is: Search for a specific author and title, and you will then get a list of all the particulars of matching titles, including publication date and physical description (size and page count), along with the suggested retail price and the discount price.

If you want to buy rather than browse, intertain.com is a wonderful service that combines the convenience of home shopping, the inventory of a book distributor, and prices of a discount chain.

Shopping on the Internet and Beyond

Exclusive Deal

intertain.com

$5 off any order of $25 or more (up to a 25 percent savings).

Exclusive deal for readers of this book only! You must mention this offer when you place your order.

Company
intertain.com (Sudbury, MA)

Where
World Wide Web

Web Address
http://intertain.com/

Email
store@intertain.com

Prices
From 10 percent to 25 percent off retail.

Shipping Fees (in the U.S.)
Actual charges. No handling fees.

International orders are accepted.

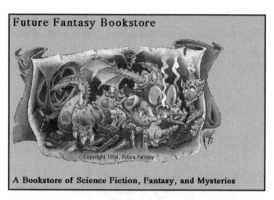

Future Fantasy Bookstore

Copyright 1994, Future Fantasy

A Bookstore of Science Fiction, Fantasy, and Mysteries

Even monsters are welcome at the Future Fantasy Bookstore.

Fantasy Books and Mystery Books

The Future Fantasy Bookstore is chock full of fantasy, mystery, and science fiction titles (12,000 in all). Such specialization allows the store to "give high-quality knowledgeable service," and enough rapport with authors to get them to sign their works.

The online catalog is extensive and searchable by all sorts of criteria. If you prefer to browse, be sure to check out their online newsletter, which gives some reviews that may guide to you to the books you will enjoy most.

In addition to books, you'll find fantasy games, Windstone Edition statues (check out the "Gargoyles Hatching from Eggs" and the "Chinese Unicorns"), T-shirts (my favorite: "Competitive? Who, Me?" with two knights hacking at each other), audio cassettes ("The Klingon language tapes"), and the famous Darwin fish bumper sticker (the "funny looking fish with legs, named Darwin"), which happens to be their biggest-selling single item.

Fantasy, Mystery Books (continued)

Company
Future Fantasy Bookstore (Palo Alto, CA)

Where
World Wide Web

Web Address
http://www.commerce.digital.com/paloalto/
FutureFantasy/home.html

Reminder! This Web address is case sensitive. Make sure you enter it *exactly* as shown.

Email
futfan@netcom.com

Prices
$2.95 and up.

Shipping Fees (in the U.S.)
Actual costs. No handling charges.

International orders are accepted.

The MIT Press
On-line Catalogs

The place to go for unMITigated cerebral core texts.

MIT Press

The MIT Press Online Catalog is the place to buy any of the 2,000 MIT Press books and 31 journals they publish. The well-organized site is complemented by a searchable electronic catalog.

The subject and titles are just as "brainy" as you would expect, focusing primarily on the sciences, although there is also a respectable collection of art and literature.

In addition to MIT Press' print offerings, you can also purchase MIT Press merchandise, which includes baseball caps, sweatshirts, tote bags, and writing implements. Talk about specialty merchandise; where else could you find the coveted "Structure and Interpretation of Computer Programs" T-shirt?

(You might note that this store is devoted exclusively to the MIT *Press*, which is not the same as the MIT *Bookstore* that serves the general campus and offers no Internet access.)

Company
MIT Press (Cambridge, MA)

Where
World Wide Web and email

Web Address
http://World Wide Web-mitpress.mit.edu/

Reminder! This Web adddress is case sensitive. Make sure you enter it *exactly* as shown.

Email
mitpress-orders@mit.edu

Instant Information
Send email to: mitpress-catalogs@mit.edu

Prices
Orders delivered to outside North America are billed 20 percent above the book prices shown.

Shipping Fees
Reasonable. Price based on destination and method.

International orders are accepted.

What happens when you go fishing for books online?
You get BiblioBytes, of course.

Electronic Books

The first question the BiblioBytes home page asks is "Have you ever bought a book from thousands of miles away and started reading it minutes later? Forget 'You Will'—You Can."

How do they accomplish this? By selling electronic versions (text files) of popular titles. This has got to be the fastest order fulfillment around. You just select your book, email them your payment information (they were one of the first to use a highly praised encryption system), and minutes later you are emailed your selection (in your choice of file format, the most common of which is ASCII). Load the file into your favorite word processor or text editor, and start reading!

BiblioBytes owns the electronic rights to over 1,000 titles and is getting them online as quickly as possible. The choices span every genre, including mystery, science fiction, romance, fantasy, erotica, and classics.

Think of how handy this can be! Did your significant other just do something unthinkable? Well then, jump online and order George Hayduke's classic *Getting Even*—and have your revenge plan plotted long before the revengee's pizza arrives.

Shopping on the Internet and Beyond

Exclusive Deal

BiblioBytes

Buy one, get one free.

Exclusive deal for readers of this book only!
You must mention this offer when you place your order.

Company
BiblioBytes (Hoboken, NJ)

Where
World Wide Web and email

Web address
`http://www.BB.com`

Email
`catalog@bb.com`

Instant Information
Send email to: `info@bb.com`

Prices
From $2.95 to $20.00.

Shipping Fees
None. All orders are fulfilled electronically.

International orders are accepted.

Look for an entire "free stuff" section loaded with previews and other goodies.

For More...

See the next page for additional sites for more great shopping opportunities related to books.

Honorable Mentions

in the category of

Books

Automotive Repair Books

Look here for how-to books on automotive repair and maintenance.

Company
S.S. Publishing

Web Address
http://www.amug.org/~a165

Books, Magazines, and Newsletters
(America Online)

Private party ads for books, magazines and newsletters on America Online.

America Online
Keyword *classifieds* then select *general merchandise boards*

Books, Magazines, and Newsletters
(CompuServe)

Private party ads for books on CompuServe.

CompuServe
Go *classifieds* then select *miscellaneous info/merchandise*

Books, Magazines, and Newsletters
(Prodigy)

Private party ads for books and magazines on Prodigy.

Prodigy
Jump *classifieds* then select *browse ads*

Business & Office

With these designer business cards, you're really in business.

Photo-Quality Business Cards

Full-color business card printing is now easy and economical with the help of Business Cards by Design. Their "standard-size business cards are printed on high-quality photo card stock and make stunning and lasting impressions."

The company provides a wide selection of designs. Choose one, input the information you want printed, upload your company logo (if you have one and want it included), and you're done.

This Web site includes samples of the company's entire product line, so you'll have an excellent idea of what *your* card will look like.

The designs (probably better referred to as backdrops) are categorized into six groups:

- Designer Series (for specific vocations—for instance, paint cans for painters, hot air ballons for travel agents, and so on)
- Executive Series (graphics intensive—solid marble backgound, for example)
- Monogram Series (graphics with large letters)
- Business Series (incorporates high-quality clip art for vocation-oriented topics, money-related topics, computers, and more)
- Scenic Series (stunning nature backdrops)
- Texture Series (extreme close-ups of everyday items—raspberry fur, dewey rose petal, and other eye-pleasing images).

Business Cards by Design offers custom orders, too. You can have *your* photo added to the card if you like, or you can specify your design. The company can also coordinate your new full-color business cards with an equally impressive, photo-quality Rolodex card or postcard.

Company
Business Cards By Design (Orlando, FL)

Where
World Wide Web

Web Address
http://www.catalog.com/business/BCBD/
Welcome.html

Reminder! This Web address is case sensitive. Make sure you enter it *exactly* as shown.

Business Cards (continued)

Email
pp001902@interramp.com

Prices
Start at $75 for 250 cards.

Shipping Fees (in the U.S.)
Actual charges. No handling fees. Start at $4.

International orders are accepted.

Office Supplies

Penny Wise Office Products is a great alternative if you don't have easy access to an office supply store. Their extensive selection includes most standard office and computer products.

These products are not the cheapest around, but they *are* fairly priced. For example, the price for the laser toner cartridge I use was more than what I pay at my supermarket-size supply house, much less than what I would pay at my "local stationers," and the same price as a chain computer store. If you are not a big supply user and if you factor in the free shipping and the time you'll save by not having to shop in person, you probably come out even farther ahead.

There are no photos, so the most efficient way to use this service is to request their free catalog and then order online by product number.

Company
Penny Wise Office Products
(Hyattsville, MD)

Where
CompuServe

Shortcut
Go *pw*

Email (via CompuServe)
70007,1242

Email (via the Internet)
70007.1242@compuserve.com

Prices
Reasonable.

Shipping Fees (in the U.S.)
Free. Delivery in the continental U.S only.

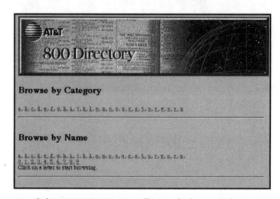

Just dial 1-800-FREECALL. (Actually, I made that up—don't try it.)

AT&T's Free Online 800 Number Directory

The AT&T free 800 number online directory is a windfall for bargain hunters and people who like to comparison shop to get the absolute best deal possible. Let's say you need to rent a car and want quotes from several agencies. Connect to the directory, choose "Automobiles—Rentals and Leasing" as your category and, *voila*, you'll get a list of companies and their 800 numbers. What's the catch? You will only get the numbers of businesses who use AT&T's 800 service. Nonetheless, this is still quite an extensive list.

For instance, the list for "Automobiles - Rentals and Leasing" included Budget, Dollar, National, Enterprise, Hertz, Thrifty, even Rent-A-Wreck *and* Rent-A-Cheap Heap. Each entry included the 800 number, company name, and the main corporate location.

You can seach by category (which number in the thousands), by specific company name, or by reverse search (input an 800 number and find out what company it belongs to). You can even enter a "search string" to find a category or specific company. The directory contains over 150,000 listings and is updated monthly, making it one of the best sources for current, national 800 listings.

Company
AT&T (Parsippany, NJ)

Where
World Wide Web

Web Address
http://att.net/dir800

Email
dir800@mail.att.net

Special Note
This entire site is a freebie.

Discount Long Distance Telephone Rates

I'm the queen of long-distance calling, with bills that have such a high page count I could publish them as a phone book. The upside is that I know good rates when I see them and AmeriCom has outstanding rates, particularly if you do a lot of daytime long-distance calling—interstate or intrastate.

AmeriCom services residential, business, and international callers. They also offer 800 service, discount calling-card plans, international callback, dedicated line service, and even ISDN connections. There are no monthly service fees, billing is based on six-second increments, and there is no surcharge for calling-card usage.

And you won't have to dial an access number, either. AmeriCom becomes your long-distance carrier just as if they were AT&T or MCI. In fact, your calls will probably be routed through one of these systems; AmeriCom basically functions as a broker. They buy huge chunks of time from these name-brand carriers and get great discounts. They then sell the time to you at a slight markup. So, you are getting high-quality fiber optic service at attractive rates.

Online you will find comparison charts, for all of AmeriCom services, which clearly show your savings over other services. Personally, I compared my "circle" plan, which had a decent per-minute charge (the best I could get with any major carrier) and found I could cut my bill an additional 35 percent by using AmeriCom for my *daytime* calling.

When you access AmeriCom's Web site, I recommend you print their guide to choosing a long-distance carrier, which I found to be informative and reasonably objective.

Shopping on the Internet and Beyond

Exclusive Deal

AmeriCom Long Distance
Debit calling card with 30 min. prepaid calls in the continental U.S. with a Domestic or Business Long Distance Service order.

Exclusive deal for readers of this book only!
You must mention this offer when you place your order.

Discount Long Distance (continued)

Company
AmeriCom Long Distance
(Salt Lake City, UT)

Where
World Wide Web and email

Web Address
http://www.xmission.com/~americom/

Email
sales@AmeriCom.com

Instant Information
residential@americom.com

business@americom.com

international@americom.com

International orders are accepted.

A free area code "decoder" database is available online, which allows you to look up local area codes, country codes, and city codes worldwide.

For that special, added touch, say it with cedar.

Wooden Business Cards

Can you imagine throwing away a solid wood business card? Well that's the idea behind CAG's

product: Give people something they'll want to hang on to or would feel guilty discarding.

Now, if you work in the wood business you can get double the impact from these cards, which is why people in construction, paper sales, cabinet making, and other similar industries are some of CAG's most frequent customers.

By the way, these cards are not just black ink slapped on a piece of pine. You have literally over 100 woods to choose from (all of which you can view at the company's Web site.) Start at the top, with the alders and ashes, and finish with weeping willows and Northern white woods. Note that the company discourages the use of porous woods, such as oak, due to the open grain, which absorbs ink from the surface.

In additon to business cards, CAG can also print wooden postcards. In fact, they also offer a special service to print on 8-1/2"×11" pieces of wood (standard paper size), which they suggest for resumes or restaurant menus. And, if you need to redo any of your imprinted wood products, you can always use the previous version as kindling!

Shopping on the Internet and Beyond

Exclusive Deal

CAG Company

15 percent off your first order.

Exclusive deal for readers of this book only!
You must mention this offer when you place your order.

Company
CAG Company (Rowlett, TX)

Where
World Wide Web

Web Address
http://www.connect.net/hollovar/ab.htm

Wooden Business Cards (continued)

Email
`hollovar@connect.net`

Prices
$110 for the first order of 200 cards. Reorders are $70.

Shipping Fees (in the U.S.)
$5

International orders are accepted.

 Free sample via snail mail with self-addressed stamped envelope.

Online Company Incorporation

In today's world of sole proprietorships and other small-business endeavors, it is imperative that owners protect their assets and cover their liabilities. For most companies, the solution is to incorporate—but doing so can be prohibitively expensive and the paperwork can be time consuming. With The Company Corporation, however, the entire process can take eight minutes to complete at a cost of $45 to $100 (plus state filing fees). And, if you incorporate in Delaware, your application can be completed in 48 hours.

The Company Corporation has been around since 1972 and has incorporated over 130,000 businesses online and offline.

Their CompuServe and Prodigy presence and World Wide Web site offer a feast of information about incorporating in general. In one visit, you will learn about the four types of corporations, the advantages of incorporating in Delaware, and commonly asked questions about the incorporation process. You can even view a sample, completed incorporation form.

Even though you have the option of registering online, The Company Corporation prides itself on its customer-focused service, and assures its clientele that a well-trained human is behind the faceless screen, handling your paperwork dependably and thoroughly.

Shopping on the Internet and Beyond

Exclusive Deal

The Company Corporation

10 percent off incorporation fees.

Exclusive deal for readers of this book only! You must mention this offer when you place your order.

Company
The Company Corporation (Wilmington, DE)

Where
CompuServe, email, Prodigy, and World Wide Web

Shortcut (via CompuServe)
Go *corp*

Shortcut (via Prodigy)
Jump *the company corp*

Web Address
`http://incorporate.com/tcc/home.html`

Email
`corp@incorporate.com`

Prices
$45 for Delaware. $100 in other states, plus the state's filing fees.

International orders are accepted.

 A Free Guide to Incorporating via snail mail is available upon request.

One of dozens of unique promotional gift ideas from Advantage Solutions.

Advertising and Promotional Specialites

If you've been considering a promotional push for your company via imprinted advertising specialities. you'll be thrilled to know about Advantage Solutions. Advantage carries all the standard promotional goodies—such as mugs, pens, magnets, and key chains—but also offer some innovative items. My three favorites are the Stress Ball, the People Feeder, and the Cuddle Socks.

Stress Balls are soft, pliable polyfoam spheres the size of a plum, which are designed to be repeatedly squashed in your hand to remedy built-up palm and "digital" tension. They come in an assortment of colors, including a globe print motif.

If you are a trade show exhibitor, the People Feeder will have attendees eating out of your hands. It's basically a hanging bird feeder that you fill with M&Ms. The feeders come in yellow, blue, and green and are a remarkably low-cost giveaway as at little as $2.40 each when purchased in large quantities. Highly recommended as promotional material for environmental or nature-related product.

If your business is in a cold-weather area, Cuddle Socks might be the perfect winter premium. They are a one-size-fits-all 16" tube sock made of synthetic fibers lined with brushed fleece. You can imprint the sole, the front of the sock (copy reads toe to heel), and/or the calf (copy reads top to bottom).

If your budget restricts your purchasing options, turn to Advantage's "Ten Best Buys" of the month for their best deals.

Shopping on the Internet and Beyond

Exclusive Deal

Advantage Solutions

One free "stress ball" *plus* 5 percent off your first order.

Exclusive deal for readers of this book only! You must mention this offer when you place your order.

Company
Advantage Solutions (Brooklyn, NY)

Where
World Wide Web and email

Web Address
http://www.bestbuys.com/bestbuys

Email
alsil@phantom.com

Prices
Quantity based.

Shipping Fees (in the U.S.)
Actual charges. No handling fees.

International orders are accepted.

Remember!

For periodic updates of this books, send email to *shop@easton.com*. See *Introduction* for more details.

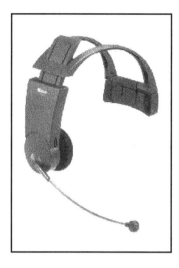

One of Hello Direct's cool communication tools: the world's only cordless heasdset.

Telephone Productivity Tools

"Stop scrunching" is the goal of Hello Direct, which offers an extensive line of what they call Telephone Productivity Tools: headsets, telephones, telephone amplifiers, cellular accessories, telephone recording devices, and more.

What makes Hello Direct stand out is their quality merchandise. Some of their products cost more than you might expect, but that's simply because everything they offer is the highest quality available. And, if you find the same product elsewhere for less within 30 days, they will refund the difference.

Hello Direct customer service is also outstanding. They have a group of representatives known as their "Custom Care Team." These are well-trained, personable folks who know their products and are honest about what they sell.

I bought a cordless headset that I thought provided good but not great sound. My friends had the same reaction. I live in a vortex of electrical power lines, which was causing interference.

What impressed me is that the Hello Direct representative I spoke to after I bought the headset told me frankly that the product didn't sound good enough to her. In fact, she insisted I return it for a (much less expensive) model whose features wouldn't conflict with the power lines. She was right. (Be sure to place your order with Loann at extension 4213.)

Hello Direct carries literally every telephone-related accessory imaginable. When you go to this Web site, you'll find most of their products represented, with pictures and comprehensive descriptions. If you crave more freedom while on the phone, you will probably find your solution at Hello Direct.

Shopping on the Internet and Beyond

Exclusive Deal

Hello Direct

10 percent off all orders (not just the first one). You must mention *keycode net3* to receive the discount. Not valid with any other discount.

Exclusive deal for readers of this book only! You must mention this offer when you place your order.

Company
Hello Direct (San Jose, CA)

Where
World Wide Web and email

Web Address
http://www.hello-direct.com

Email (via the Internet)
xpressit@hihello.com

Email (via CompuServe)
74577,425

All the paper that's fit to print on.

Specialty Paper and Presentation Supplies

In 1988, PaperDirect debuted something no one had ever seen: specialty paper. These aesthetically pleasing, professionally designed, full-color paper stocks were for use with your laser or ink jet printer (even a photocopier) to create a totally professional look without the expense of professional printing.

Today, PaperDirect remains the forerunner in a market of imitators. It's no secret why. They offer the best quality products and the most innovative designs. All of their layouts are created in-house and the company is constantly adding new items to their already impressive catalog.

PaperDirect currently has over 3,000 products, which include 1,500 papers and hundreds of predesigned styles exclusive to PaperDirect. You can choose from a host of options, including brochures, envelopes, business cards, certificates, complete presentation sets, and glossy paper frames.

The PaperDirect product line will not only grab your customers' attention, it will save you hundreds of dollars as well. This is especially true if your business has to cope with continual change. If you need only a smattering of printed materials, or if you just want the flexibility to customize all of your marketing materials so that you always have a perfect fit with your customer, PaperDirect is paper-perfect.

Shopping on the Internet and Beyond

Exclusive Deal

PaperDirect

10 percent off your first order.

Exclusive deal for readers of this book only!
You must mention this offer when you place your order.

Company
PaperDirect (Secaucus, NJ)

Where
World Wide Web

Web Address
http://mailorder.com/paperdirect

Shipping Fees (in the U.S.)
$7 flat fee per order. $1 extra for FedEx.

International orders are accepted.

Free! Free catalog upon request.

Professional Telephone Voice Prompts

Not a day seems to go by without my being subjected to at least one automatic phone answering system, which I less-than-fondly refer to as "voice jail." I'm prepared, though, because I use a legal-size pad to note the index of choices offered by the answering system. But I'll never understand the process by which companies decide *who* gets to be the voice on the line. Often these "greeters" do not reflect professionalism or stature.

The Vox Box recognized this problem and has solved it with super high-quality telephone voice productions for messages on hold, voice mail, automatic call distributiors, automated attendants, and 800 and 900 numbers.

Vox Box strongly believes that a well-produced "message-on-hold can show your callers courtesy, entertain them, and inform...while enhancing your company image, decreasing hang-ups, and answering customers' most frequently asked questions." They also point out that if you have a radio playing on hold it's not only illegal but you run the risk of a customer hearing a commerical for the competition while waiting on *your* phone line.

Vox Box's prices are quite reasonable and suited for small business. They provide a smart way to make a less-than-large company sound bigger and far more established. Conversely, if you have a large business, these messages can make you sound much more friendly and service-oriented.

If your company has an international clientele, the Vox Box can produce voice prompts and messages in English, French, Spanish, and Italian.

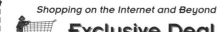

Shopping on the Internet and Beyond

Exclusive Deal

Vox Box

10 percent off your first order.

Exclusive deal for readers of this book only!
You must mention this offer when you place your order.

Company
Vox Box (Quebec, Canada)

Where
World Wide Web

Web Address
http://www.pubnix.net/~evan/

Email
evan@pubnix.net

Prices
Quoted based on job size and variety of services requested. Note that prices listed online are in Canadian dollars.

International orders are accepted.

 Free downloadable messages-on-hold and voice prompts are available.

Up-to-Date Demographic Profiles

We information-age folks often swim in a sea of statistics, and sometimes these numbers can be very helpful in evaluating the best place to establish a business, or in providing an insight into a neighborhood you are considering moving to.

UpClose publishing offers inexpenisve demographic profiles "packed with more than 250 statistics and five graphs into two letter-sized pages. The data is derived from the 1990 U.S. Census and updated with estimates for the years 1994 and 2000." Their database covers over 63,000 cities, towns, counties, metropolitian areas, and states.

As a sample, I checked out a profile of the city where I live, which I found quite enlightening. It was humbling to learn that over 50 percent of my neighbors make *significantly* more money than I do and that there are 6 percent more women than men. On the plus side, my age group has the largest population and my rent is $130 per month less than other residents.

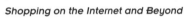

Demographic Profiles (continued)

Even if you don't have a directly applicable use for these reports, I recommend that just for the fun of it you order one for your hometown to see how you compare to the Joneses. The reports are inexpensive and instantly delivered via email or fax.

In addition to two-page profiles, UpClose sells hardbound and data-on-disk demographic digests and a statistical atlas on CD-ROM, which provides 9.5 million statistics for 123,00 areas in the U.S.

Shopping on the Internet and Beyond

Exclusive Deal

UpClose Publishing

Get a free report with your first paid report.

Exclusive deal for readers of this book only!
You must mention this offer when you place your order.

Company
UpClose Publishing (El Granda, CA)

Where
World Wide Web

Web
http://www.upclose.com/upclose/

Email
info@upclose.com

Prices
$5.95 for their two-page demographic profiles.

Shipping Fees (in the U.S.)
Electronic delivery is free. $2 for faxes.

International orders are accepted.

Free demographic summaries available for any state, metro area, country, or city with a population more than 10,000.

*Now that we've got a virtual law firm, what's next?
Virtual courts and virtual jails?*

Law Firm Online

When Mark Theirman graduated from the Harvard Law School, little did he imagine how he would apply his degree from this prestigious university to technology.

Mark is now the head of The Virtual Law Firm, the first law firm on the Web that literally functions online. You can submit your case online, correspond with your attorney via email, even retrieve legal articles that may pertain to your case.

This is no gimmick. The Web site is beautifully designed and packed with information. In fact, it's got such a professional law-firm feel you can almost smell the weathered wood paneling and oversized leather chairs.

Like any notable law firm, The Virtual Law Firm employs well-educated, experienced attorneys who are sought out for their specialties. However, given the firm's Internet connection, they are able to cover many more jurisdictions than a standard firm ever could, including foreign countries. (Also note that they do not accept personal injury cases, a fact which, in my mind, buttresses their credibility even further.)

The advantages of an electronic firm are quite notable. This team of attorneys uses technology to serve their clients using the latest database research tools, transcript summary software, and electronic mail "to help solve legal problems quickly, creatively, and cost effectively."

Law Firm Online (continued)

When visiting their site, check out the Internet Arbitration section. Here you will find information and forms for Low Cost Dispute Resolution so you can avoid costly litigation.

Now all we need is a virtual Judge Ito.

Shopping on the Internet and Beyond
Exclusive Deal

The Virtual Law Firm

One free answer (in overview form) to any legal question submitted via email. One per person, please. A $68 value.

Exclusive deal for readers of this book only!
You must mention this offer when you place your order.

Company
The Virtual Law Firm
(San Francisco, CA)

Where
World Wide Web

Web Address
http://www.tvlf.com/tvlf

Email
hub@tvlf.com

Prices
Rates range from $135 to $275 per hour.

International orders are accepted.

Free, downloadable legal forms.

Remember!

For periodic updates of this book, send email to *shop@easton.com*. See *Introduction* for more details.

Even the chair fits inside.

Mobile Office

The manufacturers of The Office™ describe this furnishing as "an Electro-entopic Satellite OffiCenter (e-soc). The term Electro-entopic describes ergonomically correct placement, within the unit of electric, electronic, and mechanical components, as well as functional tasks areas."

My description reads like this: The Office is basically a fully contained armoire-looking unit that houses everything you need in an office, including all the electronic and electrical connections, even an ergonomic chair. All you need to supply is a 110-volt electrical plug and one phone jack for complete operation. Since it is housed as a single unit, it is easily mobile. It is truly an extraordinary achievement in furniture, efficiency, and technology.

Mobile Office (continued)

What impresses me most about this concept is the care that has gone into the design and construction. For example, the ergonomic chair is not only beautifully designed, it is virtually guaranteed to stave off any repetitive stress ailment, while also providing support in key areas. If you were to buy a similar chair, if you could even find one, it would cost several hundred dollars.

The Office is especially well-suited for heavy computer users, and includes such features as automatic intake and exhaust fans to prevent computer overheating and a powerful APC BackUPS uninterruptable power supply to protect your computer against power failures.

Although the Summerland Company could have made this unit much cheaper, they wanted to build the highest-quality, most durable unit possible—and with this unit, you get what you pay for.

To fully appreciate the breadth of features, visit their Web site or email them for a brochure.

Shopping on the Internet and Beyond

Exclusive Deal

The Summerland Group

$100 off the purchase price.

Exclusive deal for readers of this book only!
You must mention this offer when you place your order.

Company
The Summerland Group (Summerland, FL)

Where
World Wide Web

Web Address
http://www.gate.net/the-office/

Email
summer@gate.net

Prices
Starting at $3,495.

Shipping Fees
$200 to anywhere in the continental U.S.

International orders are accepted.

For More...

For more great business shopping opportunities, see the next page.

Honorable Mentions

in the category of

Business & Office

Advertising and Promotional Materials

Private party ads advertising and promotional materials on CompuServe.

CompuServe
Go *classifieds* then select *business services/investment*

Business Equipment and Services

Private party ads for business equipment and services on CompuServe.

CompuServe
Go *classifieds* then select *business services/investment*

Business Opportunities

Private party ads offering money-making opportunities on Prodigy.

Prodigy
Jump *classifieds* then select *browse ads*

Business Opportunities

Private party ads for business services on Prodigy.

Prodigy
Jump *classifieds* then select *browse ads*

Career Opportunities

Private party ads, on Prodigy, offering career opportunities.

Prodigy
Jump *classifieds* then select *browse ads*

Consulting Services

Private party ads for consulting services on CompuServe.

CompuServe
Go *classifieds* then select *business services/investment*

Employment

Private party ads offering employment opportunities on Prodigy.

Prodigy
Go *classifieds* then select *business services/investment*

Events, Seminars, and Conferences

Private party ads for events, seminars, and conferences on America Online.

America Online
Keyword *classifieds* then select *general merchandise boards*

Financial Services

Private party ads for financial services on CompuServe.

CompuServe
Go *classifieds* then select *business services/investment*

Home-Based Businesses

Private party ads, on CompuServe, promoting home-based businesses.

CompuServe
Go *classifieds* then select *business services/investment*

Home-Based Businesses

Private party ads for work-at-home opportunities on Prodigy.

Prodigy
Jump *classifieds* then select *browse ads*

Investments, Credit, and Money Services

Private party ads for financial services on CompuServe.

CompuServe
Go *classifieds* then select *business services/investment*

Legal and Investigative Services

Private party ads for legal and investigative services on CompuServe.

CompuServe
Go *classifieds* then select *business services/investment*

Marketing Opportunities

Private party ads for multi-level marketing opportunities on CompuServe.

CompuServe
Go *classifieds* then select *business services/investment*

Phone Services

Private party ads for business phone services on Prodigy.

Prodigy
Jump *classifieds* then select *browse ads*

Publishing, Mailing, Phone and Fax

Private party ads for standard office products on CompuServe.

CompuServe
Go *classifieds* then select *business services/investment*

Selling Businesses

Private party ads for those wanting to sell established businesses on CompuServe.

CompuServe
Go *classifieds* then select *business services/investment*

Catalogs & Department Stores

This attractive feeder from the Nature Company is a great draw for our tiniest of feathered friends.

The Nature Company

If you're looking to enhance "your observation, understanding, and appreciation of the natural world," then The Nature Company's online catalog is the first place you should browse. In keeping with their naturalist theme, they feature high-quality telescopes, nature videos, and field vests, in addition to some fun bird products.

For example, if you want hummingbirds to flock to your home, consider their "bright red plastic feeder that mimics the color of the tubular flowers they like best." Since a hummingbird breaks for only 15 minutes between meals (a concept adopted by many cruise ship companies), they will immediately gravitate to your hanging buffet.

If you care to display the end result of your generous nourishment, consider The Nature Company's Bird Droppings T-shirt. This sarto-

rial homage "bears the distinctive signatures of twenty bird species and graphically illustrates the humorous side of bird lore."

The prices for The Nature Company products online are the same as those in their catalog. As with all purchases from catalogs in the 2Market section of America Online, your order is processed and shipped directly from the company whose catalog is online.

Company
Nature Company

Where
America Online

America Online
Keyword *2market*, select *collections* then *nature*.

10,000 Free Catalogs

The Catalog Mart has no problem justifying their claim that they are the "easiest, fastest, and most direct way to receive just about any catalog offered in the United States today." With over 800 topics representing more than 10,000 catalogs, they must be the hands-down winner.

And they've made the ordering process incredibly simple. Sashay over to their Web site, complete the six-line customer questionnaire, and start clicking on categories that interest you.

These three features help make this service exceptional:

- *Well-delineated categories.* For example, instead of a general Home Building and Improvement category, they've broken this broad area into 17 sub-categories. This way, if your interest is strictly paint or paneling, you won't get pelted with catalogs for siding or stucco.

- *The depth of the selection.* You can find catalogs on virtually any topic, including such hard-to-find groupings as boccie, boomerangs, chair caning, choir gowns, left-handed golf equipment, matchbook covers, seashells, soap making, sundials, weather vanes, and wirecrafting.

- *The cost.* Perhaps the most amazing feature is that the catalogs are really free. There's no service charge, no handling fee.

Company
Internet Catalog Mart
(Port Washington, NY)

Where
World Wide Web

Web Address
http://catalog.savvy.com/

Email
catalog@savvy.com

Hot Tip!

For 100 percent subjective reviews and opinions of popular consumer products, take a look at ther Usenet Group *misc.consumers*.

Keep your home and family toxin-free with test kits from ESP.

Environment-Friendly Products

It makes sense that Environmentally Sound Products (ESP) is publishing their catalog of environmentally friendly products on the paperless World Wide Web.

This site features their most popular merchandise, focusing on the family and home. Examples include "Indoor Pollution Solutions" (water filters and air fresheners), "Premium Natural Cleaning Products" (soaps for laundry and dishwashing and cleaners for carpet and glass), baby products ("un-petroleum" jelly, talc-free powder), along with an assortment of buttons, bumper stickers, books, and bags promoting environmentalism.

I found ESP's Healthy Home Improvements section especially intriguing. The products they offer in this area neutralize what are often considered highly toxic concoctions, such as paint, furniture wax, thinner, wood stain, sealer, and floor oil.

"Unique" is the operative word at Morley House, which features this tire pressure gauge and portable beach chair, among dozens of other great products.

Environmental Products (continued)

What motivates ESP is their desire to sift through what they consider deceptive and unclear marketing claims to offer "a wide variety of products assured to be the best possible environmental choices"—all of which helps to make *us* the solution, rather than just contributors to the problem.

Shopping on the Internet and Beyond

Exclusive Deal

Environmentally Sound Products

On your first purchase of $7 or more, get 3 months free membership in the ESP Buyers Club.

Exclusive deal for readers of this book only! You must mention this offer when you place your order.

Company
Environmentally Sound Products (Towson, MD)

Where
World Wide Web

Web Address
http://virtumall.com/ESP/ESPmain.html

Email
73770.2127@compuserve.com

Prices
From $1.00 up to $150 (for premium water filters).

Shipping Fees (in the U.S.)
Minimum of $3.50, up to 7 percent of order total.

Direct from Australia

Morley House is an online Australian catalog selling items to complement every aspect of your life: fashion, car care, household, office gadgets, even picnicking paraphernalia.

Among their more unusual products are an authentic Australian personalized port crock, a 16-gauge vinyl, inflatable kayak, a suction cup dent puller, and a USSR mint coin collection.

Morley's Web pages have good clean photos, which are accompanied by plenty of description to help you make accurate purchasing decisions—this level of detail becomes a heck of a lot more important when your purchases are literally traveling halfway around the world to get to you.

With over 21 different areas to navigate, it's worth a trip to Morley House, especially if you are in the mood to browse and want to see what is basically an Australian version of a standard, American direct marketing catalog.

Remember, since this site does originate from down under, the prices quoted are in Australian dollars.

Direct from Australia (continued)

Company
Morley House (Victoria, Australia)

Where
World Wide Web

Web Address
`http://www.sofcom.com.au/Morley/index.html`

Reminder! This Web address is case sensitive. Make sure you enter it *exactly* as shown.

Still a household staple in the 90s, Tupperware is now on the Web, with more containers than you can shake a leftover turkey leg at.

Tupperware

KingsInc, a Tupperware representative, is the first to present the Tupperware Online Catalog.

This staple of American ingenuity and food storage remains on the cutting edge, online and off. Take advantage of their cyberspace presence by hosting your own online Tupperware party.

KingsInc will send you catalogs and order forms or you can have your friends visit the Web site. They simply email you their orders or indicate to KingsInc that you are their "virtual party host."

Once orders are in, via email or Web site, KingsInc will calculate your hostess credit, good for valuable gifts like Tupperware or appliances such as electric carving knives, blenders, and, if you really haul in the orders, a Krups Espresso/Cappuccino machine.

Online, you'll find roughly the entire catalog, pictures and all. And, if this author's request is honored, you'll also find a sound file of the chart-topping Tupperware "burp."

Company
KingsInc (Temple City, California)

Where
World Wide Web

Web Address
`http://www.webcom.com/~kingsinc/Tupperware/`

Reminder! This Web address is case sensitive. Make sure you enter it *exactly* as shown.

Email
`kingsinc@aol.com`

Prices
Same as the catalog prices.

Shipping Fees (in the U.S.)
Actual cost. No handling charges.

International orders are accepted.

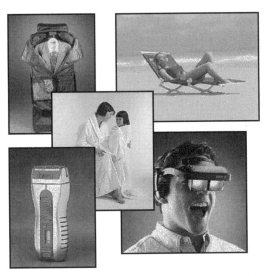

If you've got the money, Hammacher Schlemmer's got the goods.

Hammacher Schlemmer

"Since 1848, Hammacher Schlemmer has been offering products as unique as their name" is how the company defines itself. The products are certainly unique and of outstanding quality. The prices are also steep—not overpriced, just expensive because these are high-quality goods. Shopping at Hammacher Schlemmer is about overall value.

Because you are buying premium merchandise, which they consider the best available, Hammacher Schlemmer backs their products with an "Unconditional Guarantee of Satisfaction...you can return any product, any time for a full refund of your purchase price." And they mean *anytime*—even years later.

To give you an idea of the level of merchandise they carry, take a look at this description of a Genuine Turkish Bathrobe: "...imported exclusively for Hammacher Schlemmer from the ancient city of Bursa, Turkey, famous for its baths and centuries-old towel making industry. Our bathrobe is made of thirsty 100 percent cotton and each square yard of fabric weighs a full 16 ounces and contains 612,000 individual loops to absorb water faster, helping conserve body heat." Price: approximately $100.

Okay, so you can get a high-quality bathrobe elsewhere for half the price. However, if you want the best one in the world (according to Hammacher Schlemmer), this Turkish number has got to be your bath-time buddy.

Hammacher Schlemmer's online catalog is really fun to visit. After awhile, though, you might start to feel as if everything you own—for which they have a counterpart—is simply inferior. On the other hand, this site's a great way to learn about product features you've never considered—like how many loops per inch you should look for in a bathrobe.

Company
Hammacher Schlemmer (Chicago, IL)

Where
World Wide Web, CompuServe, Prodigy, America Online

Web Address
`http://www2.pcy.mci.net/marketplace/hamshlem/`

Shortcut (America Online)
Keyword *2market* then select *collections* then select *hammacher schlemmer*

Shortcut (CompuServe)
Go *hs*

Shortcut (Prodigy)
Jump *hammacher*

Prices
Steep, but fair.

The dancing frog candlestick holder and guitar-shaped CD storage rack are just two of the cleverly designed products available from Spiegel.

Spiegel

The Spiegel catalog, infamous for engraving the ZIP code 60609 into the skulls of Americans born pre-1965, has set its sights on a new address: cyberspace.

Spiegel is currently in two online locations: the World Wide Web and Prodigy, with a slightly different selection at each site.

On the Web you'll find seasonal offerings and gift-oriented items. The selections are separated into toys, holiday, sporting life, pets, fashion, and electronics. By clicking on a particular item, you can see a full-color photo and complete description. Ordering is done offline through an 800 number.

Spiegel on Prodigy allows for electronic ordering. The selection on the national service is a bit different, though. Here you choose from these categories: women's, men's, electronics, home, kitchen, bedding, bath, and luggage.

Also on Prodigy you'll find a Best Bets section, which "offers some key items at their absolute lowest price of the season." Among the sale items

I found Levi 501 jeans at 20 percent off, and an Emerson clock radio at 33 percent off. These are good but not great deals once you figure in the shipping costs, handling fees, and sales tax, which in Spiegel's case applies to 44 out of 50 states in the U.S.

Company
Spiegel (Chicago, IL)

Where
Prodigy and World Wide Web

Shortcut (Prodigy)
Jump *spiegel*

Web Address
`http://cybermart.com/spiegel/`

Prices
Varies by product and category—same as their catalog.

Shipping Fees
Varies based on method (ground, air, freight).

For the snorer who has everything, including a really loud uvula, this snore control device gently wakes up your partner to encourage him or her to shift to a less vocal position.

The Sharper Image

Digital auto drive tie racks. Fingertip pulse massagers. The Deadball. Five-motor relaxor mats. What do these out-of-the-ordinary products have in common? They're all part of the

The Sharper Image (continued)

online Sharper Image catalog in the 2Market section of America Online.

Sharper Image is renowned for their high-tech gadgetry. They can take any life-essential item and revamp it into something electrified, motorized, or computerized.

For example, check out their Sonicare Quadpace toothbrush. No manual, four-bristle row of plastic here. This is the "first high-frequency toothbrush that not only cleans, it programs your brushing...in four distinct zones of your mouth (quadrants). Every 30 seconds, a beep and an interruption in brushing action alert you to move to the next quadrant. Now every area receives carefully timed, consistent attention for improved plaque removal." Sounds effective to me. When you find out this dental wonder costs $149, your gaping mouth will probably never shut—making it all that much easier to properly scour your oral quadrants.

Even though you are shopping on America Online, all items are shipped directly from Sharper Image, therefore when you check out, the amount shown will be for the product only. The shipping charge (based on the option that you choose) and any appropriate taxes will be added when the order is processed by Sharper Image.

Company
Sharper Image

Where
America Online

Shortcut
Keyword *2market*, select *click on collections* then *sharper image*.

Prices
High-end products with high-end prices.

Shipping Fees (in the U.S.)
Varies by order size and method of delivery.

The Yummy Yummy talking fork and spoon can help make those peas and carrots go down a bit easier.

Talking Products

The Speak to Me Catalog is probably the noisiest site on the World Wide Web—as it should be. This collection of clocks, calculators, and other electronics all have something in common: they talk.

This site is the perfect example of how shopping online is better than perusing paper catalogs. The Speak to Me company has taken full advantage of your computer's sound card—and the option to play audio via most Web browsers—by including sound files for all their products.

Interested in the talking Hippo Alarm Clock, but want to hear it first? Click on the sound demo button next to the description, and within moments you'll listen to exactly what you would hear if the actual product were in front of you.

Talking Products (continued)

"Speak to Me" has six sections:

- Personal Electronics (like keychain recorders, talking picture frames)
- Clocks and Watches (including a talking Star Trek alarm clock)
- Calculators and Scales (my weight is one area where I avoid multimedia)
- Fun Novelties ("no smoking" and swearing keychains)
- "Bargain Basement" (close-out deals)
- Things for Kids

In the "Things for Kids" area, I succumbed to the "Yummy Yummy Talking Fork and Spoon" ($9.95) for my toddler-aged nephew. This technological marvel spares parents the tedious task of announcing every inbound bite. By pushing on the utensil's handle, Yummy rotates one of the following four phrases: "Um, that's good," "Open wide, here comes Yummy," "Yummy Yummy special friend...I love you," and "Hey, that tickles. You're so silly."

Actually, you could think of Yummy as one in a series. When you are ready to complement the talking fork and spoon, you can always get the "Brushy Brushy Musical Singing Toothbrush."

Shopping on the Internet and Beyond

Exclusive Deal

Speak To Me

Get a free reusable candle that plays "Happy Birthday" as it burns, plus 5 percent off your first order of $50 or more.

Exclusive deal for readers of this book only!
You must mention this offer when you place your order.

Company
Speak To Me (Renton, WA)

Where
World Wide Web

Web Address
`http://www.clickshop.com:80/speak/`

Email
`seth@halcyon.com`

Prices
From $5.99 to $179.99.

Shipping Fees (in the U.S.)
From $4 to $9, based on order total.

Free paper catalog upon request.

Licensed Merchandise on Sale

Logos Online carries only officially licensed products tied into sporting events, sports teams, or entertainment enterprises (such as movies).

This concept of "officially licensed" is an important point. Because the company must get approval from the license owners (the sports team, the movie company, and so on) to use identifiable artwork, the merchandise is generally of higher quality in styling, durability, and quality.

Hot Tip

Go *emn* on CompuServe for CompuServe's "Mall News," which features updates on special offers from their Electronic Mall merchants. Jump *shopping* to get to Prodigy's "Bargains Galore" menu—a listing of special deals offered by their online merchants.

Licensed Merchandise (continued)

Their prices for this merchandise are (in my opinion) overpriced—except for their close-out items, which are a real deal. Fore example, I found World Cup T-shirts selling for $10 (the youth size was a mere $7), a PageMaster two-piece flatware set for $3.95, and a Lion King hanging globe for $2.25.

For a current list of Logos Online fire-sale items, click on Clearance in their shopping section.

Company
Logos Online (Rye, New York)

Where
Prodigy

Shortcut
Jump *logos*

Prices
High for "non-clearance" items, but clearance merchandise is an excellent value.

Shipping Fees (in the U.S.)
$3.75-$5.50 for UPS Ground. Second day available.

International orders are accepted.

For More...

See the next page for additional sites for more great shopping opportunities related to catalogs.

Honorable Mentions
in the category of
Catalogs & Department Stores

Eclectic Bargains

Outlet for a wide range of quality consumer merchandise.

Company
Good Stuff Cheap

Web Address
http://www.onramp.net/goodstuf/

Email
gsc@onramp.net

Free Catalogs

Browse extensive CompuServe listings of free catalogs. Every topic covered!

Company
Concord Direct

CompuServe
Go *ca*

Email
70007.4600@compuserve.com

Home Shopping Club

The online version of the Home Shopping Club specializing in discounted clothes, jewelry, and housewares on CompuServe.

Company
Home Shopping Values

CompuServe
Go *hsv*

Home Shopping Club Outlet

Great buys on leftover lots from the Home Shopping Network on Prodigy.

Company
Home Shopping Club Outlet

Prodigy
Jump *hsc outlet*

JC Penney Online

Online catalog includes name brand clothing, electronics and housewares.

Company
JC Penney

Web Address
http://www.jcpenney.com/

Prodigy
Go *jcp*

CompuServe
Jump *jc penney*

Marshall Field's Online

Choice gift selections for all occasions and all ages from this renowned department store.

Company
Marshall Field's

Web Address
http://www.shopping2000.com/shopping2000/fields/

Online Superstore

CompuServe outlet for a wide range of quality consumer merchandise. "250,000 items from 1,700 top manufacturers all at up to 50 percent off."

Company
Shoppers Advantage

CompuServe
Go *sac*

Online Superstore

Electronics, sporting goods, housewares, and more.

Company
Damark

Web Address
http://www2.pcy.mci.net/marketplace/damark/

Sundance Institute

Online version of Robert Redford's famed Southwestern themed catalog.

Company
Robert Redford's Sundance Organization

Web Address
http://cybermart.com/sundance/

Email
sales@sundance.net

Clothing

This shirt definitely has the write stuff.

Write-With-Light T-Shirts

In 1979, Seattle artist Steve Voorhees created a truly interactive piece of clothing: The Neo-Video Write-With-Light T-shirt that "lets you wear your own idea in glowing neon light."

"Each Neo-Video shirt is printed with a non-toxic, non-radioactive, light-sensitive ink. By running a lighted pen across the surface of the special video screen, you can draw an endless number of glowing pictures and messages, which slowly fade to make room for more fun with light...a sensation where there's laughter in the dark."

You can use these shirts in two ways: to create light art and shadow art. Light art occurs when you use the supplied penlight flashlight and draw by running the tip over the special surface on the front.

Shadow art is achieved by masking "part of the screen with fingers or objects, exposing it to a bright light, then taking it to a darkened area. Great for shadow puppets and stencils."

The imprints last about five minutes. The inventor likes to think of it as a "personal etch-a-sketch that you don't have to shake to erase."

Perhaps this has a higher calling—the means by which you can play glow-in-the-dark pictionary.

Company
NeoVideo (Seattle, WA)

Where
World Wide Web and email

Web Address
http://adware.com/mall/neovideo/neoshirt.htm

Email
neovideo@adware.com

Price
$19.95

Shipping Fees (in the U.S.)
$2 in the U.S.

International orders are accepted.

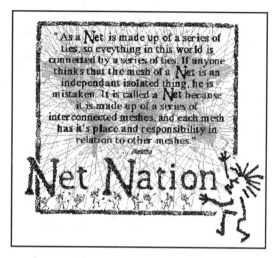

Mighty Dog's philosophy of the Net on the back of their new T-shirt.

Web and Rock Climbing T-Shirts

Mighty Dog T-shirts celebrate the two favorite activities of this business' owners: surfing the World Wide Web and rock climbing.

In the Web category, you will find the Net Surfer logo and a World Wide Web motif that has the Mosaic "S" running through it.

Mighty Dog Designs' Climbing Catalog portion of their Web site includes shirts with titles like "Church of the Rock," and "Only the Hard Survive." There is a philosophy behind these shirts; the company is "committed to producing quality products that reflect the real spirit of the adventurer on this Rock we call Earth!"

Apparently orders are pouring in from around "the rock." Mighty Dog has sold its wares in over 15 countries and 43 states.

Other interesting facts: They sell only sizes large through extra, extra large, citing too little demand for small and medium sizes. "Sorry," they say, "WebWear is for big dogs only."

If you don't have Web access, you can still see Mighty Dog's designs. Simply send them email with the words "send me GIFs" in the subject line, and they will email you GIF pictures of their designs.

Shopping on the Internet and Beyond

Exclusive Deal

Mighty Dog Designs

Three shirts for $39.

Exclusive deal for readers of this book only!
You must mention this offer when you place your order.

Company
Mighty Dog Designs
(Clemson, NC)

Where
World Wide Web and email

Web Address
http://sashimi.wwa.com/~notime/mdd/
mddhome.html

Email
mighty_dog@wwa.com

Prices
$15 for large and extra large sizes. $17 for extra, extra large.

Shipping Fees
$3 in the U.S.

International orders are accepted.

Propellor heads beware: The way-cool crowd is taking over the Net.

Internet Apparel

Net Sweats and Tees have three divisions of Internet clothing: Cyber Wear, Net Rageous, and Web Gear.

Cyber Wear and Net Rageous are similar concepts. Cyber Wear celebrates the Internet in general with such concepts as the "Cybernaut" T-shirt/sweatshirt, which they are establishing as the first official design for Cybernauts Anonymous; the "Windsurfer...a classic, understated expression of the surf metaphor;" and "Navigator...for the Infonaut who can find anything."

The Net Rageous choices are more humorous: "Binocular...a low tech solution for high-speed access," "Penguins," with the expression "Where's the Party," and "Easter Island...remote location is no excuse."

Net Sweats and Tees, as with other T-shirts sites, are an evolving collection. Be sure to stop by periodically to stay current on their new designs.

Company
Net Sweats and Tees (Salt Lake City, UT)

Where
World Wide Web

Web Address
`http://www.icw.com/netsweat/netsweat.html`

Email
`duenorth@icw.com`

Prices
$12.95 to $26.95.

Shipping Fees (in the U.S.)
From $3 to $4.

International orders are accepted.

Tailored Men's Clothing

On their home page Menswear Unlimited starts by citing all the reasons that you should shop with them:

- "Why travel to a store if we can send it to your door?"
- "No hassle returns."
- "Prices lower than sale prices elsewhere...always 25 percent or more below retail."
- "We work hard to please you."

Tailored Men's Clothing (continued)

Tailored clothing online is certainly a new frontier, but this company is happy to take on the challenge. They take a detailed inventory of your size and style requirements and apply them to the custom products you select: suits, rainwear, wool coats, blazers, trousers, and shirts.

All of this is very handy when you need something out of the ordinary such as an unusual size, an extra pair of pants for a favorite suit, or to mix and match sizes (large pants, medium shirt).

But Menswear Unlimited doesn't stop there. They also equip you with all necessary accessories, such as cufflinks, collar bars, suspenders, gloves, scarves, and earmuffs. And, to make sure you're totally satisfied, they encourage special requests.

Buying a tailored suit online might sound a bit risky, but Menswear Unlimited has certainly considered every detail and ordering this way is probably as reliable as having one of their tailors come directly to your door.

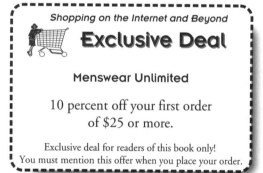

Shopping on the Internet and Beyond

Exclusive Deal

Menswear Unlimited

10 percent off your first order
of $25 or more.

Exclusive deal for readers of this book only!
You must mention this offer when you place your order.

Company
Menswear Unlimited (Baltimore, MD)

Where
World Wide Web and email

Web Address
http://www.clark.net/pub/menswear/suits.html

Email
menswear@clark.net

Prices
From $2 to $250 and up.

Shipping Fees
$5 flat. Varies with international orders.

International orders are accepted.

If the 1994-1995 baseball strike has disillusioned you to the game, send a stern message to the boys of summer with the Salary Cap.

The Official Salary Cap

"What brought baseball to its knees? What's standard equipment in pro football and basketball? What's the one thing the owners always call for?" A salary cap!

However, in this case, the cap is literally a hat. The front has an emblem comprised of a large dollar sign and the words "salary cap." The back of the cap reads "What all the pros play under!"

Remember!

For periodic updates of this book, send email to *shop@easton.com*. See *Introduction* for more details.

The Official Salary Cap (continued)

If you agree with this sentiment, why not wear it? At least that was the thought process for Adam Rockmore, a die-hard sports fan who designed and now sells the hat.

For those of you who share his opinion, the Salary Cap is "one-size-fits-all, and is available in any color as long as it's black. Constructed from a rugged cotton-poly blend, the Official Salary Cap is perfect for professionals and amateurs alike."

The cap is a steal at $9.95 (which includes shipping). Now sports lovers can make a statement using their head with the Official Salary Cap.

Shopping on the Internet and Beyond

Exclusive Deal

Salary Cap!

Buy 12 (for the whole team)
and get one free.

Exclusive deal for readers of this book only!
You must mention this offer when you place your order.

Company
Salary Cap! (Westport, CT)

Where
World Wide Web and email

Web Address
http://www.frymulti.com/thecap/

Email
adamrock@frymulti.com

Price
$9.95

Shipping Fees
Shipping is included in hat price. Additional charges for international orders.

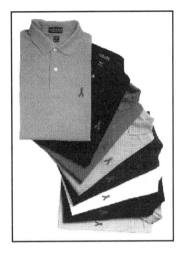

These shirts not only look good, part of the proceeds go toward a good cause.

AIDS Awareness Shirts

"Wear It, Where It Belongs—Over Your Heart." The reference to "It" is a red, AIDS-awareness ribbon that is embroidered on the left side of these high-quality, polo-type shirts.

This is a straightforward deal. These AIDS ribbon shirts come in two styles and eight colors. They all have the red ribbon over the heart against colored fabric of black, navy, jade white, natural, coral, turquoise, or forest green. You can choose between 100 percent cotton mesh (honeycomb appearance) or 100 percent cotton interlock (extremely soft) fabric.

You might consider these shirts more like dressy sportswear. "Both shirt styles include superior detailing with a 2 1/2" spread collar; taped neck and shoulder seams; top-stitched two-button placket; pearl buttons; welted cuffs; and longer tennis tails so they stay where you put them."

Five percent of every purchase goes toward AIDS research. Customers are asked to specify their national AIDS charity of choice when ordering. Note that orders originating from this book will get an extra 5 percent donation. So buy by the dozen!

AIDS Awareness Shirts (continued)

Shopping on the Internet and Beyond

Exclusive Deal

Stonewall Partners

A 5 percent extra donation will
be made on your behalf.

Exclusive deal for readers of this book only!
You must mention this offer when you place your order.

Company

Stonewall Partners (Chicago, IL)

Where

World Wide Web and Email

Web Address

`http://branch.com:1080/united/united.html`

Email

`stonepart@aol.com`

Prices

$29.95 each ($31.50 for XX-L). Minimum order of two shirts required.

Shipping Fees (in the U.S.)

$4.75 each. $1 for each shirt more than two.

International orders are accepted.

Hot Tip

If you stand on the tall side, be sure to visit TallWeb. Here you'll find an international listing of retail and mail-order clothing shops that are not online, but cater to tall men and women. TallWeb is located at:
http://www.planet.net/tallweb/shops.html

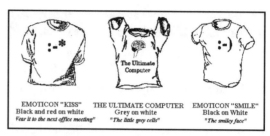

EMOTICON "KISS"
Black and red on white
Wear it to the next office meeting"

THE ULTIMATE COMPUTER
Grey on white
"The little grey cells"

EMOTICON "SMILE"
Black on White
"The smiley face"

A smile is the ultimate universal message, and so are these shirts.

"Smiley" Fashions

Perhaps the biggest difference between people online and those who have never logged on is an appreciation and understanding of "smileys"— punctuation marks that form faces when you turn your head at a 90-degree angle. The most famous and ubiquitous of the bunch is the standard happy face :-)

Smileys, also known as "emoticons" ("emotions" and "icon"), are the centerpiece of the Elswear collection, which celebrates the joys of computing.

While you can get the standard "happy face" smiley imprinted on any of the above, Elswear features some slightly less known emoticons such as the kiss: :-* This white shirt has the colon and dash printed in black with a bright red asterisk. "Wear it to your next office meeting," suggests the manufacturer.

Both the "Happy Face" and "The Kiss" are available on T-shirts, hats, tote bags, sweatshirts, and polo shirts. Keep in mind that these are international symbols. Elswear has shipped orders to Hong Kong, Australia, Switzerland, and Norway.

Of course, wearing or carrying smiley merchandise has the added benefit of identifying true Internauts. If people approach and ask "Why are you wearing a shirt with punctuation marks?" you'll know exactly on which side of cyberspace they dwell.

Company
Elswear (Charlotte, Vermont)

Where
World Wide Web

Web Address
http://branch.com/shirts/shirts.html

Email
elswear@aol.com

Prices
Up to $17 for the T-shirts.

Shipping Fees (in the U.S.)
From $3.50 to $7.50, based on order size.

International orders are accepted.

High Fashion African Clothing

Ujamaa Fashions are high in taste and style but low on price—a combination you just can't beat.

Ujamaa (which means "cooperative economics" in Swahili) is dedicated to creating the finest in African heritage clothing. Their line includes Dashikis with or without embroidery and batik print pants sets for men and women.

Their Unisex Batik print shirt ($15) is really beautiful. It is available in green, purple, or brown as the predominant color, with your choice of varying neckline shapes. Matching pants and hats are also available. All items are 100 percent cotton.

If you are a man in need of an Agbada Suit, Ujamaa offers an elegant four-piece ensemble complete with an embroidered buba for much less than you would expect to pay.

The company is extraordinarily service-oriented. Sylvia Small, one of the principals, guarantees great descriptive information and the best customer attention online or offline.

Company
Ujamaa Fashions (Landover, MD)

Where
World Wide Web

Web Address
http://www.ip.net/shops/Ujamaa_Fashions/

Reminder! This Web address is case sensitive. Make sure you enter the address *exactly* as shown.

Prices
From $15 to $300.

Email
ulamaa@cais.com

International orders are accepted.

That Einstein! What a big palooka!

Hats for Jugheads

"From Jughead to the Dead End Kids, fashion leaders have always appreciated the classic styling of the Palookaville hat. Whether juggling rubber chickens in a brightly colored felt Palookaville, or juggling business meetings in a dressy black leather one, you will always be regarded as a true fashion individual."

Stacey Rosenbaum custom makes these one-of-a-kind hats, and she only makes the Palookaville. They can be constructed from felt, leather, or "cool Guatemalan fabric." Sizes are Big (24"), Mid-sized (22"), and Not Very Big at All (20").

The choices improve with respect to fabrics. If you go for the felt, you can choose up to six colors because the hat is comprised of six panels (although only two or three colors are recommended). Leather fans choose between black and brown (unless you can find a purple cow), while the Guatemalan orders are filled based on the fabrics available at the time of your order. Felt hats cost $20, while leather and Guatemalan hats go for $40.

These classic hats are certainly a novelty. If you like to be the center of attention or if you just want to see if you can revive a fashion trend, consider these Palookaville hats your chance to create your own *haute couture.*

Shopping on the Internet and Beyond

Exclusive Deal

Palookaville Hats

Free shipping on your first order or a $2.50 international shipping credit.

Exclusive deal for readers of this book only! You must mention this offer when you place your order.

Company
Palookaville Hats
(Stacey Rosenbaum, Los Angeles, CA)

Where
World Wide Web and email

Web Address
`http://www.primenet.com/~hanibal/hat.html`

Email
`hanibal@primenet.com`

Prices
From $20 to $40.

Shipping Fees (in the U.S.)
$1.50 each. $2.50 for leather.

International orders are accepted.

Remember!

If you have full Internet access, you also have access to the World Wide Web. All you need is a Web browser, such as Mosaic or Netscape.

If they're too cute to be geeks, they must be Greek!

"Greek" Clothing

You better have some idea of what you want before you visit the Going Greek site. They have such a tremendous selection of fraternity and sorority wearables, you might feel like you're being hazed by the selection.

This is exactly how Going Greek wants it. Their passion is Greek everything. Their custom garment design shop is outstanding. They carry ten types of sweatshirts in 15 colors and five sizes, hats in six styles and 15 colors, shorts and boxers in ten styles and four sizes, even two different Kangaroo Jackets. Add to this their slew of jerseys, long sleeve shirts, tanktops, T-shirts, and tote bags and you get the idea.

It's doesn't matter which sorority or fraternity you hail from, either. "From Alpha Alpha Alpha to Omega Omega Omega, Going Greek has the lettering, colors, and styles to match your chapter traditions." According to the company "...never before have Greeks had such a wide selection of customized merchandise at such incredible savings."

Company
Going Greek (New Brunswick, NJ)

Where
World Wide Web

Web Address
`http://virtumall.com/GoingGreek/custom.html`

Reminder! This Web address is case sensitive. Make sure you enter the address *exactly* as shown.

Prices
From $2 to $200.

Shipping Fees
$4 for the first item and $1 for each additional.

International orders are accepted.

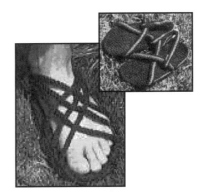

The best in open-air footwear, from the sandal capital of the U.S.— San Diego.

Rope Sandals

Here's something I bet you didn't know: Sandals are one of the most effective ways to take the shape out of your feet. Of course, they are also a cool footwear alternative on hot summer days.

Thanks to The Sandal Dude, you can order hard-to-find rope sandals online, during any season, at a respectable savings of at least 20 percent.

Imported from Mexico, the Dude's sandals come in two-strap and six-strap models. The difference

Rope Sandals (continued)

between them is strictly a matter of taste, as both designs are made of "100 percent polypropylene, are durable, last for years, even with daily use, and are ideal for comfortable casual wear."

The color choices are tan, red, black, and denim. Sometimes their discontinued inventory sports some extra color choices such as blue, red, or pink.

The sizes offered have a wide range. Kids' sizes are available for either gender. Men's sizes go as big as 13 and women's sizes go up to 10 (with the option of converting to men's footwear for the big-footed gal.)

If you're looking for open-air footwear that is somewhat more sophisticated than a plastic "flip-flop," fling yourself over to the Sandal Dude's Internet emporium for the latest in rope shoes.

Company
Sandal Dude (San Diego, CA)

Where
World Wide Web and email

Web Address
http://mmink.cts.com/mmink/kiosks/sandals/ropesandals.html

Email
rdegel@cts.com

Prices
$23.99

Shipping Fees
$3.50.

International orders are accepted.

You'd smile too if you were this comfortable.

Canton Fleece Tops and Bottoms

Werger's cotton apparel offers something I had never heard before: *Canton* fleece. I knew all about polar fleece through my beloved Patagonia collection, so I was intrigued.

According to the company, "100-percent cotton Canton fleece garments have been brushed inside for warmth and comfort and gently dyed. Using the natural elements of water, soft heat, light, and oxygen, garments are woven for durability and processed for comfort." Talk about a pampered fabric.

If you want this quality but don't want to be quite this "soft," Werger offers *textured* Canton fleece garments with a "nubby" feel to them. All the clothing is dyed after it is sewed. You can go the *natural* white route, or opt for a color or a pigment (the pre-washed look).

The Werger inventory is quite extensive. They offer tops and bottoms (shirts, pants, sweatshirts, and so on) in "long" styles for autumn and winter and "short" styles for spring and summer.

Fleece Tops, Bottoms (continued)

If you love to feel like the outside of a stuffed animal, then Werger apparel will be your Teddy Bear line of clothing.

Shopping on the Internet and Beyond
Exclusive Deal

Werger

5 percent off your first order of $25 or more plus a free sample of Zobell moisturizer.

Exclusive deal for readers of this book only! You must mention this offer when you place your order.

Company
Werger (Gilford, CT)

Where
World Wide Web and email

Web Address
http://branch.com/werger/werger.html

Email
werger@aol.com

Prices
From $20 to $34.

Shipping Fees (in the U.S.)
Actual cost of shipping with no handling charges.

International orders are accepted.

Remember!

Access the Web from any major online service. On AOL, keyword *web*. On CompuServe, go *netlauncher*. On Prodigy, jump *web*.

No need to wait until they get their Hanes on you. They're already on the Web, ready to order and ready to wear.

Hanes and L'eggs Outlet

This Hanes/L'eggs site is one of the best deals online. It is actually an offshoot of an extremely popular mail-order catalog that I, and other people I know, have been ordering from for years.

Though the prices are the same as the catalog, the selection does differ a bit from site to site, the most complete being their World Wide Web location. At the time of this writing, CompuServe is offering all the hosiery and intimate apparel but only part, if any, of the Hanes clothing collection.

In terms of hosiery, you'll find the entire Hanes line of pantyhose, which actually encompasses four brands: Hanes, L'eggs, Just My Size, and Color Me Natural. The savings vary by the quantity you order. Overall, however, the discounts go as high as 55 percent on 12 or more pair—but you can buy as few as three pair at a slightly lesser savings.

Hanes and L'eggs Outlet (continued)

Why so cheap? By definition these pantyhose are "imperfect." Now, the company doesn't exactly define imperfect but don't worry. In the years I've been buying from the outlet, I have yet to find even one aberration with any pair of "imperfects."

In addition to pantyhose, you'll find bras made by Bali, Champion, and Playtex, Hanes undies for men and women, and even Isotoner gloves. If you are a fan of Hanes ActiveWear (T-shirts, sweatshirts, sweatpants), you can find these at good prices. Note that all of these items are *perfects,* so the savings are not nearly as substantial.

Company
Hanes (Winston-Salem, NC)

Where
America Online, CompuServe, Prodigy, and Web

America Online
Keyword *hanes*

CompuServe
Go *lh*

Prodigy
Jump *leggs*

Web Address
http://www.shopping2000.com/shopping2000/
sara_lee/index.html#13

Prices
Up to 55 percent off retail.

Hi-Style Men's Undies

It wasn't until I visited the 2(x)ist Underwear for Men home page that I understood how guys

Guys will find this site to be a great place to order, but their significant others will probably enjoy it even more.

must feel the first time they see a Victoria's Secret catalog. Ladies, start your modems.

If the aesthetics of the models—I mean photos—is indicative of the quality of the products, expect to be wearing these undies well into the next millennium.

Research has proved time and time again that underwear has the highest brand loyalty of any retail item, clothing or otherwise. On the chance, however, that you will consider deviating from your beloved BVDs, 2(x)ist is a great place to start.

They offer traditional styles (boxers, button fly boxers, classic fly-front briefs), as well as somewhat racier choices. In this category you will find the Y-back thong and contour pouch brief, the latter being one of their best-sellers (undoubtedly bought by significant others).

According to the company, 2(x)ist products have a different fit, accomplished by means of a three-way gusset that maintains the shape of the rise while allowing the leg opening to conform to the leg size.

All of the products are made of 100 percent cotton and come in basic colors of white, black, or heather grey, depending on the style—but this is the only standard aspect of this fabulous looking line.

Company
Underwear 2(x)ist (New York, NY)

Where
World Wide Web and email

Web Address
`http://www.digex.net/2xist.html`

Email
`2xist@access.digex.net`

Prices
From $8 to $24.

Shipping Fees (in the U.S.)
From $3.50 to $9.50.

For neat feet, try the invincible, indestructible Sea Gull fasteners.

Shoelace Fasteners

Sea Gull lace fasteners have one function: eliminate the need to tie and retie shoelaces—for any brand and any style of shoe.

How they work: "The fastener has back-to-back hinged buckles that fasten laces firmly and neatly. To tighten laces, pull loops; to release, raise Sea Gull's 'wings' and the laces release instantly."

Of course, these fasteners are a great timesaver for the able-bodied, especially athletes. But also consider the advantages for people with arthritis or a disability where tying shoelaces is a cumbersome, perhaps even painful task.

In addition to their functionality, the fasteners can enhance your footwear fashion statement. The fasteners are sold in pairs of three, with four different color combinations:

- Fluorescent green, hot pink, and yellow
- Soft pink, purple, and sky blue
- Dark red, blue, and green
- Black, white, and grey

Even though Sea Gull lace fasteners are made of plastic, they are cited as indestructible. The company dares you to "yank on them, pull on them…beat them with a hammer…remembering of course to remove your foot first."

Company
Sea Gull Lace Fastener
(Honolulu, Oahu, HI)

Where
World Wide Web and email

Web Address
`http://www.pixi.com/fii/home.html`

Email
`seagull@pixi.com`

Prices
$9.95 for three pair.

Shipping Fees (in the U.S.)
$1.50

International orders are accepted.

Shoes fit for a queen, or at least queen-sized feet.

Ladies Shoes Made from Men's Soles

Big-footed women have a real problem. Even if they can find shoes in their size, they are rarely wide enough. The Giallombardo sisters recognized this problem and solved it. Their secret? They use a man's shoe form, which is not only wider, but flatter and generally more accommodating.

Even though men's soles are the basis of the Queen Cushion shoe line, this footwear is as feminine as you can get. Among the company's offerings are: pumps, spikes, boots, flats, ankle straps, sandals, open-toe, mules, evening shoes, even wedding shoes for big-footed brides.

Leather shoes come in nine different colors. The suede ones are available in five colors, including orange, purple, green, and fuchsia pink. Queen Cushion Shoes can also accent any style with extras like beading, feathers, and fake fur trim. A line of matching purses and belts is in the works.

The French-made shoes are distributed to over 17 countries. Cher owns eight pairs from this designer (though not from the large-size line).

In terms of size range, Queen Anne footgear fits gals up to a size 16. (To put this in perspective, the average American woman wears a size 7 or 8.) Many of the styles are available in half-sizes as well.

By the way ladies, keep this site in mind come Halloween. If you've been dying to dress up your guy as a gal, Queen Cushion Shoes will sell you any of its styles in a true men's fit from size 7 to 14.

Shopping on the Internet and Beyond

Exclusive Deal

Queen Cushion Shoes

On your first order, $5 off orders of $125 or less. $10 off orders of $126 or more.

Exclusive deal for readers of this book only!
You must mention this offer when you place your order.

Company
Queen Cushion Shoes (Buffalo, NY)

Where
World Wide Web

Web Address
`http://199.170.0.46/qcs/qcs.html`

Prices
From $125 to $175.

Shipping Fees (in the U.S.)
$7 for up to five pair.

International orders are accepted.

For More...

For more great clothes shopping oportunities, see the next page.

Honorable Mentions
in the category of
Clothing

Clothing, Cosmetics, and Jewelry

Private party ads on America Online for clothes, cosmetics, and jewelry.

America Online
Keyword *classifieds* then select *General Merchandise Boards*

Consignment Clothing

Look here for pre-owned, well-cared-for fashions.

Company
Nine Lives Consignment Store

Where
http://www.los-gatos.scruznet.com/

Dress Shirts for Men

Fine dress shirts for men in every size.

Company
Paul Fredrick

CompuServe
Go *pfs*

Prodigy
Jump *paul fredrick*

Fashion Dos and Don'ts

Look here for videos on fashion-related topics.

Company
InfoVid Outlet

Web Address
http://branch.com:1080/infovid/c306.html

Flyfishing Apparel

Find flyfishing and outdoor clothing and accessories.

Company
Upstream Flyfishing

Web Address
http://www.los-gatos.scruznet.com/los_gatos/
businesses/upstream/storefront.html

Professional Apparel

Find custom business and personal apparel.

Company
Namark Cap & Emblem

Web Address
http://www.accessnv.com/namark/

Sports Insignias

Find insignia wear for all pro and college teams.

Company
TransAmerica Sports Clothing

Web Address
http://www.ceainc.com/TransAm/index.html

Tennis Accessories

For tennis clothing and accessories.

Company
Tennis Shop

Web Address
http://www.cts.com/~tennisa1/

Watersport Fashions for Women

Find a full line of sailing and watersport-related items for women, including wetsuits, clothing, and gloves.

Company
She Sails Catalog

Web Address
http://www.aztec.com/pub/aztec/shesails

Coffee & Tea

Let Ruta Maya take you to the Cuba of long ago.

Cuban-ish Ecuadoran Coffee

The Ruta Maya Coffee Company sells two types of coffee: Ruta Mayan—an Altura, Arabica bean grown by cooperative farmers in the Chiapas region of Mexico—and Cubita, a sun-dried, hand-sorted bean from the Andes Mountains of Ecuador. In fact, Cubita coffee is grown at an elevation of 2,000 meters, which is the closest distance to the sun at the Equator.

Packed in burlap bags, the Cubita coffee is reportedly very similar in taste and aroma to that served in Cuba long ago, hence the name "Cubita."

"Each bag of Cubita contains reproductions of works by famous Cuban artists and brief accounts of other Cubans who have won international acclaim for their achievements in such diverse fields as sports, science, music, and medicine."

The Ruta Mayan coffee is available in a medium roast (smooth, sweet flavor) and espresso roast (less bitter than most espressos), and is sold as whole beans only.

For each pound of coffee that you buy, 2.5 cents is donated to the Ruta Mayan Foundation, and 2.5 cents to the University of Texas Maya Seminar.

Company
Ruta Maya Coffee Company (Austin, TX)

Where
World Wide Web

Web Address
http://www.onr.com/maya.html

Email
ctcexprt@onr.com

Prices
From $7.15 to $9.45 per pound.

Shipping Fees
No handling charges. Quotes based on destination.

International orders are accepted.

Thirty percent of Ash Creek Orchard's earnings are paid directly to the CaPulin coffee laborers in the jungle region of Mexico.

Jungle Coffee

CaPulin coffee, also known as jungle coffee, is like nothing you've ever tasted, according to this company.

Jungle Coffee (continued)

"Capulin is the traditional name given to a particular condition of coffee, coffee that has never been touched by water. None of the finest, most subtle flavors and alkaloids have been dissolved away."

Their coffee comes from a plantation in the Mexico jungle "left almost untouched by modernization, chemical fertilizers and toxic spray techniques."

Thanks to Seth Appell, who lives in a peach orchard in Arizona, people around the world are enjoying this remarkable coffee. In fact, many of his Chinese and Japanese customers are giving up tea for this joyous jungle java.

CaPulin comes in two roasts: Vienna (medium roast) and French (dark roast). Your beans are roasted *only after your order is received*, ensuring that you are shipped the finest, freshest coffee beans possible.

In addition to great flavor, proceeds from CaPulin coffee purchased from Ash Creek Orchards support families directly involved in the "harvesting and handling of these exotic beans. For each pound of coffee sold, at least 30 percent is actually paid toward the labor before any other costs are incurred." The result is one approach designed to help stabilize the economy in this region of Mexico, in the hope that it will deter further forest devastation for short-term profits.

Shopping on the Internet and Beyond

Exclusive Deal

Ash Creek Orchards

Free shipping on your first prepaid order. Or a $6 credit towards international shipping.

Exclusive deal for readers of this book only! You must mention this offer when you place your order.

Company
Ash Creek Orchards (Pima, AZ)

Where
World Wide Web

Web Address
`http://emall.com/AshCreek/AshCreek1.html`

Reminder! This Web address is case sensitive. Make sure you enter it *exactly* as shown.

Email
`capulin@zekes.com`

Prices
Average is $12 per pound.

Shipping Fees (in the U.S.)
$6 per pound for 2nd day air.

International orders are accepted.

NaKuma's Kauai coffees make great gifts.

Estate-Grown Kauai Coffee

You've probably heard of Hawaii's famous Kona coffee from the Big Island, but few people are familiar with the robust pleasures of coffee grown on Kauai. Known as the "Garden Island," Kauai is a much smaller Hawaiian island and probably is most famous as the location used to film *Jurassic Park*.

It's possible that Steven Spielberg chose this Hawaiian land dab just for the phenomenal cof-

Kauai Coffee (continued)

fee produced on its west side? The coffee is grown and harvested at the Koloa Estate, the largest coffee plantation in Hawaii and the largest irrigated coffee estate in the world. In fact, in 1845, Kauai became the first Hawaiian island to have a coffee processing plant.

According to the NaKuma company, the distributors of Kauai Coffee, "most Hawaiian coffees, even when 100 percent, come from several estates that may co-op their coffees. Before it becomes Kauai Coffee, it must meet Hawaii's rigid grading standards, and be 'cupped,' or tasted, by experts who make the final determination on quality."

Only high-quality Arabica beans are used. Quantities can be purchased from a 2.5-ounce trial size up to 5-pound bags of whole beans.

If you are a breakfast coffee drinker, you might consider elaborating on your Hawaiian coffee theme with a jar of Aunty Lilikoi's Incredible Passion Fruit Jelly, also offered at the NaKuma Web site. A far taste from Smucker's, this island morning delicacy is the perfect toast topper to complement your steaming mug of "aloha."

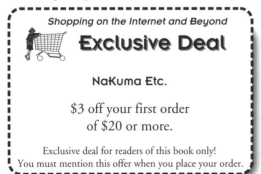

Shopping on the Internet and Beyond

Exclusive Deal

NaKuma Etc.

$3 off your first order
of $20 or more.

Exclusive deal for readers of this book only!
You must mention this offer when you place your order.

Company
NaKuma Etc. (Hanapepe, Kauai, HI)

Where
World Wide Web

Web Address
`http://hoohana.aloha.net/~nakuma/`

Email
`nakuma@aloha.net`

Prices
Average $12 to $13.50 for a 10-ounce bag (other quantities are available).

Shipping Fees (in the U.S.)
All prices include shipping by Priority mail.

International orders are accepted.

Straight from paradise: Hawaii's best coffee.

Hawaiian Coffee and Espresso

When Bob and Arminda Alexander boarded a plane for their Hawaiian honeymoon, little did they know they'd find a new home and a new business. If necessity is the mother of invention, then Maui's need for a good espresso shop was enough encouragement for these now former Seattle residents to invent one. They realized many other island visitors probably feel the same.

Hawaiian Coffee, Espresso (continued)

Shortly after opening their store, the couple decided to open a "virtual" shop on the World Wide Web. The need they anticipated locally extends well beyond the shores of Maui, because their online enterprise has been so successful that they now exclusively sell their coffee on the Internet.

What they offer are "the best coffees from paradise at the best prices."

A sampling of their coffee from the Big Island of Hawaii includes Kona Prime Special (economically priced), Kona Fancy (aromatic, distinctive, and smooth), Kona Peaberry (small round beans that produce an exceptional brew), Kona Organic (certified organic), and Kona Wailapa Organic Kona Estate (voted the best tasting coffee in Kona).

From the island of Maui, you can buy Pure Maui Kaanapali (a limited supply of these Maui beans makes this a unique brew) and Pure Maui Ono Farms Organic Estate (considered the "Rolls Royce" of Hawaiian coffees, grown in the lush Maui region of Hana and priced at $25.99 per pound).

All of the coffees are available in regular or decaffeinated and light roast or dark. "The light roasted coffees are toasted just long enough to lose their graininess but retain the richly toned and sweet flavor. The dark roasts are like the classic European brews; sharp, tangy, and bittersweet."

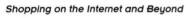

Company
Hawaii's Best Espresso Company (Maui, HI)

Where
World Wide Web

Web Address
`http://hoohana.aloha.net/~bec`

Email
`bobalex@aloha.net`

Prices
From $10.99 to 25.99 per pound.

Shipping Fees
Based on location and quantity. Automatically calculated for you online.

International orders are accepted.

At the Celestial Seasonings Web site, you can order tea, and tea accessories like this attractive tea rack.

Celestial Seasonings Online

Everyone's favorite Sleepytime bear is taking a nap on the World Wide Web. Celestial Seasonings, the forerunner of mass-produced herbal teas, is now brewing in cyberspace, offering all the teas in their popular line.

There are so many choices that the selections have been split into five categories:

- Basic herbal teas
- The newest herbal teas
- After-dinner tea
- Black tea
- Iced tea bags

Because most grocery stores do not stock all of Celestial Seasonings selections, the "newest teas" section should be your first stop. At the time of this writing, I found such hidden treasures as Emerald Gardens ("a mellow green tea with plum and passion fruit"), Orange Mango Zinger ("a tangy burst of sweet orange straight from the grove"), and Country Peach Passion ("an orchard-sweet taste of real peaches with spice").

If you don't mind a little caffeine, you'll probably enjoy Celestial's black teas. Some are fairly mainstream, such as Earl Greyest and Organically Grown Orange Pekoe, while others are quite unique, such as Vanilla Maple and Firelight Orange Spice.

The Iced Tea choices are really fun. In the herbal category you'll find such snappy boxes as Cranberry Razz, Lemon Lime Splash, and Caribbean Oasis. Celestial's flavored black iced teas (with caffeine) include Waikiwi Peach, Sgt. Puckers, and The More Berrier.

Also at the Web site, I discovered Celestial Seasonings merchandise in the form of gift items and apparel. For mugs, tea racks, tea bag holders, sampler packs, and note cards, head to the "gift collection." For Sleepytime nightshirts, Sleepytime bears, Celestial sport caps, and T-shirts, click on Celestial Apparel.

Company
Celestial Seasonings (Salt Lake City, UT)

Where
World Wide Web

Web Address
`http://usa.net/celestial/seasonings.html`

Prices
Prices are the same as in retail stores.

Shipping Fees (in the U.S.)
Vary on order size, starting at $4.50.

Take a tour of the black tea world, all courtesy of Todd & Holland.

Rare Loose-Leaf Teas

If you are ready to venture beyond your routine Lipton, then Todd & Holland tea merchants will be more than happy to expose you to an international selection of the finest choice, rare, loose-leaf teas available. Well known to serious tea drinkers around the world, the company also enjoys serving tea newbies.

Todd & Holland stock over 250 teas, including black teas, assams, niligiris, yunnans, ceylons, darjeelings, oolongs, pouchongs, and green teas.

Loose Leaf Teas (continued)

They also offer some "very special teas," a few of which cost as much as $200 per quarter pound!

But don't let the prices scare you. A quarter pound yields far more than you might think.

"The price reflects their rarity and scarcity. Compared with varietal wines and gourmet coffees, estate teas are very reasonable. Using a very conservative yield of 80 cups per quarter pound, a $40 rare tea costs only 50 cents per cup." That's far less than a mug of joe at Starbucks or a glass of mid-level Chardonnay.

If you're new to the tea world and want to dip your spoon a bit further, consider one of Todd & Holland's four tea tours. A tour works like a tea-of-the-month club, with either a quarter-pound or eighth-pound (your choice) shipped once a month for six months.

One tour ships six black teas over the six months, while another delivers five darjeelings and one sikkim. Yet another focuses on green teas and oolongs. For adventurous tea travelers, Todd & Holland has even put together a year-long "itinerary" that covers every major tea region, including South Georgia black tea (from Old Russia, not the Old South), estate teas from Kenya and Java, choice black tea from Argentina, and even white tea from China.

Since the backbone of Todd & Holland's business is customer service, browse their site first, then email or phone them. They will spend as much time with you as necessary to make sure that your tea fantasies are fulfilled.

Shopping on the Internet and Beyond

Exclusive Deal

Todd & Holland Merchants

10 percent off your first order of $50 or more.

Exclusive deal for readers of this book only! You must mention this offer when you place your order.

Company
Todd & Holland Tea Merchants
(River Forest, IL)

Where
World Wide Web

Web Address
http://branch.com:1080/teas/teas.html

Email
teaman@tea-merchant.chi.il.us

Prices
$20 to $200 (per quarter pound)

Shipping Fees
$4.50 for up to 1.5 pounds (Priority). Quotes for international orders are based on weight and destination.

International orders are accepted.

Remember!

Access the Web from any major online service. On AOL, keyword *web*. On CompuServe, go *netlauncher*. On Prodigy, jump *web*.

Meditate on coffee and be one with the bean—as long as it's certified organic.

Organic Coffee

On his Web site, Jim Cannell, the founder and President of The Organic Coffee Company, lists all the reasons that he went into the organic coffee business. His foremost motivation was to be the best organic coffee distributor in the world, to do so with a conscience, and to have fun while doing it. And when it comes to roasting these pristine beans, he likes to think of it "not as a science, but an art form involving all five senses."

"Dark roasting is an art unto itself. By roasting longer, you burn off coffee's delicate, acidic qualities (and thus more caffeine) and are left with the more full bodied, bolder characteristics. The trick is to know what to burn off and how much. Each coffee we select for dark roast has an optimum dark roast level; once we decipher that (based on taste), we name the roast."

If the depth of the company's inventory is any indication of their progress, The Organic Coffee Company is a rousing success. You can choose from varietals, dark roasts, coffee blends, and decaffeinated coffees, all of which are available retail and wholesale. (A wholesale order requires a minimum of one case of 12 packages or two five-pound bags.)

With respect to the varietals, The Organic Coffee Company "looks for the best organic coffee each region has to offer, batch roasting them to bring out the best possible character." Look for entries from Mexico, Guatemala, Costa Rica, Indonesia, Peru, and Colombia (minus Juan Valdez).

The "Coffee Blends" section is fun to visit, if only for the names and descriptions. The Zen Blend is a combination of Mexican and Costa Rican coffees "roasted full city and balanced for a sweet-tasting brew with a smooth, velvety finish. A dharma coffee experience. Jahva Love is an international, harmonious blend of light and dark roast coffees; exotic and syrupy with a tangy finish...[the] answer to mocha java." And the New Age-type descriptions go on from there.

All orders are roasted and shipped on the same day. All coffees are whole bean; grinding is available for a minimal service charge.

Company
The Organic Coffee Company
(Wareham, MA)

Where
World Wide Web

Web Address
`http://www.bid.com/bid/cybercafe/occ.html`

Organic Coffee (continued)

Email

orgcofco@aol.com

Prices

$5.30 to $17 per pound.

Shipping Fees (in the U.S.)

Based on order price, starting at $4.25.

International orders are accepted.

Need a quick lift? Call Cafe Mam.

"Socially Responsible" Coffee

Cafe Mam (pronounced "mom") wants to do more than just sell coffee. This company wants to hasten the good fight for pesticide reform while helping cooperative farmers in Mexico.

To succeed in "breaking the circle of poison," a percentage of profits is donated to the Northwest Coalition for Alternatives to Pesticides, a leader for more than 15 years in reducing poisons on the planet."

To help the people growing and harvesting the beans they sell, Cafe Mam works with ISMAM (Indigenous Peoples of the Sierra Madre of Motozintla), a cooperative of native Mayan farmers living in the highlands of Chiapas, Mexico.

"ISMAM is organized on egalitarian democratic ideals that stress responsibility to the co-op, hard work and high standards." Have I mentioned that their coffee is also organically certified?

Now that you know the social basis of Cafe Mam's coffee, take a look at what's available. You have a choice of four roasts:

- French, the darkest roast available
- Italian, their original roast
- Espresso, their breed, which is slightly lighter than Italian
- Light Roast, with a "medium body and herbal, flowery aftertaste"

They also offer two blends: Tango, an equal combination of Italian and French coffees, and Viennese, which is three parts espresso/one part French roast.

All blends and roasts are available in regular and decaf (Swiss water process) and are packed in bags that are "natural kraft lined with glassine (recyclable as kraft paper or cardboard.)"

If you prefer to eat your beans instead of brewing them, Cafe Mam also offers chocolate covered espresso beans for a quick perk-me-up on the go!

Company

Cafe Mam (Eugene, OR)

Where

World Wide Web and email

Web Address

http://mmink.cts.com/mmink/dossiers/cafemam.html

Prices

$13.50 for a sample pack. Up to $37.75 for five pounds of decaf.

Shipping Fees (in the U.S.)

Based on destination. There is a chart of shipping fees online.

International orders are accepted.

Settle down, guy. Baltimore Coffee & Tea also offers decaf.

(Almost) 31 Flavored Coffees

The Baltimore Coffee & Tea Company sells plenty of the finest green coffee and more than 500 varieties of bulk and packaged teas. What will amaze you most, however, is their unequaled selection of flavored coffees, 29 of them at last count.

You can select from Amaretto Royale, Apricot, Butter Rum, Cappuccino, Chocolate Cherry, Chocolate Macadamia Nut, Chocolate Raspberry, Chocolate, Strawberry, Coconut Cream, Dutch Chocolate, Egg Nog, French Vanilla, Gran Marnier, Hazelnut Cream, Irish Cream, Peaches and Cream, Pralines and Cream, Seville Orange, Snickerdoodle, Southern Pecan, Rainforest Crunch, Streusel Cake, Swiss Chocolate Almond, Tiramisu, Toasted Nut Fudge, Toasted Almond, Toasted Caramel, and Viennese Cinnamon.

You could think of this company as the Jelly Belly equivalent of coffee (except they don't offer watermelon or cotton candy flavors). And just like Jelly Bellys, you can combine flavors for limitless options. (Egg Nog and Butter Rum might be a good combo.)

All flavored coffees are available in "caf" and "decaf." The decaf is made using the Swiss water process, which "uses no chemicals to remove 99.9 percent of coffee's caffeine. This patented process retains all of the coffee flavor."

Over 40 percent of this company's java sales are from flavored coffees, even though they carry beans from Brazil, Tanzania, the Island of Sumatra, and Ethiopia, as well as other more traditional coffee-growing countries such as Costa Rica, Colombia, and Jamaica.

If you want to add flavor to any of these premium beans, inquire about their selection of world-famous San Marino flavoring syrups.

Company
Baltimore Coffee & Tea Company, Inc. (Baltimore, MD)

Where
World Wide Web

Web Address
`http://www.charm.net/~davew/BCT/BCT.html`

Reminder! This Web address is case sensitive. Make sure you enter it *exactly* as shown.

Email
ucyb80a@prodigy.com

Flavored 31 Coffees (continued)

Prices

Average per pound price is $6 to $9 (except for the highest grades).

Shipping Fees

Actual charges with no handling fees. Shipping fees are quoted when you order.

International orders are accepted.

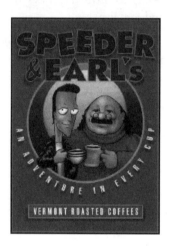

You, too, can benefit from the adventures of Speeder and Earl and the unearthly coffee they've unearthed from around the world.

Exotic Vermont-Roasted Coffees

"It is our heartfelt philosophy that coffee roasting is an artistic endeavor that is the result of interaction between a person, their subject, tools and environment," cites Gordon Blankenburg, President of Speeder & Earl's Roastery. "Vermont has given us a place to practice our art that is inspiring in its purity and beauty and nurturing in its people, many of whom also came here to live a simpler, more principled life."

Speeder & Earl's roasting curve goes from Cinnamon Roast (sometimes called American Roast), which they consider "typical of canned coffees...the taste is usually weak and watery," all the way to Espresso/Italian Roast. ("The heaviest, darkest roast. Almost carbonized.") They will not roast any darker than French roast "because it tastes like burnt toast."

Even though they feel they have perfected their roasting process, the search for the perfect bean continues. Their philosophy is: "We'll go anywhere and try anything. In fact, we try *everything*. That's our job."

Given the origin of some of the coffees these folks sell, you can only imagine how far they've traveled.

In addition to familiar coffee types such as Colombian and Costa Rican, Speeder & Earl's "regular" coffee listings include such hard-to-pronounce varieties as Papua New Guinea Sigri, Yemen Mocha Mattari, Indian Monsooned Malabar, Sumatra Mandheling, and Wiseacres Pluma Hidalgo. You can even find a Sumatra Gayo Mountain Organic (whatever that means).

Also at this well-designed and highly informative Web site you'll find tips on coffee brewing, history, and grinding, as well as extensive listings of everything the company offers.

Shopping on the Internet and Beyond

Exclusive Deal

Speeder & Earl's
Custom Built Coffees

10 percent off your first order.

Exclusive deal for readers of this book only!
You must mention this offer when you place your order.

Vermont-Roasted Coffees (continued)

Company
Speeder & Earl's Custom Built Coffees
(Burlington, VT)

Where
World Wide Web

Web Address
http://www.gryffin.com/speeders

Email
speeder@gryffin.com

Prices
$8.49 to 12.99 per pound.

Shipping Fees (in the U.S.)
Actual charges with no handling fees. Exact amount is quoted when you order.

International orders are accepted.

For More...

For more great coffee and tea shopping opportunities, see the next page.

Honorable Mentions

in the category of

Coffee & Tea

Black Teas

Look here for full-leaf black and black-blended teas. 10 percent of the profits are donated to help children in the fight against cancer.

Company
Republic of Tea

Web Address
http://emall.com/Republic/Tea.html

California Wine Country Roaster

A custom roaster for over 350 restaurants, country inns, and grocery stores throughout California's wine country. Environmentally and socially conscious.

Company
Thanksgiving Coffee Company

Web Address
http://www.northcoast.com/unlimited/
product_directory/thanksgiving/
thanksgiving.html

Chef's Blend

Rich blends and varietal coffees roasted by a gourmet cook.

Company
Jax Gourmet Roasted Coffees

Web Address
http://www.callamer.com/~mwinfo/jax.html

Elite Coffees

The finest elite coffees—premium straights, blends, and flavored.

Company
Cafe Gourmet Coffees

Web Address
http://www.usit.net/cafegour

Email
gbc@uist.net

Espresso Machine

The Formosa espresso machine—the smallest, commericial unit available. All the bells and whistles of its bigger counterparts.

Company
Salvatore

Web Address
http://www.internet-cafe.com/salvatore

Gourmet Coffees

A complete line of regional and flavored coffees, and a variety of blends.

Company
Java Byte

Web Address
http://www.computek.net/jb

Email
javabyte@computek.net

Green Bean Importers

On CompuServe, family owned business in San Francisco—a pivotol import location for green coffee beans.

Company
Coffee Anyone??

CompuServe
Go *cof*

Hawaiian Coffees

A selection of Hawaiian grown coffees.

Company
The Coffee Store

Web Address
http://www.maui.net/shop/mauicofe.html

Hawaiian Coffees

Kona coffee and Kona and Maui blends come to you directly from an Hawaiian coffee plantation.

Company
Maui Coffee Company

Web Address
http://www.maui.net/~kona/mauicof.html

London's Finest

Fresh coffee and teas from the heart of London's world-famous Portobellow Road Market.

Company
The Tea & Coffee Plant

Web Address
http://www.demon.co.uk/london-calling/coffront.html

Roasters

Since 1912. Custom Arabica coffee roasters. Designers of one of the world's most popular roasting machines.

Company
Diedrich Coffee

Web Address
http://www.diedrich.com/

Spinelli Coffees

Quality coffee and tea from their world renowned stores.

Company
Spinelli Coffee Company

Web Address
http://www.bid.com/bid/cybercafe/
spinelli.html

Venezuelan Coffee

100 percent Venezuelan "Tachira" coffee from their plant in Barcelona, Venezuela. So potent you only need three heaping tablespoons for a 10-cup pot.

Company
El Presidente

Web Address
http://www.interlog.com/~drock/ep.html

Collectibles, Crafts, & Hobbies

The one-stop Web shop for all your dragon needs.

Dragons Are Us

"Discover Dragons and satisfy your ultimate dragon fantasy with the world's only all-dragon catalog. Ancient symbols of power, knowledge and inspiration, dragons bring good fortune wherever they appear." And if you want them to appear everywhere, Dancing Dragons has a depth of inventory to accomplish just that goal.

Their selection includes books, posters, puzzles, masks, sculptures, jewelry, and T-shirts as well as personal and household items. Their prints are mystical and engaging, their masks some of the most interesting I've seen.

If your dragon fantasies remained long after hearing of Puff and his friends in Honalee, you probably are a "dracophile," and the Dancing Dragons' Web site will have you fire-breathing with delight.

Company
Dancing Dragons (Arcata, CA)

Where
World Wide Web

Web Address
```
http://www.northcoast.com/unlimited/
product_directory/dancing_dragon/
dancing_dragon.html
```

Email
```
dragon@northcoast.com
```

Prices
From $5 to $3,700.

Shipping Fees
From $4.50 to $14.50, depending on the order size. International shipping fees vary.

Email them for a free color catalog.

If you've ever wanted to clog dance and eat peanut butter at the same time, Auntie Q can help get you started.

Affordable Collectibles

Affordable, neat old stuff is my description of Auntie Q's Antiques and Collectibles.

The emphasis here should probably be more on collectibles than antiques because these are fun items that have as much sentimental value as they do potential monetary merit.

This is especially true in their Advertising Specialties section, which features such memorable pieces as a Shedd's Peanut Butter pail and a Heineken wooden shoe (circa 1950s).

Keep in mind that Auntie Q's usually has only one or two of any particular collectible, which means if you see something you like, grab it.

In addition to packaging and promotional items from times long past, Auntie Q's specializes in depression-era glassware, dinnerware, and lanterns. Other categories include holiday, lighting, paper, and metal antiques.

If you know what you want but don't find it on the Auntie Q's Web site, let them know. "We especially enjoy searching out specific items that people are looking for," boasts their home page, "so send us a detailed list of your antique and collectible wants." In fact, this policy works in reverse as well. Auntie Q's has its own collectibles wish list, and you might just have exactly what *they* want.

By the way, if you're wondering whether there's a *real* Auntie Q (as I did), you probably haven't yet noticed that the company's name is actually a play on the word "antique."

Company
Auntie Q's Antiques and Collectibles
(Albany, OR)

Where
World Wide Web

Web Address
http://www.teleport.com/~auntyq/

Email
auntyq@teleport.com

Prices
From $10 to $150.

Shipping Fees (in the U.S.)
Actual cost plus a small handling fee.

Remember!

For periodic updates of this book and additional discounts, send email to *shop@easton.com*. See *Introduction* for more details.

Now you can use your modem to go dialing for dollhouses.

Dollhouses, Miniatures, and Related Supplies

The Enchanted Dollhouse may be a part of the world-wide network we call the Internet, but this group still maintains its "Mom and Pop" feel. And if you can't make the journey to the retail store nestled in an 1850s Vermont farmhouse, let the World Wide Web bring it to you.

There is something for every room of your dollhouse. In fact, you can visit over 19 different "rooms."

If you build you own dollhouses, you'll find the Lighting Shop and the Village Carpenter & Lumber Yard areas of particular interest, you'll also want to take a look at Electrifying Possibilities and Miniature Toolshop areas too.

In fact, if you know exactly what type of dollhouse you want, but don't have the skill or desire to build it yourself, the Enchanted Dollhouse will put it together for you from blueprints you supply.

If you've already built your dream dollhome, or if your dollhouse interests favor interior deco-

rating, allow yourself plenty of time to browse. You can start with Carpets, continue on to Colonial American Kitchen, and then head upstairs to Bedroom Furniture. After you finish decorating, it'll be time to move in the family. To choose the family members, stop by the Angel Children and Dolls for Sharing Love areas.

Many of these miniatures are genuine one-of-a-kinds and must be seen to be fully appreciated. But any dollhouse lover with fall in love with the Enchanted Dollhouse.

Company
Enchanted Dollhouse
(Manchester Center, VT)

Where
World Wide Web

Web Address
`http://www.together.com/dollhouse/`

Email
`76745.2041@compuserve.com`

Prices
From $1.50 to $2,300.

Shipping Fees (in the U.S.)
Actual costs. No handling fees.

International orders are accepted.

Norma Jean, everybody's favorite poster girl, is now a British West Indies postage girl.

Marilyn Monroe Postage Stamps

Direct from the island of St. Vincent in the British West Indies comes a set of nine postage stamps designed to pay "a worldwide and lasting tribute to Marilyn Monroe, the controversial actress and model, by issuing a limited edition set of legal tender stamps commemorating the starlet's life and career."

As is true for its Elvis stamp offering, the International Collectors Society is selling the Marilyn stamps for $9.95 per set, even though, according to the company, the stamps are believed to be far more sought after and desirable than the Elvis issue from Antigua and Barbuda. The St. Vincent's Marilyn issue is about four times the size of an ordinary U.S. postage stamp, has a face value of $1.00, and is legal for postage in St. Vincent and accepted by postal authorities worldwide. You'll also get a certificate of authenticity along with a free pocket guide, *99 Little Known Facts About Marilyn Monroe.*

Limited quantities are available.

Company
International Collectors Society
(Owings Mills, MD)

Where
World Wide Web

Web Address
`http://www.kiosk.net/marilyn/`

Prices
$9.95

Shipping Fees (in the U.S.)
$3 per order.

International orders are accepted.

Remember!

For periodic updates of this book and additional discounts, send email to *shop@easton.com*. See *Introduction* for more details.

You ain't nothin' but a postage stamp.

Collectible Elvis Stamps

"Elvis has been sighted in Antigua and Barbuda!" And, thanks to the International Collectors Society, you can get the entire set for under $10.

"These are larger, more colorful, and much rarer than the widely collected U.S. Elvis issue. While the U.S. Post Office was trying to decide between the young and the old Elvis, these tiny nations issued *nine* different stamps showing Elvis in every stage of his career—and the U.S. Postal Service is all shook up over it." Over 500 million U.S. Elvis stamps were sold. Compare that number to the mere thousands of sets in the Antigua and Barbuda issue, and their uniqueness quotient increases exponentially.

These stamps are about four times the size of the U.S. Elvis stamp. They have a face value of $1, are legal for postage in Antigua and Barbuda, and are accepted by postal authorities worldwide. A certificate of authenticity is included with each order.

There is a limit of six sets per person, available while supplies last. As a bonus with each order, you'll receive a free pocket guide, *99 Little Known Facts About Elvis Presley.*

Shopping on the Internet and Beyond

Exclusive Deal

International Collectors Society

10 percent off any order.

Exclusive deal for readers of this book only! You must mention this offer when you place your order.

Company
International Collectors Society
(Owings Mills, MD)

Where
World Wide Web

Web Address
`http://www.kiosk.net/elvis/homepage.html`

Prices
$9.95

Shipping Fees (in the U.S.)
$3 per order.

International orders are accepted.

Anne of Green Gables Memorabilia

Prince Edward Island is the mecca for Anne of Green Gables merchandise. "Anne of Green

Anne of Green Gables (continued)

Gables" is one of Canada's most celebrated fictional characters. Through the writings of Lucy Maud Montgomery, people from all over the world have enjoyed the charm and enthusiasm of Anne as she grew up on rural Prince Edward Island.

Anne of Green Gables Mercantile may be the only company in the world that sells Anne merchandise exclusively. Virtually all of their figurines and porcelain dolls are made by local artisans on Prince Edward Island. The dolls are hand painted and garbed in a traditional dress, and each doll has a number each one to verify authenticity.

The figurine sizes average 8 to 12 inches; the dolls are about 12 to 19 inches in size. Great attention is shown to detail, with the artisans making sure that her hair is just the right color red and that she has the mandated seven freckles.

Selected products are shown on the Anne of Green Gables Mercantile Web site, but the company stocks over 100 items. Special requests are encouraged.

If you haven't read the eight-book series about the young girl "with the romantic soul and adventurous spirit," you can buy it here. In fact, the Anne stories were translated into Japanese in the 1950s and were so popular that they since have been integrated into Japan's secondary school curriculum.

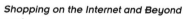

Shopping on the Internet and Beyond

Exclusive Deal

Anne of Green Gables Mercantile

10 percent off your first order.

Exclusive deal for readers of this book only!
You must mention this offer when you place your order.

Company
Anne of Green Gables Mercantile
(Charlottetown, Prince Edward Island, Canada)

Where
World Wide Web

Web Address
http://www.peinet.pe.ca/homepage/anne/
homepage.html

Email
anne@peinet.pe.ca

Prices

From $6 to $300 (Canadian dollars).

Shipping Fees (in the U.S.)
$8.95 (ground shipping).

International orders are accepted.

Two celebrated rebels: one with a cause and one without.

John Lennon and James Dean Postage Stamps

For over three years, the International Collectors Society heard rumors that there were issues of John Lennon and James Dean postage stamps.

The buzz among collectors was rampant, but there was one problem: Nobody had actually seen these stamps.

Eventually they *were* discovered, and what was once a rumor is now reality: authentic, legal tender stamps of John Lennon and James Dean direct from the Republic of Malagasy.

"Each stamp is surrounded by a deluxe souvenir sheet that portrays various highlights from their legendary careers." A certificate of authenticity accompanies each order, but supplies are severely limited with this issue, so Lennon and Dean fans should probably act quickly.

Shopping on the Internet and Beyond

Exclusive Deal

International Collectors Society

10 percent off all orders.

Exclusive deal for readers of this book only! You must mention this offer when you place your order.

Company
International Collectors Society
(Owings Mills, MD)

Where
World Wide Web

Web Address
`http://www.kiosk.net/stamps/homepage.html`

Prices
$8 per set or $13 for both.

Shipping Fees (in the U.S.)
$3 per order.

International orders are accepted.

World-Wide Collectors Digest is a cybercollector's dream site.

Free Collectible Dealer Listings

Attention: If you collect trading cards, comic book memorabilia, pogs, figurines, toy trains, or toy planes, you'll go berserk over the World-Wide Collectors Digest service available free on the World Wide Web. This site lets you choose a category (from those mentioned above) and instantly links you to a listing of dealers that specialize in your favorite collectible. And to make the service efficient, the directories are also sorted by state.

This site also gives you instant access to price guides to help you determine an item's value before you even contact a dealer.

In addition to dealer listings, the World-Wide Collectors Digest site lists upcoming national trade shows, Star Trek conventions, sports schedules, professional sports standings, and new product releases.

If your collectible interests are sports-oriented, you'll appreciate the professional team listings, along with the Hall of Fame roster and stadium and arena seating charts, statistics, and information.

The folks at this site also provide Theft and Forgery reports to help you prevent a collectible catastrophe.

When I showed this site to collectors, they said they would willingly *pay* for the information that's being given away here. But since the site is free (and always will be according to one of the company's vice presidents), you'll have that much more dough to augment your collection.

Collectible Dealer Listings (continued)

Company
World-Wide Collectors Digest
(Glydon, Maryland)

Where
World Wide Web

Web Address
http://www.wwcd.com

Email
office@www.wwcd.com

Prices
Free!

For some complex bead designs, the silversmith may require as much as a month to complete it.

Handmade Balinese Beads

Nina Cooper gets to spend a lot of time in Bali. Unlike most visitors who loaf under the Indonesian sun, Nina is checking in with her Balinese silversmiths, who make the stunning silver beads she sells on her World Wide Web site.

These are no ordinary beads. "Working with silver is an extremely labor-intensive process...The silversmiths and carvers display superb technique and immense patience. Each bead is carefully made with exquisite detail. Every silver dot is individually placed, each turtle shell patterned by hand. Each bead is a work of art. No two are exactly alike."

If you want to know more about the process, the Web site has pages that navigate you through the entire procedure, complete with photos.

Nina Designs carries the full spectrum of beads, including oendants, carved beads, clasps, cones, spacers, buttons, chains, watch band tops, and more.

The entire online catalog displays about 300 of these handmade Balinese beads. "Click on any bead for description, price, and magnified image. Once you have magnified a bead you can add it to your order the continue to browse with the arrow buttons." So, not only are Nina's beads well-designed, her site is too.

Shopping on the Internet and Beyond
Exclusive Deal

Nina Designs

5 percent off your first order.

Exclusive deal for readers of this book only!
You must mention this offer when you place your order.

Company
Nina Designs (Sante Fe, NM)

Where
World Wide Web

Web Address
http://www.nets.com/nina

Email
nina@nets.com

Prices
14 cents to $22 per bead. $100 minimum order.

For More...

For more great collectibles, craft, and hobbies shopping opportunities, see the next page.

Honorable Mentions

in the category of

Collectibles, Crafts, & Hobbies

Aircraft Models

Original producer of the world's finest military, civilian, and commercial aircraft models; choose from over 200.

Company
Pacific Aircraft

Web Address
http://www.dash.com:80/netro/sho/ema/
pacific/pacific.html

All Things Collectible

Private party ads on CompuServe for collectibles of all varieties.

CompuServe
Go *classifieds* then select *tv/misc/hobbies/collecting/cooking*

Antiques

Private party ads on America Online for antiques and collectibles.

America Online
Keyword *classifieds* then select *general merchandise boards*

Antiques and Auctions

Private party ads on CompuServe for antique and auction supplies.

CompuServe
Go *classifieds* then select *tv/misc/hobbies/collecting/cooking*

Arts, Crafts, and Gifts

Private party ads on Prodigy for arts, crafts, and gifts.

Prodigy
Jump *classifieds* then select *browse ads*

Arts and Crafts Supplies

Private party ads on America Online for arts and crafts supplies.

America Online
Go *classifieds* then select *general merchandise boards*

Automobilia

An online source for automobilia in the USA including car miniatures.

Company
EWA / Miniature Cars

Web Address
`http://shops.net/shops/EWACARS/`

Card Dealer Directory

A complete, searchable directory of trading card dealers, including dealers involved in sports cards, non-sports cards, and telephone cards.

Company
Trading Card Dealers Directory

Web Address
`http://www.webshop.com/collectors/cards/dealers/`

Comic Books

Buy comic books directly from other collectors via the Net.

Usenet Address
`rec.arts.comics.marketplace`

Comic Books and Coins

Private party ads on CompuServe for comic book and coin collecting supplies.

CompuServe
Go *classifieds* then select *tv/misc/hobbies/collecting/cooking*

Craft Supplies

Crafts and related supplies for sale among crafters from around the globe.

Web Address
`rec.crafts.marketplace`

Dilbert

Dilbert and Dogbert apparel, books, and screen savers on America Online. Free samples.

Company
Dilbert and Dogbert Merchandise

America Online
Keyword *dilbert*

Doll Clothes

All styles of doll clothes with special emphasis on 18-inch dolls. Outfits can be ordered separately or with a matching girl's outfit.

Company
Kinikia Kreations

Web Address
http://199.170.0.46/kk/dolls.html

Gifts and Collectibles

Private party ads on Prodigy for gifts and collectibles.

Prodigy
Jump *classifieds* then select *browse ads*

Graphic Design and Art Supplies

Private party ads on America Online for graphic design and art supplies.

America Online
Go *classifieds* then select *general merchandise boards*

Hobby Supplies

Private party ads on CompuServe for hobby supplies.

CompuServe
Go *classifieds* then select *tv/misc/hobbies/collecting/cooking*

Hollywood Collectibles

Official merchandise and apparel from popular feature films and television shows on America Online.

Company
Hollywood Online

America Online
Keyword *hollywood* then select *hollywood online store*

Licensed Collectibles

Fully licensed collectibles on CompuServe, ranging from Broadway plays to limited edition Hirschfeld lithographs of entertainment legends.

Company
E-Drive

CompuServe
Go *estore*

Mail-Order Antiques

Impressive collection of antique china, clocks, glass, jewelry, and a whole lot more.

Company
Incredible Collectibles

Web Address
http://rivendell.com/antiques/stores/IC/

Model Railroad Equipment and Supplies

Everything a model railroad fan could ever need from this world-famous company.

Company
Atlas Model Railroad Co., Inc.

Where
http://www.atlasrr.com/atlasrr/

Photography Equipment

Private party ads on CompuServe for cameras and other photography equipment.

CompuServe
Go *classifieds* then select *tv/misc/hobbies/collecting/cooking*

Photography Equipment

Private party ads on the Internet for photography supplies.

Usenet Address
rec.photo.marketplace

Photography Equipment

Buy and sell equipment and supplies with America Online subscribers.

America online
Keyword *classifieds* then select *other ad areas*

Hot Tip!

Be sure to check out the Internet Usenet Group *alt.comsumers.free-stuff* for listings of fabulous free offers found by freebie freaks from around the world.

Pictures on Disk

Have your photos put on a floppy when your film is processed. For less than $14 you get one roll of 24-exposure film processed *and* put on a floppy *plus* a free replacement roll of film.

American Online
Keyword *komando*

Prodigy
Jump *photoworks*

Rolling Stones Memorabilia

Official Rolling Stones merchandise, including hard-to-find items such as leather jackets.

Company
The Rolling Stones

Web Address
http://www.stones.com/

Sports and Non-Antiques

Private party ads on America Online for sports and non-antique-related items.

America Online
Go classified then select *general merchandise boards*

Sports Memorabilia

Authenticated, autographed memorabilia from the biggest names in sports.

Company
Upper Deck

Web Address
http://www.shopping2000/upperdeck/

Sports Celebrity Photos

Lucite protected 8×10 photos of favorite sports figures, signed and authenticated.

Company
Sports Memoribilia Plaques

Web Address
`http://www.webscope.com/plaques/homepage.html`

Sports Stuff

Private party ads on Prodigy for sports goods and memorabilia.

Prodigy
Jump *classifieds* then select *browse ads*

Stamps

U.S. postage stamps available on Prodigy.

Company
US Stamps

Prodigy
Jump *us stamps*

Stamp Collecting

Stamps and stamp collecting supplies.

Company
Seaside Book & Stamp

Web Address
`http://www.nstn.ca/cybermall/biz-subject/bookstores/seaside/seaside.html`

Star Trek Card Game

Specialists in the official *Star Trek: The Next Generation* customizable card game.

Company
Sarasota Sports Collectibles

Web Address
`http://iquest.com:80/~tstevens/sarasota/`

Trading Cards and Fine Art

Private party ads on CompuServe for trading cards and fine art.

CompuServe
Go *classifieds* then select *tv/misc/hobbies/collecting/cooking*

Trading Cards Galore

This Internet newgroup is a haven for any trader.

Usenet Address
`rec.games.trading-cards.marketplace`

Warner Bros. Merchandise

Classic Warner Bros. character merchandise on America Online, including clothing, animation art, even kitchen accessories.

Company
Warner Bros. Studio Store

America Online
Keyword *2market* then select *collections* then select *warner bros. store*

Computer Hardware and Software

Virus-Deterring Magical Vortex Energy Charged Crystals

Straight from the New Age capital of the world come magical vortex energy charged crystals for warding off viruses and other hardware evils from your beloved computer.

"Sedona's new age metaphysical community has gotten a lot of attention. Vortex energy is abundant and it has been rumored that computers are repaired by waving magical vortex energy charged crystals over them while chanting religious mantras."

Each crystal set includes The Wise One's Sacred Instructions, a not-so-religious mantra for chanting, and one magical vortex energy charged crystal (for repairs and preventive virus protection).

Now here's the not-so-small print: "No money back guarantee. If your computer problems persist after using these magical crystals and you are not 100 percent satisfied, you will absolutely *not* get a refund, guaranteed. These magic crystals have not been tested nor verified as to their authenticity."

Okay, results are a little shaky for virus protection and computer malfunctions, but perhaps they can prevent mathematical errors resulting from my mutant Pentium!

Company
Sedona Online (Sedona, AZ)

Where
World Wide Web

Web Address
http://www.sedona.net/crystal.html

Email
arnie@sedona.net

Price
$19.95

Shipping Fees (in the U.S.)
Shipping is included in the price.

International orders are accepted.

*Give me an M!
Now give me
an M&M!
What've you
got? 3M,
of course!*

Bargains on 3M Media and Diskette Duplication

3M's media are considered to be some of the most durable and dependable media available, which is why Disk-O-Tape specializes in the 3M line.

If it is a form of magnetic media and 3M makes it, Disk-O-Tape carries it at rock bottom prices, including hard-to-find formats. If it's 8mm tape you want, Disk-O-Tape is your place.

If your media requirements are more mainstream, you'll find fabulous values on everything from data cartridges (all formats) to diskettes to flopticals to optical disks.

If you desire disks with something on them, Disk-O-Tape has you covered, offering both duplication equipment and duplication services.

They sell "state-of-the art Rimage duplication and labeling equipment" with models for small needs (such as 50 diskettes) to more industrious

duplicating equipment (up to 50,000 diskettes at a pop). Especially noteworthy: This line of equipment is modular and can be expanded as your requirements grow. Most formats are supported, including DOS, Mac, and Unix.

If your duplication needs are somewhat sporadic, contact Disk-O-Tape. They will be happy to duplicate anything you want on a per-order basis.

Shopping on the Internet and Beyond

Exclusive Deal

Disk-O-Tape

On your first order of $50 or more, get one free box of 3M high-density diskettes or a $3 credit toward shipping charges.

Exclusive deal for readers of this book only!
You must mention this offer when you place your order.

Company
Disk-O-Tape (Cleveland, OH)

Where
World Wide Web and email

Web Address
http://branch.com/disko/disko.html

Email
disk.o.tape@pcohio.com

Prices
Extremely competitive. They constantly update their price list to reflect price reductions.

Shipping Fees (in the U.S.)
Actual cost with no handling charge. Shipping fees on orders under $50 run $3.

International orders are accepted.

CD-ROM Services

Digital Dynamics' service is simple: They offer CD-recordable services to "write" your information on a CD-ROM disk for easy access or to archive data on this high-volume format.

One CD-ROM holds approximately 650 megabytes of data; that's the equivalent of about 450 high-density 3.5" diskettes. That's a lot of storage, especially for text files. If, for example, you have piles of backup disks of old word processing, database, or spreadsheet files, this is a fabulous way to archive them. No need to plow through stacks of floppies to find the file you want from six years ago; just pop in the CD-ROM and do a quick search.

Or, egad, suppose you have backup and archived files in multiple formats, such as 3.5" and 5.25" floppies, perhaps some on SyQuest cartridges and other files on DAT tapes. Now you can centralize them onto one CD-ROM. This company can even convert data from different software sources to one common denominator. For example, if you have word-processing documents from three different programs, you can convert them all to one format.

In addition to making archives and backups, Digital Dynamics offers another great service: They can use a CD-ROM to create electronic documents from your hard copies (such as timecards, canceled checks, or purchase orders).

You will find personal uses for their services as well. For example, one coin collector compiled scanned images of his collection on disk to create a permanent, electronic record. Such an inventory record is useful for insurance purposes and for showing his collection without risking theft or damage.

Because CD-ROMs can store images, text, sound, and video files, it is a great medium for preserving family history archives for future generations.

You can also forget about operating system compatibility issues, because Digital Dynamics can produce CD-ROMs for several platforms including Windows, DOS, Macintosh, and Unix.

Company
Digital Dynamics (Ann Arbor, MI)

Where
World Wide Web

Web Address
`http://branch.com/dd/dd.html`

Email
`cd@rom.com`

Prices
$125 to $200 for the first CD-ROM, $75 for each additional copy of the first CD-ROM (the master).

Shipping Fees
Actual cost. No handling fees.

International orders are accepted.

Insight's PCI P60 Pentium system, Ergo Computing's DX4 Powerbrick, and Insight's Reveal MFX-03 Multimedia Kit are just three of hundreds of hardware deals available from PC Catalog.

Free Computer Pricing Comparison Charts

If you are shopping for *anything* computer related, the PC Catalog on America Online, Prodigy, CompuServe, and the World Wide Web is a great place to start—and probably finish.

PC Catalog is an umbrella for 175 mail-order companies and manufacturers. Choose the type of equipment you want (modem, printer, monitor) and you'll then receive a comparison listing of the prices from various mail-order companies and manufacturers. Click on the cheapest price for the product you want, and you'll see a complete spec list along with the name and toll-free phone number of the dealer, from whom you buy directly.

To try the system, I chose to comparison shop for a particular Sony monitor I've been panting for. I found two listings for the model I wanted, and the price difference was staggering. One dealer's quoted price was $539, while another dealer's price was $429. The $429 offer is the lowest sale price I found in Los Angeles. The $539 price is closer to the suggested retail price, which makes me wonder on which planet the $539 dealer is located.

Speaking of price, according to PC Catalog many of the prices listed in the comparison charts are slightly lower than the company may list in other advertising media. For this reason, the company encourages you to mention to the vendors that you saw their information in PC Catalog.

PC Catalog's listings for over 2,000 products are updated every week.

Company
PC Catalog (Lincoln, NE)

Where
America Online, CompuServe, Prodigy, and World Wide Web

Shortcut (America Online)
Keyword *marketplace* then select *pc catalog*

Shortcut (CompuServe)
Go *pca*

Shortcut (Prodigy)
Jump *pc catalog*

Web Address
gopher://pccatalog.peed.com

Remember!
For periodic updates of this book, send email to *shop@easton.com*. See *Introduction* for more details.

Mr. Upgrade is ready to sell you top-grade computer parts at bottom-basement prices—as soon as he changes out of his pajamas.

Upgrading Hardware Products and Services

Mr. Upgrade may be the only virtual retailer in cyberspace that offers name-brand parts and components specifically for people who want to specifically upgrade of their hardware.

Their parts menu includes cases, CPUs, motherboards, disk drives, controllers, memory, modems, multimedia—literally anything that is supposed to be encased.

This is a tricky business because potential compatibility problems abound. Mr. Upgrade recognizes this, and according to their president, the company has one of the most knowledgeable sales staffs in the industry. "We can prevent hardware conflicts by teaching the customer what is compatible and what is not, and we will even review current hardware with customers, if they wish."

If for some reason you need to return a part, Mr. Upgrade offers a generously low re-stocking fee of 7 percent if the goods are returned within 10 days (compared to the more typical 15 percent). There arent any credit card surcharges, and they double-box all shipments for extra protection.

As both a parts distributor and manufacturer's representative, Mr. Upgrade can also sell you all the computer guts required to build your own system. Using nothing but top-quality, name brand products, you could assemble your own machine at a savings of up to 15 percent.

Be sure to check out the "specials" section on this Web site for even greater savings.

Shopping on the Internet and Beyond

Exclusive Deal

Mr. Upgrade Computer Products

Free shipping on your first order (U.S.) or an $18 shipping credit for non-U.S. destinations. A free Mr. Upgrade mousepad will be included if your first purchase is $50 or more.

Exclusive deal for readers of this book only! You must mention this offer when you place your order.

Company
Mr. Upgrade Computer Products (a.k.a. Motherboard Discount Center) (Gilbert, AZ)

Where
World Wide Web

Web Address
http://www.primenet.com/~jimb/mrupgrad.html

Prices
$34 to $5,000 for a full system

Shipping Fees (in the U.S.)
Average of $18.

International orders are accepted.

The Internet Shopping Network is truly vast—these are just the vendors that sell hard drives!

Hardware and Software for Everyone

The statistics related to the Internet Shopping Network (ISN) computer offerings are staggering. ISN sells over 24,000 hardware and software items for PCs, Macs, and Unix systems—with over 1,000 participating companies. More than 95 percent of the products are in stock and available for delivery on the next business day. The combined inventory of this company totals more than 500 million dollars.

You must become a member to buy from ISN. The membership is free, but you must provide a credit card number when you join. Furthermore, you must keep track of yet another I.D., which they refer to as a "user code." You can browse the site as much as you like before joining. Membership is required only if you want to buy.

Once you are registered, the Internet Shopping Network offers you downloadable programs and demos, and their biggest-selling product

category is hard disks. Prices for hard disks are about 5 to 10 percent below the average street price (what you'd pay at a national chain such as CompUSA) or mail order house. As of this writing, ISN does not offer any price guarantees or price matching.

If you find that a software product you've purchased is not compatible with your system (or you have some other equally compelling problem), ISN will let you exchange your purchase for another item in the same category. (However, in most cases they do assess a 20 percent re-stocking fee.)

The Internet Shopping Network is owned by The Home Shopping Network, which accounts for their extensive inventory and high profile. Because of their size, ISN is one place you want to be sure to check when comparing hardware and software prices.

Company
Internet Shopping Network
(Palo Alto, CA)

Where
World Wide Web

Web Address
http://www.internet.net/

Email
info@internet.net

Prices
Competitive.

Shipping Fees (in the U.S.)
Based on weight. No handling charges.

 Some downloadable demos are available.

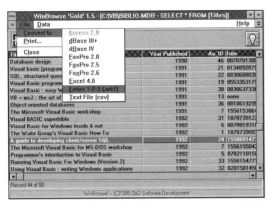

WinBrowse is one of hundreds of shareware programs available from Q&D. WinBrowse lets you display files created in most PC and Windows database formats, and lets you convert files from one database format to another.

Interactive Shareware Catalog

Someone has finally figured out an efficient way to distribute shareware both interactively and with easy access to free upgrades and free support.

At the Shareware Central Web site, you begin at the table of contents, where you can peruse a list of Windows-based shareware. The list includes a description of each program, written by the software's author to ensure accuracy.

Downloading is the easy part. Simply click on the program of your choice, and the site will automatically start downloading the requested program.

There is no charge for this, and you have 30 days to evaluate the program. If you are still using the software after one month, you are expected to pay a "modest" registration fee, which varies by program. Registered users then get free support and free upgrades.

Some of the programs include an online interactive demo, which enables you to try the program online before you even download it.

All types of shareware are offered, including programs for business, databases, education, games, sports, Windows icons, networking, personal information managers, programming and development tools, printer applications, and other utilities.

The company running this site is a member of the Association of Shareware Professionals "and as such, assures you of the highest-quality software and support."

Company
Q&D Software Development
(Shareware Central)

Where
CompuServe (via Library 1 of the WINAPD forum) and World Wide Web

Web Address
http://www.intac.com/~dversch/swc.html

Email
dversch@intac.com

International orders are accepted.

Recycled Diskettes for a Quarter

I never realized it was possible to help the environment while backing up my hard disk, but EnviRoMedia(tm) has found a way: by recycling high-grade floppies.

According to the company, this is how the service works: "Major software publishers buy only the finest-quality diskettes [they have to in order to endure the rigorous duplication process]. When versions of their software are upgraded, there are always millions of diskettes, non-biodegradable plastic waste thrown into landfills. That's where EnviRoMedia comes in." They rescue the abandoned media before they're discarded, reformat and overlabel the disks, then sell them at substantial savings.

How big a bargain are these diskettes? Try as little as 25 cents each (at the time of this writing) in quantities of 1,000. If you only need 100, you pay a mere 29 cents. Compare that to 80 cents apiece for new ones bought in boxes of ten at discount stores.

The 3.5", high-density disks are preformatted and file ready. The company sells both PC and Macintosh formats with unconditional guarantees.

EnviRoMedia is anxious to prove to you how good these diskettes are, and will send one free of charge with no obligation to buy. Requests can be made via email.

Company
EnvirRoMedia™ (Wakefield, MA)

Where
World Wide Web

Web Address
http://www.shore.net/~crazybob

Email
sales@crazybob.com

Prices
Price is determined by the quantity of purchase. Prices are extremely low.

Shipping Fees
Based on shipping weight. No handling fees.

International orders are accepted.

 Free sample diskette upon request.

Whether you want to buy printers that work or you want to repair printers that don't, Printer Works is the place to check out.

Laser Printer Sales, Service, and Parts

At the Printer Works, laser printers are their only business. They sell 'em whole, they sell 'em in parts, they sell 'em used, they sell 'em new.

They've been at it since 1982 and remain one of the largest printer-only repair facilities in North America. This company is a Canon Authorized Service Facility, and since Canon manufactures the engines for the Hewlett-Packard and Apple laser lines (among others), they can service and supply just about any laser printer made.

The Printer Works is unique because they're one of the few companies in the world that will sell you laser printer *parts*.

If you know the source of problem—let's say a broken corona wire—they'll sell you the subassembly you need to replace it, saving you lots of money in labor charges and the hassle of taking the printer into a repair facility. In fact, the Printer Works even offers a repair exchange option. In this case, they'll ship the new part immediately, even before the broken mechanism is sent to them.

Laser Printer Sales, Parts (continued)

If you're squeamish about repairing your own machine, you can always ship the unit to the Printer Works and have their experts resuscitate it.

The Printer Works also sells used printers. These completely refurbished printers are a real steal. For example, a 4-year old $3,500 printer model can be bought from them today for a mere $400.

On the other end of the printer spectrum, new models, manufacturer by the Printer Works, are available at substantial savings. While an Apple Laserwriter might go for $1,800, the Printer Works' equivalent is priced $500 less at $1,299.

Servicing of less-than-common printers is also a specialty; they repair and sell lasers for the NeXT line of computers. The company is also the exclusive manufacturer of the StepWriter product line.

For the full scope of all they offer, email them for their 160-page data book and part catalog.

Company
Printer Works (Hayward, CA)

Where
World Wide Web

Web Address
http://www.stepwise.com/Developers/
ThePrinterWorks.html d/index.html

Reminder! This Web address is case sensitive. Make sure you enter the address *exactly* as shown.

Email
tpw@td1.com

Prices
From 10 cents to $5,000.

Shipping Fees (in the U.S.)
Based on weight, by UPS.

International orders are accepted.

A cloudy mind, some airy thoughts, and thou.

CD-ROM Cloud Art

Judy Collins may have looked at clouds from both sides, but professional photographers Michael and Mary Bartnikowski have seen them from every angle imaginable.

These self-professed cloud lovers have traveled the globe for over 20 years shooting hundreds of rolls of film, capturing more than 10,000 images. From this astounding collection, they've selected what they consider to be their 32 finest images, which they've compiled on one CD-ROM, called the Cloud Gallery.

The Cloud Gallery is great for special effects, backgrounds, charts, newsletters, brochures, flyers, and of course, screen savers for a serene view of a sometimes unforgiving world.

"Each TIFF image is fully accessible and ready to download onto your hard disk. Flip, twist, filter, and whirl these pups to your heart's delight...Name them. Change them." Use these files anyway you want. They are royalty-free, and

CD-ROM Cloud Art (continued)

the only minimum requirement is a Macintosh II with a CD-ROM drive and 8 Mb of RAM.

The quality of these photographs is remarkable. To their credit, the Bartnikowskis make it look simple, but we should realize that cloud images are one of the most difficult types of photography to do well. Accurately capturing the essence and emotion of clouds requires painstaking and extensive lighting considerations—all done to perfection by these fine photographers.

"Sit back, and enjoy these inspiring glimpses of heaven...from the lush cloud fields of Tahiti to the banks of puffs rolling by Upstate New York, Cloud Gallery is your one stop shopping for dramatic backdrops."

Note: For more art on CD-ROM, be sure to check out Loretta DeMars' Sea Art in the *Art* chapter.

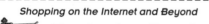

Shopping on the Internet and Beyond

Exclusive Deal

Cloud Gallery

Enjoy $28 off your first order
(a 30 percent discount).

Exclusive deal for readers of this book only!
You must mention this offer when you place your order.

Company
Cloud Gallery (Palo Alto, CA)

Where
World Wide Web

Web Address
http://www.commerce.digital.com/palo-alto/
CloudGallery/home.html

Reminder! This Web address is case sensitive. Make sure you enter the address *exactly* as shown.

Email
terrasoul@aol.com

Prices
$96 (see the coupon for a special discount).

Shipping Fees (in the U.S.)
$3

International orders are accepted.

Komando Komputer Klinic

Talk show host, TV commentator, syndicated newspaper columnist, and author—Kim Komando is a ubiquitous computer personality. She has one of the most popular areas on America Online—The Komando Komputer Klinic—a similar version of which is also available on the World Wide Web.

Due to Kim's popularity and expertise, people buy what she recommends. Realizing this, Kim now buys directly from manufacturers on behalf of her swelling fan base, then offers substantial savings on the computer-related merchandise she likes most.

For example, $19.95 computer books often sell for $14.95 in the Komputer Klinic. Given the popularity of computer titles these days, they're rarely discounted, so the 25 percent off that Kim offers has added meaning.

In addition to books, The Komando Mall offers some spiffy deals on software, hardware, even computer-related clothing.

If you're shopping for a used computer (any make or model) or pre-owned peripherals such as a printer, note that Kim includes the NACOMEX Used Computer Price Guide on her Web site.

Komando's Klinic (continued)

For virtually any name-brand piece of equipment, you'll learn the current high price, low price, and "closing" price. For example, if you want a used Toshiba laptop, simply locate the model number in the well-organized chart and you'll know the fair asking price when perusing the classifieds. These listings are updated frequently and are considered extremely accurate.

Kim Komando: computer powerhouse and a great bargain hunter, too! Thanks, Kim.

Company
Kim Komando's Komputer Klinic (Scottsdale, AZ)

Where
America Online and World Wide Web

Shortcut
Keyword *komputer klinic*

Web Address
http://www.komando.com

Email
komando@aol.com

Prices
Vary, but are always excellent.

Hot Tip!

To look at private party ads from individual online-service subscribers, use these shortcuts:

America Online: Keyword *classifieds*
CompuServe: Go *classifieds*
Prodigy: Jump *classifieds*

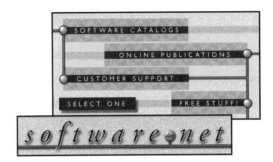

Get caught up in the Software.net.

Just Software...and Lots of It

Software.net carries so many software titles that I can safely say if you don't find it here, you probably don't need it. With over 8,200 titles in 38 categories for Windows/DOS, Apple, OS/2, and Unix platforms, no other single company can better satisfy your software needs. Responding to the environment in which they do business, Software.net (pronounced "software-dot-net") is "the first independent Web site that allows software buyers to download commercial products electronically."

While only a small portion of their catalog can be downloaded, the downloadable feature is so popular that it accounts for a significant percentage of the company's sales. Software.net has over eight different categories of products from which to choose.

The programs available for immediate downloading are some of the biggest selling titles around. These name-brand packages include Mecca's TaxCut (especially handy on April 14th); Norton's PC Anywhere, Anti-Virus, and its infamous utility package, along with other celebrated titles.

Just Software (continued)

Electronic delivery is not limited to full packages. There are oodles of demos and trial versions of equally desirable programs—all for *free*. In addition to these freebies, Software.net has a section devoted exclusively to free stuff.

Software.net is also extremely respectful of their customers. The company guarantees "you will receive the lowest price available on any product. If you find a product elsewhere at a lower price, simply email or call them and give the details to their customer support rep. They will match any in-stock price."

Company
Software.net (Menlo Park, CA)

Where
World Wide Web

Web Address
http://software.net/

Email
info@software.net

Prices
Extremely competitive. Will match competitors' prices.

Shipping Fees
Actual charges with no handling fees.

International orders are accepted.

 Plenty of downloadable demos and trial versions are available.

Quite possibly the world's first cyberoo.

Novelty Australian WAV Files

Makin' Waves' novelty Australian sound files have many uses. You can use them as startup and shutdown sounds for Windows, turn them into talking greeting cards, or copy them onto a cassette and use them as greetings for your telephone answering machine.

"Here's how it works. You choose a voice, male or female, decide on a character or particular accent, and what you want the voice to say. For example, you might want to have a Paul Hogan voice say 'G'day (your name here). Good ta see ya' each time you start up Windows."

While Makin' Waves' specialty is Australian-flavored sound files, other characters and accents are available. Their credo: "You name the character and we supply the voice."

The company is able to produce just about anything from a simple sound byte to a full 30-second commercial with broadcast-quality pro-

Australian WAV files (continued)

duction values. Makin' Waves stresses that they use "professional voice-over talent along with a sound engineer whose imagination and ability with sound effects defies description."

Although Makin' Waves normally uses the WAV file format, the company can generally supply your personalized sounds in the format you prefer.

Now that you know where to go for Australian voice-over work, why not "put another shrimp on the bar-bie, and then go tie your digereedoo down.

Company
Makin' Waves Studio
(Blackwood, South Australia)

Where
World Wide Web

Web Address
`http://cyberzine.org/html/Waves/`
`wavepage.html`

Reminder! This Web address is case sensitive. Make sure you enter it *exactly* as shown.

Email
`kjones@adam.com.au`

Prices
Personalized message ($30 Australian dollars— about $22 U.S. dollars).

Shipping Fees
None. All deliveries are made electronically.

International orders are accepted.

 Several fun and free WAV files are available.

For More...

For more great computer shopping opportunities, see the next page.

Honorable Mentions

in the category of

Computer Hardware & Software

General Usenet Private Party Ads

misc.forsale.computers.memory
misc.forsale.computers.other.software
biz.marketplace.services.computers
pdaxs.ads.computers
misc.forsale.computers.other.misc
aus.ads.forsale.computers
misc.forsale.computers.discussion

Peripheral Usenet Private Party Ads

misc.forsale.computers.modems
misc.forsale.computers.storage
misc.forsale.computers.printers
misc.forsale.computers.monitors

Mac Usenet Private Party Ads

biz.marketplace.computers.mac
misc.forsale.computers.mac-specific.misc
misc.forsale.computers.mac-
   specific.portables
misc.forsale.computers.mac-
   specific.systems
misc.forsale.computers.mac-
   specific.software
misc.forsale.computers.mac-
   specific.cards.misc
misc.forsale.computers.mac-
specific.cards.video
misc.forsale.computers.other.systems

Non Mac or PC Usenet Private Party Ads

comp.sys.mext.marketplace
biz.marketplace.computers.other
misc.forsale.computers.workstation
comp.sys.amiga.marketplace
comp.sys.apple2.marletplace
misc.forsale.computers.net-hardware

PC Usenet Private PartyAds

misc.forsale.computers.pc-specific.cards.misc
comp.sys.ibm.pc.games.marketplace
biz.marketplace.computers.pc-clone
misc.forsale.computers.pc-specific.portables
misc.forsale.computers.pc-specific.systems
misc.forsale.computers.pc-specific.audio
misc.forsale.computers.pc-specific.motherboards
misc.forsale.computers.pc-specific.cards.video
misc.forsale.computers.pc-specific.software
misc.forsale.computers.pc-specific.misc

Buyers

Marcus Associates purchases used computer and communications equipment. They even pay for shipping.

Company
Marcus Associates

Web Address
http://branch.com/marcus/marcus.html

Computer Equipment

Computer hardware, software, and accessories.

Company
Reveal Computer Products

Web Address
http://www2.pcy.mci.net/marketplace/reveal/

DATs

Famous maker computer-grade DATs up to 60 percent off.

Company
Cassette House

Web Address
http://www.edge.net/ch/index.html

Digital PC Equipment

Digital brand PC products available to CompuServe members.

Company
Digital's PC Store

CompuServe
Go *dd*

Free Software

Free demos of commercial software packages.

Company
Free Software Shack

Web Address
http://www.pic.net/uniloc/

Hardware and CD-ROMs

Prodigy members have online access to hardware and CD-ROMs from Sears.

Company
Sears

Prodigy
Jump *sears*

IBM Computers

IBM computers available online to Web surfers and Prodigy members.

Company
IBM PC Direct

Web Address
`http://www.pc.ibm.com`

Prodigy
Jump *ibm pc direct*

Mac Equipment

Macintosh hardware, software, and accessories available to CompuServe members.

Company
MacWarehouse

CompuServe
Go *mw*

Mac Equipment

Software for less than $1/program. Available to CompuServe and Prodigy members

Company
Shareware Depot

CompuServe
Go *sd*

via Prodigy
Jump *shareware depot*

Magazines

Discount subscription offers to Prodigy members for *Computer Life, Computer Shopper, MacUser, PC/Computing, PC Magazine*, and *Windows Sources*.

Company
Ziff Davis

Prodigy
Jump *ziff davis*

Mapping Software

Mapping software and databases for consumer, education, business, and government markets.

Company
DeLorme Mapping

Web Address
`http://www.delorme.com/`

Email
`webmaster@delorme.com`

Software

Action, adventure, fantasy, and simulation software available to CompuServe members.

Company
Mission Control Software

CompuServe
Go *mcs*

Software

CompuServe members now have access to software for many fields, including financial, business, productivity, personal improvement, church, and genealogy.

Company
Parsons Technology

CompuServe
Go *pa*

Software and Demos

Prodigy members can download software and free demos. Check out the "Bargain Bytes" section for super buys.

Company
Download Superstore

Prodigy
Jump *download superstore*

PC Equipment

Values for the PC enthusiast. Available to CompuServe members.

Company
JDR Microdevices

CompuServe
Go *jdr*

PC Equipment

Hardware, sofware, and accessories available to CompuServe members.

Company
MicroWarehouse

CompuServe
Go *mcw*

PC Equipment

PC components and supplies available to CompuServe members.

Company
DALCO Computer Electronics

CompuServe
Go *da*

Destinations in Travel

Fly With Us describes the MIG-25 as the world's fastest combat plane, and claims that the aircraft accelerates "so fast that you could light a cigarette on the cockpit window!" Now that's hot.

Russian Fighter Pilot for a Day

Sooooo, you're a daredevil, eh? You've memorized *Top Gun* and seen *Hot Shots* and *Hot Shots Part Deux* more times than you can count. You spent your childhood with your arms at 90-degree wing formation, jumping off sofas and dive bombing your little sister, and you landed on your head so often you actually think you're Tom Cruise.

Why grow up now? If you still long to know the pure exhilaration of taking tight turns at up to nine Gs, check into "Fly With Us," the original Russian purveyor of military flights for civilians.

"If you're ready for the thrill, the challenge of a lifetime, you can take the controls of a high-performance fighter jet in Moscow and break the speed of sound with one of the best pilots in the world as your co-pilot."

You'll fly to a Russian airbase, where you'll be driven to a flight center to meet your pilot, be fitted for your G-suit, and take a basic physical before taking the throttle. You must also go through a rigorous Russian security clearance, though, so Norman Schwartzkopf need not apply.

You can choose to fly an L-39 advanced fighter trainer, a MIG-21 Supersonic Combat Trainer, a MIG-25, a MIG-29 or an SU-27 "Hook Cobra." I'm not sure what these planes do, but their names sure sound impressive. And remember, when you're flying faster than the speed of sound, you can't stop screaming because your panic might actually catch up with you.

Sure, these are Russian jets, so the company's boasts of having the "world's finest flying machines" seems a little much, but then again, the U.S. is a little busy with their F-16s, so these Russian machines will have to do.

Company
Fly With Us (Moscow, Russia)

Where
World Wide Web

Web Address
`http://www.mig29.com/mig29`

Prices
From $6,300 to $50,000.

Home Swapping

Eek! There's a stranger in your house! Then again, you're a stranger in theirs. Huh?

It's all part of the International Home Exchange Network and no, it's not a way for squatters to take over your property while you're on vacation. This Web site allows you to post your house for a vacation trade with another person or family who wants to visit your part of the world.

You can swap homes altogether, usually at no cost to either party and with no involvement from the producers of the Web site. Or you can participate in something called "hospitality exchange," where travelers agree to trade hospitality in their homes. One family stays with you for a period of time, and then you stay with them for a similar period in their home.

You can also broker your home to paying guests for a fee, place a vacation home or empty home up for rental, or browse a list of bed and breakfasts, country inns, youth hostels, and those seeking traveling companions.

Best of all, you get to stay in a real home, instead of a square box with an ice machine grinding outside your door. By swapping instead of lodging, you can visit places that you never dreamed you could afford. No hotel bills. No snotty desk clerks. Just a great place, in exchange for returned kindness.

Available locations include small towns in Colorado to historic cities in Israel to the French Riviera to all parts in between. Locations change frequently, so there's always a chance you'll stumble across the dream vacation bargain of a lifetime.

Home is where the heart is. And thanks to the International Home Exchange Network, you can leave your heart in San Francisco, New York, Paris, or anywhere else in the world!

Company
The International Home Exchange Network (Orlando, FL)

Where
World Wide Web

Web Address
http://www.magicnet.net/homexchange

Email
linda@magicnet.net

Prices
From $29.95 per year, per listing.

Here on Mexico's Pacific coast is the best of worlds old and new: the modern resort of Ixtapa, with its luxury hotels, restaurants and lively night spots; and five minutes away the quaint fishing village of Zihuatanejo, with cobblestone streets and shops selling Indian handicrafts. At your feet is the sound of the surf on a long beach; behind you, green mountains and all the romance of Mexico.

Ixtapa, Mexico, one of Club Med's great vacations for the stress in your head.

Club Med

Club Med—their middle name is "relaxation." But sometimes, thanks to the avalanche of brochures the company offers, planning your trip can be more of a workout than an exciting holiday anticipation.

Thanks to the World Wide Web, you can do your Club Med vacation shopping online. Browse through information on virtually all their villages, including those located in the United States, Bahamas, Caribbean, Mexico, French Polynesia, and elsewhere.

Each area has detailed information on the local Club Med village, including the types of tours available and a listing of what each site is best known for. For example, Cancun is listed as a destination for scuba diving and Mayan temples, and it's listed as ideal for singles and couples (in other words, families with small children may find a better match at another Club Med resort).

But if you'll be toting tots, that problem is solved, too. At the time of this writing, a "criteria" database was under construction to help you deter-

mine the destination features most important to you. After you've identified the specialties you and your family are looking for, a list is generated of the clubs that best match your parameters. For example, if you clicked on "earthquakes," "floods," and "riots," Club Los Angeles might pop up. (That doesn't actually exist, but you get the point).

By the way, if you've got a slower modem, Club Med cares. They allow you to sift through their site in either text or graphics mode. So, if you're reading through the history of Club Med and you're not interested in what their founder looks like, you can blow through the graphic and read the words. But if you like to look at pretty views of sunsets, Club Med's site has plenty, including QuickTime videos with "interviews of Club Med guests interviewed during their trip to Club Med's villages."

Club Med has more than 110 villages on six continents in 33 countries—"each reflecting the architecture, culture, and cuisine of the host nation." Many of the clubs are specifically for singles, couples, or families. If you think a break is just a rarely used key on your keyboard, then perhaps you need to consider the "antidote for civilization."

Company
Club Med

Where
World Wide Web

Web Address
http://www.clubmed.com/

Prices
Something for every budget.

Vinland Ltd. won't leave you out in the cold, although they'll be happy to take you there.

Greenland Cruises with Internet Access

Picture this: You're sailing by a majestic Greenland glacier that's floating along a pristine landscape the next moment. In the evening, you're emailing your family, telling them of the extraordinary sites you've seen in this Arctic wilderness.

If this scenario appeals to you, then navigate yourself to the Vinland Ltd. home page for details of their North Atlantic adventure cruises, complete with onboard Internet access.

To accommodate weather and ice conditions, there are basically two itineraries: Iceland in the months of June and July, and the fiords of Greenland in August and September. In the off months, the boat is chartered to organizations that perform research missions, such as the Icelandic Marine Research Institute expedition to tag six whales and to put them in direct satellite contact with computers at the University of Missouri.

The vessel, Leifur Eirksson, holds up to 24 passengers in 5 cabins. It was built in 1980 as a fishing trawler, but four years later was converted to a "Survivor Safety Standby" vessel for the offshore British oil industry. The boat was named after the famed explorer, but the company likes to point out that their cruises, unlike Eirksson's, "are both shorter and more peaceful."

Since the ship can only accommodate 24 people max, you can essentially charter the boat for small clubs or a large family. Vinland Ltd. will be happy to work with you to design a custom itinerary based on what your group would most like to experience.

The trip lasts for five to seven days and stresses nature sightseeing and as much fishing as time permits in the seas and nearby rivers and lakes. According to the company, "experienced salmon and trout fishermen who have fished in these areas state that they have never in their lives experienced so many fish."

The onboard Internet access connection is courtesy of cellular-type connection and is available to any passenger who feels a need to recharge his or her electronic connections. By doing so, Vinland Ltd. has added another dimension to the metaphor "cruising the Web."

Company
Vinland Ltd. (Reykjavik, Iceland)

Where
World Wide Web

Web Address
http://www.centrum.is/com/vinland.html

Email
siggi@centrum.is

Prices
About $150 per day, per person.

Now you don't have to kill yourself to travel to Dead shows. Tickets and Travel can get you there fast and inexpensively.

Sports and Entertainment Travel

A few weeks ago, a friend of mine called and wanted to know the best way to get from Des Moines, Iowa to Cleveland, Ohio, because he and a buddy wanted to see the Screaming Headless Torsos in concert. Now this was a problem.

Rather than asking me to crawl around CompuServe, Eaasy Sabre, and dozens of other online niches, he could have simply webbed into Tickets and Travel Inc. Devoted to creating entertainment-based packages, Tickets and Travel has been sending people on journeys to see their favorite rockers and sporting events since 1985, and is one of the few companies that provides such a service—and the only one online.

Tickets and Travel puts together truly customized trips, complete with show tickets, hotel, airfare, and ground transportation. The company is currently preparing excursions to see the Grateful Dead, Bruce Springsteen, REM, and several other bands now on tour.

Their most popular packages, however, are race related—Indy 500 and Daytona 500 trips that include everything you need to see that rare and thrilling car crash.

Their Indianapolis 500 package, for example, includes three nights hotel accommodations, reserved Terrace race tickets, a choice of attending the Drivers Meeting or the Festival Parade, admission to the Speedway Museum, choice of pre-race races, and a commemorative IndyCar Souvenir Program. Prices for a recent package ranged from $699 to $1,199 per person, depending on the luxury level you want.

For those who love sports and like to cruise, Tickets and Travel has got your boat. They offer basketball cruises complete with NBA players, free-throw shooting competitions, and other once-in-a-lifetime opportunities.

Whether you want to slam dunk or see punk, Tickets and Travel has your ticket to excitement.

Shopping on the Internet and Beyond

Exclusive Deal

Tickets and Travel

$30 per person off your first purchase off a complete travel package.

Exclusive deal for readers of this book only!
You must mention this offer when you place your order.

Company
Tickets and Travel (Indianapolis, IN)

Where
World Wide Web

Web Address
http://www.inetdirect.net/tnt

Email
tnt@inetdirect.net

Prices
From $499 to $2,495 per person.

Welcome to paradise, now go home. Just kidding! Stay, sip a julep by the pool, sun yourself on the beach.

Interactive Travel Service

So, you and your significant other can't seem to identify a mutually agreeable vacation destination. *You* want to take in a gourmet wine tour of France, but your beloved would prefer to spend a week at a dude ranch in the Marble Mountain Wilderness.

While you might not choose to spend your holiday together, you can at least research your "separate but equal" vacations with each other, through the help of The Travel Source, an interactive travel guide with 400 categories for every type of travel manner or destination you can shake a ticket at.

With 19 categories and counting, The Travel Source should consider renaming their company The Travel Re-Source. It's stocked with information and pictures in a beautifully laid out Web site that loads fast and takes you quickly to where you want to be.

The travel categories include:
- Exotic Resorts
- Cruises
- Scuba Diving
- Sports Tours
- Specialty Tours
- Hotels
- Yacht Charters
- Trekking
- Golf Getaways
- Bed & Breakfasts
- Spa Resorts
- Guest Ranches
- Safaris
- Wine Tours
- Villa Rentals
- Ski Vacations
- Cycling
- River Rafting
- Travel Info

The last category is quite handy. Considering a trip to the land-locked former Soviet Social Republic of Belarus? You might think again after you read the State Department advisories for world destinations, which are linked to the Travel Source Web site. Along with the CIA World Fact Book—which provides detailed country information and maps—the two combined could literally save your life if you tend to venture to destinations off the well-beaten path.

From the major topic listings, you click and point yourself to a menu of sub-choices. For example, if you select Villa Rentals, you'll get a list of companies that service this travel objective. Select the one that best fits your vision and you'll be shown a background on the companies and their properties, along with an opportunity to get a full brochure via snail-mail (with a simple email request).

There's nothing to buy on the Travel Source, except time. This efficient service can direct you to where you want to go and then help get you on your way without the hassle of a research trip to the library or a stuffy afternoon in a travel agent's office.

Travel Service (continued)

Company
The Travel Source (San Diego, CA)

Where
World Wide Web

Web Address
http://www.travelsource.com

Email
info@travelsource.com

Prices
Free service

Fly Dirt Cheap

"If you can beat these prices, start your own airline" is the simple motto of Air-Tech Ltd, purveyors of dirt-cheap airline tickets.

Usually, deep-discount travel companies conjure up images of fly-by-night operations out for a quick buck and with the inevitable plethora of stranded passengers. Not the case with Air-Tech. They've been in business since 1988, with 12 offices in the United States and Europe. Furthermore, they have unconditional endorsements from such notable travel guide series as Let's Go and Frommers. Even *Consumer's Digest* recommends Air-Tech as a source for unbeatable tickets prices.

How do they do it? Well, by offering three unique types of service: Space Available, Confirmed Reservation, and Courier Fares.

According to Air Tech's president Mark Cole, Space Available should be your first choice. "Air-Tech Ltd. has agreements with various carriers to accept their Air-Tech FlighPasses on a space-available basis. The staff locates seats that airlines are unable to sell at full fare." You are then notified of such openings up to a week in advance of your trip. Air-Tech likes to think of it as "a green approach to recycling airline seats."

The Space Available program operates on a first come/first served basis for one-way or round-trip tickets. When you are advised of your departure date and time, you exchange your flightpass for a boarding pass and away you go. If you fly under the Space Available approach, you must have some flexibility in your travel plans and a departure window of about one to four days. You might not know *exactly* what day and time you are outbound, but Air-Tech will get you there on a major carrier at otherwise-impossible prices.

"If you want a specific flight on a definite date to an exact destination somewhere in the world," then you want Confirmed Reserved tickets from Air-Tech. They work with ticket consolidators and tour companies to find you the cheapest ticket to your destination.

And then there is the Courier option. Okay, so you give up your check-in luggage allowance and agree to carry-on baggage only, but you do receive a confirmed date and destination at discounted fares. These are round-trip flights, with a return date set when you book your flight. You can stay in European destinations for up to several weeks and up to three months for the South Pacific packages. Prices are quoted at the time of booking and are limited to particular routes, but consider the lucky fellow who flew round-trip from New York to Hong Kong for only $200.

"Air-Tech is open to everyone and caters to independent, resourceful travelers." Much of their clientele are people with a lot of flexibility in their travel plans, such as students, senior citi-

Fly Dirt Cheap (continued)

zens, and "Kerouac-types." For example, if you're dying to go to Paris, Air-Tech may discover that you're better off flying to a destination nearby, such as Amsterdam, and then taking a short bus or train trip to Paris, which can save you loads of loot off their already extraordinary low fares.

In addition to plane tickets, Air-Tech offers Eurail passes, Europasses, and car rentals in Europe and the Caribbean.

The company's mission is clear and well-stated: "Air-Tech delivers planet Earth to you."

Shopping on the Internet and Beyond

Exclusive Deal

Air-Tech Ltd.

$5 off your first ticket purchase and $10 off your first purchase of two or more Eurail passes.

Exclusive deal for readers of this book only! You must mention this offer when you place your order.

Company
Air-Tech Ltd. (New York, NY)

Where
World Wide Web

Web Address
http://campus.net/aerotech

Email
dirt-cheap@aerotech.com

Instant Information
info@aerotech.com

Prices
From $129 to $999.

International orders are accepted.

See India the way the locals see it. Of course, the "locals" include a few of the four-footed variety.

Low-Key Adventure Travel

If your idea of a vacation is to hike among civilizations most people only read about in *National Geographic*, then Canadian Himalayan Expeditions is your Club Med.

What they offer are unique trips to Nepal, India, Pakistan, and Asia, "designed to be genuine explorations for travelers (not 'tourists') who are looking for the advantages of a well-organized adventure holiday, yet also desire some individual freedom to do things on their own."

In what they refer to as the antithesis of the "If it's Tuesday, it must be Belgium syndrome," Canadian Himalayan Expeditions offers an "active, participatory type of experience with hiking, rafting, climbing, or some other kind of physical activity on many of the days. You do not have to be a marathon runner or mountaineer to participate—you simply have to be the kind of person who enjoys walking the outdoors and the opportunity of cross-cultural contact in exotic lands." The endurance level of each trip is rated from a low of "good rhythm to pumping nicely to pounding to racing."

Low-Key Adventures (continued)

Most of their trips are limited to 15 people, with a typical group number from 8 to 12 people. Your fellow travelers are generally well-educated with a mix of half men, half women, and half married, half single in an average age range of 25 to 40.

In business since 1983, the company organizes about 14 trips per year—five each in fall and summer, and four in springtime. The costs quoted for each trip are for land only, which includes all meals; major equipment; "porters/yaks/mules" to carry equipment and personal gear; a group leader, sherpa, and cooks; local transportation from city of origin; and hotel accommodations when you and your group aren't on the trail.

And now a personal note: According to my mother, who works at a prestigious Los Angeles travel agency, Canadian Himalayan Expeditions prices are so good they're "almost scary." I described one of their itineraries to her and asked what she thought the trip would cost. Her answer was double the actual price.

In my interview with the company, they made two key points about their prices. First, they've been doing this a long, long time and have developed relationships with locals, which helps them get the best prices; and second, they don't incur the marketing expenses most tour companies do since they don't offer a several page, four-color, glossy brochure. Their advertising is through word of mouth and testimonials (along with email addresses of those quoted, which can be found on the company's Web pages).

Admittedly, I am more a vacationer than a traveler. A week on a beach with a Chi Chi in one hand and a John Irving novel in the other is my idea of a relaxing holiday. However, these adventure trips do sound invigorating without being taxing and the just might be the perfect way to get way, way, away from it all.

Company
Canadian Himalayan Expeditions
(Toronto, Canada)

Where
World Wide Web

Web Address
http://www.netpart.com/che/

Email
venice@io.org

Prices
From approximately $950 (U.S. dollars) to $1,725 (U.S. dollars), land only.

International orders are accepted.

For More...

For more great travel shopping opportunities, see the next page.

Hot Tip!

To book your own plane tickets and for fare and route information, Eaasy Sabre—a light version of the reservation system that Travel Agents use—is available on all the major online services. The lowest fare feature is quite useful.

America Online: Keyword *eaasy sabre*
CompuServe: Go *ezs*
Prodigy: Jump *eaasy sabre*

Honorable Mentions

in the category of

Destinations in Travel

Air France Vacations

Tour booking and information.

Company
Air France

CompuServe
Go *af*

Air, Land, and Sea

Private party ads on America Online for all modes of travel.

America Online
Keyword *classifieds* then select *general merchandise boards*

Air Travel and Cruises

Private party ads on CompuServe.

CompuServe
Go *classifieds* then select *travel*

Archaeological and Culture Trips

Offers unique adventures "for adventure, education, camaraderie, and a new understanding of the world's cultures."

Company
Far Horizons

Web Address
http://rt66.com/coach/far/far.html

Email
75473.3100@compuserve.com

Arctic Adventures

Expeditions and explorations in the Arctic area, from Norway to Northern Russia.

Company
Avid Explorer

Web Address
http://www.explore.com

Email
webmaster@explore.com

British Airways

Special offers and free brochures for trips to England, Scotland, Wales and Northern Ireland.

Company
British Airways

Prodigy
Jump *british airways*

Cathay Pacific Holidays

Asian travel packages to the airlines' premiere destination.

Company
Cathay Pacific

Web Address
http://www.cathay-usa.com

Cruise Specials

"Amazing cruise specials...choose from 100s with the best cruise rates guaranteed."

Company
Rosenbluth Vacations

CompuServe
Go *ros*

Discount Dining Nationwide

Members get 2-for-1 deals, with 20 percent off subsequent visits to more than 9,000 restaurants.

Company
Premier Dining Club

America Online
Keyword *premier dining*

CompuServe
Go *pd*

Prodigy
Jump *premier dining club*

Discount Vacations

Focusing on popular destinations, look for special offers, brochures, and travel auction house.

Company
Preview Vacations

America Online
Keyword *vacations*

Email
auctiongal@aol.com

Embassy Suites and More

Database with pictures and detailed descriptions of Promus Company lodgings.

Company
Promus Companies

Web Address
http://www.promus.com

Freighter Cruises

Choose from an impressive selection of world-wide destinations, in this less-than-luxurious but economical travel opportunity.

Company
Freighter World Cruises

Web Address
`http://www.gus.com/travel/fwc/fwc.html`

Hawaii Video

"Award winning series" of videotapes on all aspects of vacation and travel in Hawaii NTSC and PAL versions.

Company
The VRC Collection

Web Address
`http://sirius.pixi.com/g_store/video/vrc`

Email
`vrc@pixi.com`

Hostelling Options

With a focus on Northern California, get information pertaining to hosteling.

Company
American Youth Hostels

Web Address
`http://cyber.cclims.com/comp/ayh/ayh.html`

Hotels and Camping

Private party ads on CompuServe.

CompuServe
Go *classifieds* then select *travel*

Internet Travel Club

Rebates, discount certificates, and special cruise and accommodation deals.

Company
Costa Travel Online

Web Address
`http://mmink.cts.com/mmink/kiosks/costa/costatravel.html`

Email
`costatvl@aol.com`

Luggage

"Fine-quality famous maker luggage collection and travel accessories."

Company
Lieber's Luggage

Web Address
`http://www.cyspacemalls.com/lieber/index.html`

Email
`service@cyspacemalls.com`

Maps

Maps and travel guide books. Covers everything on earth. Map reviews on their Web site.

Company
World of Maps

Web Address
`http://www.magi.com/~maps`

Email
`maps@magi.com`

Maine Coast Nature Trips

Join Captain Patterson for birdwatching trips, nature cruises, and sightseeing trips along the "real Maine coast."

Company
Bold Coast Charter Company

Web Address
http://www.maine.com/afp

Email
afp@maine.com

Northern Arctic Adventures

Expeditions and explorations in the Arctic area...from Northern Norway to Northern Russia.

Company
Arctic Adventures

Web Address
http://www.oslonett.no/adv/AA/AA.html

Rentals and Time Shares

Private party ads on CompuServe.

CompuServe
Go *classifieds* then select *travel*

Hot Tip!

For best buys on Prodigy, jump *shopping* to get to Prodigy's "Bargains Galore" menu—a list of special deals offered by their online merchants.

Select European Accomodations

Make direct contact with hotels, B&Bs, and cottage renters in England, Wales, Scotland, Ireland, France. No fees or commissions.

Company
AccomoDATA

Web Address
http://www.cityscape.co.uk/users/eb19

Email
tech@accomodata.co.uk

Southwest Accomodations

Complete arrangements for destinations in the Southwest from a Company specializing in the area since 1978.

Company
Arizona Accommodations Reservations

Web Address
http://www.indirect.com/www/scott

Email
scott@indirect.com

Time Shares and Vacation Homes

Private party ads on Prodigy.

Prodigy
Jump *classifieds* then select *browse ads*

Travel

Private party ads on America Online.

America Online
Keyword *classifieds* then select *general merchandise boards*

Travel Accessories

Travel-related hard-to-find products.

Company
Traveler's Checklist Catalog

Web Address
http://www.ag.com/travelers/checklist

Email
travelers.checklist@ag.com

Travel and Tours

Private party ads on Prodigy.

Prodigy
Jump *classifieds* then select *browse ads*

Travel Arrangements

A good source for all types of travel, including major cruise lines, "value" vacation packages, and popular tour companies.

Company
The Avid Explorer

Web Address
http://www.explore.com

Travel Deals

If you're hankering to skip town on a budget ,log onto the internet on your way out.

Usenet Group
rec.travel.marketplace

Travelers Advantage

Members get low price guarantees, 5 percent cash bonuses, special, car rental discounts, and saving at over 2,500 hotels.

Company
Travelers Advantage

America Online
Keyword *travelers advantage*

CompuServe
Go *ta*

Prodigy
Jump *travelers advantage*

Travel Videos

Travel videos from Hilton Head Golf to Howe Caverns, the Great Smoky Mountains, and more!

Company
Video Postcards

Web Address
http://www.coolsite.com/tapes1.html

Hot Tip!

America Online members, be sure to periodically stop by "Product Spotlight—Featured Items & Great Deals" in the 2Market shopping area for a list if items on sale. Keyword *2market*.

Vacation Specials

Full travel service with last minute vacation specials.

Company
Air Waves Travel

Web Address
`http://www.xnet.com/~creacon/AWT/`

Wholesale Airline Tickets

"Save 20 to 35 percent off domestic airfares above $250 guaranteed...and still qualify for mileage credit and reserved seating."

Company
Travel Discounters

Web Address
`http://www.tagsys.com/Ads/NetSale/`
`index.html`

Email
`td3@ix.netcom.com`

Education

Scholastic books—for the elastic minds of fantastic kids.

Scholastic Books

Scholastic is the largest publisher of children's books in the English-speaking world. So, just how big is "largest?" Well, if you gave every child in the United States *four* books *every year* from Scholastic publishing, you would still have thousands remaining from the 125 million copies that Scholastic publishes each year.

The company publishes books, software, videos, and magazines; 9 out of every 10 schools in the country are clients Their products are geared for kids ranging in age from pre-schoolers through secondary school.

Scholastic's Internet Center offers a generous selection of these ubiquitous products via their Ultimate Education Store. Here you'll find hundreds of trade books, technology products, reference texts, and instructional publishing materials.

If you're a teacher (or parent), you can also jump on the Scholastic school bus. Their Professional Bookshelf section offers teaching aids for such subjects as critical thinking, math, and science, as well as multilingual and multicultural books.

This site's handy search feature also lets you quickly find what you're looking for by using such criteria as grade level, topic, or educational approach.

Scholastic has certainly achieved its goal of providing an "online shopping center that takes the pain out of buying K through 12 educational materials."

Company
Scholastic Inc. (New York, NY)

Where
World Wide Web

Web Address
http://scholastic.com:2005

Email
info@scholastic.com

Shipping Fees
Based on weight and destination.

International orders are accepted.

Remember!

For periodic updates of this book, send email to *shop@easton.com*. See *Introduction* for more details.

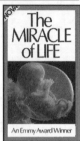

When it comes to science, NOVA covers the full spectrum, from an up-close and personal look into a womb with a view to a couple of guys with their view of a tomb.

NOVA Videos

The NOVA series of Emmy award-winning programs have been broadcast on PBS for years. If you've missed any of these notable education documentaries, you can buy the videos via the Internet.

The NOVA sites features three of their most popular series:

- *The Miracle of Life.* This program could probably be renamed "A Womb with a View." Using extraordinary cinematographic techniques, you can witness the "incredible voyage through the human body as a new life begins" through the "entire birth process."
- *The Old Pyramid.* A 90-minute special relating the "the history and development of pyramid building techniques." Using the Great Pyramid of Giza, a noted Egyptologist and a professional stonemason examine the "bizarre construction theories" used to build this architectural wonder.

- *In Search of Human Origins.* A three-part series tracing the "the origins of the family, the development of intelligence, and the emergence of culture" The program focuses on Don Johanson, the man responsible for finding "Lucy," the skeleton believed to be our "oldest ancestor."

The quality of NOVA programming is the standard by which other science programming is often compared. These educational programs are superb additions to the library of scientific information and are highly recommended for any family's video library.

Company
WGBH Television (Boston, MA)

Where
World Wide Web and email

Web Address
http://branch.com/nova/nova.html

Email
nova@branch.com

Prices
From $19.95 to 59.85.

Shipping Fees
Based on order size and method.

International orders are accepted.

Parliamentary Procedure Resources

Parliamentary Procedures are the formal rules by which meetings of deliberative assemblies and clubs are formally conducted.

Parliamentary Resources (continued)

These procedures are paramount in ensuring orderly conduct in a government or corporate environment. More importantly, attorneys, city clerks, or other parliamentarians "have a legal responsibility to see that public business meetings are conducted according to Parliamentary Authority."

The rules, however, are not simple and sometimes can cause legal problems if not heeded.

In response to this potential problem, Robert McConnell has produced a series of books and videotapes to educate those who must have this information, as well as for those who would find it helpful in conducting more effective and time-efficient meetings. The system is called "Robert's Rules of Order" (a sample of which is available on the Web site).

The video is especially helpful. In the first 60-minutes, you get "clear, step-by-step instructions on how to follow Robert's Rules. At the end there is a 20-minute simulated meeting to explain the major points." The video is intended for adults and high school students (just make sure you at least have a quorum in your treehouse before you begin). Included with the video is a "handy printed reference booklet containing key definitions, terms, and concepts. An officer can conduct a meeting with the printed handbook at the podium."

The best testimonial of the video comes from a North Carolina attorney who said "The video lets everybody benefit from orderly meetings, neither wasting time nor ignoring a full discussion and the rights of the minority opinion."

Shopping on the Internet and Beyond

Exclusive Deal

Robert McConnell Productions

$5 off your first order of $49 or more.

Exclusive deal for readers of this book only!
You must mention this offer when you place your order.

Company
Robert McConnell Productions
(Muncie, IN)

Where
World Wide Web

Web Address
`http://cyberzine.org/html/Parliamentary/mainpage.html`

Email
`pp001042@interramp.com`

Prices
From $49.50 to $152.50.

Shipping Fees
Included in product price. Shipping fees for foreign orders are higher than U.S. fees.

International orders are accepted.

Being dogged by the law? Be your own legal beagle and bite back.

Self-Help Legal Information

Question: How many lawyers does it take to change a light bulb?

Legal Information (continued)

Answer: How many can you afford?

Court TV and the People's Court have convinced a lot of us that just about anyone can handle his her own legal affairs. So, if you're looking for do-it-yourself legal information, Nolo Press likely publishes at least one book (and probably more) to help you wade through any legal quagmire.

As "America's leading source of self-help legal information," Nolo Press is "dedicated to the simple proposition that the American legal system should be affordable and accessible to all."

"Nolo's mission is far from a radical idea. Every American's right to know the law—without paying for a lawyer—is a cornerstone of our democracy," and they state that "making the process easier is what we are here for."

Nolo accomplishes this through books, software, and audiotapes in the following categories: Business and Workplace, Estate Planning, Family Matters and Seniors, Homeowner/Landlord/Tenant, Immigration, Intellectual Property, Money and Consumer Matters and, of course, Representing Yourself in Court.

Nolo Press also has a sense of humor about the profession, offering such books as "29 Reasons Not to Go to Law School" and "Poetic Justice: The Funniest, Meanest Things Ever Said About Lawyers."

If you're looking to re-stock your lawyer-joke arsenal, Nolo offers a free section on their Web site chock full of their favorite lawyer jokes and quotes—updated pretty frequently.

Company
Nolo Press' Self-Help Law Center
(Berkeley, CA)

Where
World Wide Web

Web Address
http://gnn.com/gnn/bus/nolo/

Email
cs@nolopress.com

Prices
From $4.95 to 160.96.

Shipping Fees
Based on order size.

Vic Sussman, U.S. News and World Report's head cybersurfer, is one of hundreds of personalities available to speak at your company's next engagement.

Speakers On-Line

Live lecturing remains one of the most effective ways to educate people—assuming that the speaker is experienced, engaging, and informative. That's the concept behind Speakers On-Line: Give people easy access to the top public lecturers in the country for corporate and social event planning—big names that pull in big numbers, such as One Minute Manager Kenneth Blanchard, NBC's Tom Brokaw, sales wizard Zig Ziglar, NFL Hall of fame player and coach Mike Ditka, and other notables in their respective fields.

Speakers On-Line is a well designed site and will help you contact exactly who you need for your organization's next speaking engagement. You can search based on topic, budget criteria, or location. (If you need to consider travel costs for your speaker, it's often cheaper to "hire local.")

For the topic sections available, you can choose from Voices in the 90s, Performing Arts, Conducting Business, What Tomorrow Will Bring, How's Your Health, and Internet Pioneers & Proponents.

Regarding that last topic, I can vouch for the speaking skills of Vic Sussman, Cyberspace Editor at *U.S. News and World Report* and one of the country's most highly praised lecturers.

Vic's beat primarily deals with the legal, cultural, and social implications of cyberspace. He can speak extemporaneously about all that is online, including hysterically funny anecdotes guaranteed to be retold at the water cooler long after his visit. His informative, insightful, and wildly entertaining style is irresistible.

If Vic Sussman's lectures are any indication of the overall quality of the Speakers On-Line roster, you'll find no better resource for locating a speaker for your next business or social function.

Company
Speakers On-Line

Where
World Wide Web

Web Address
http://www.clark.net/pub/speakers/web/speakers.html

Email
speakers@clark.net

Prices
Under $5,000 to over $20,000.

Okay, so you couldn't get into Princeton. Maybe you'd have done better if you'd gone to Princeton Review first.

Achievement Test Tips

I have yet to meet a college-bound teenager who isn't nervous about the alphabet soup of tests for which he or she has to prepare: the PSAT, SAT, SAT II, or ACT—not to mention the array of exams students face for graduate school applications, including the LSAT, GMAT, GRE, and MCAT.

The Princeton Review is one of the nation's leaders in preparing students for these rigorous standardized tests via books, audiotapes, videos, and computer software—the last of which is called RevieWare. This educational software is extremely handy because it actually scores the tests for you, thus eliminating the tedious job of calculating your results manually, which can easily result in errors.

Many of the Princeton Review books available for purchase online also include disks. As part of their "Cracking the System" series, you can find book/software combos for the SAT, PSAT, GRE, LSAT, and GMAT—with more titles on the way.

To give you an idea of what you get when you purchase one of these products, let me quote from the PSAT/SAT guide. The disk included with the book uses "CAT (computer-adaptive testing), which adjusts the level of difficulty of a problem based on your answers. This allows the computer to evaluate your performance in one hour versus three. The CATs are great tools because they can give you a fast, accurate idea of your progress while you practice the techniques. You can spend more time learning and less time checking your performance, although the RevieWare does give you the option of taking timed, full-length exams."

Now, if they could just do something about those essay questions.

Company
Princeton Review

Where
World Wide Web

Web Address
http://www.review.com/

Email
info.tpr@review.com

Prices
From $16.00 to 29.95.

Shipping Fees

Based on order size.

Learning English

If a picture truly says a thousand words, then learning words through pictures makes a lot of sense. That's the idea behind The English Learning Store (ELS), which offers vocabulary-building videos for kids and adults who are learning English—in its spoken form as a second language.

ELS has two programs: Open Door is geared for pre-school through grammar school and Stage One is designed for grades six through adult.

The Stage One series approaches English through music. "The program consists of 32 lessons, with each lesson introducing 32 words. "The lesson

is presented in a stage setting and in story form by four children and their mentor." Note that the "mentor" is neither purple nor Jurassic.

The underlying concept of Stage One is that, by singing "catchy tunes, the lyrics will help listeners become fluent in the use of English sounds, while the rhythms aid their retention of the new vocabulary." Said one teacher from a school that uses these tapes, "I can always tell what unit the other classes are working on by the songs I hear floating down the hall."

The Stage One video series is a 12-tape compilation, with each video running about 30 minutes. The lessons are totally in English and help students recognize the sounds and meanings of 1,000 frequently used English words. Each lesson contains seven, five-minute segments featuring mimes, artists, field trips, and skits. "The skits show real life situations. They create models for role playing. The scene sets and props show students a cross-section of life in the United States."

If you want to preview either of these series, you can do so via a five-minute demonstration tape available for a nominal fee.

Shopping on the Internet and Beyond

Exclusive Deal

The English Learning Store

$10 off your first order
(excluding demo tapes)

Exclusive deal for readers of this book only!
You must mention this offer when you place your order.

Company
The English Learning Store
(Alexandria, VA)

Learning English (continued)

Where
World Wide Web

Web Address
`http://www.ip.net/shops/English_Learning_Store/`

Reminder! This Web address is case sensitive. Make sure you enter it *exactly* as shown.

Email
`sissonva@aol.com`

Prices
From $12.00 to $359.50.

Shipping Fees (in the U.S.)
$10

International orders are accepted.

Uh oh! Tommy Tyrannosaurus is going after Sammy Slug! Who do you think will win this one, boys and girls?

Educational Software for Kids

I can't tell you how many crazed parents I see wandering the aisles of software stores trying to figure out which titles are best suited for their kids. While Mom and Dad pore over the fine print on each box, little Russell is usually "oh-ing and ah-ing" over the "less-than-educational" choices. The supermarket cereal battles have carried over into the software store.

Enter Children's Software Company, which solves these parental dilemmas. First, you can buy and view everything online, bypassing CompUSA and the inevitable parent-child "war to the death." Second, all the software in their catalog is educational and has passed a stringent evaluation process that helps take the quality issue out of the buying process.

Everything at the Children's Software Company site is for pre-school through high-school aged folks. The company carries both Mac and PC formats, as well as a slew of CD-ROMS.

At last count, I found eleven software/CD-ROM categories total, and you can browse via an alphabetical index (if you know exactly what you want).

When you find something that strikes you, click on the title to get virtually all the same information, and then some, that you'd get from the back of the box—including a photo, a list of system requirements, and the price, which is discounted. In addition, you also get a comprehensive review of the software, which provides enough information for you to make a sensible decision.

If your child tends to plow through programs, you can stay on top of the latest titles via the Children's Software Company electronic newsletter (free—subscribe at their site).

Educational Software (continued)

Company
Children's Software Company
(Chevy Chase, MD)

Where
World Wide Web

Web Address
`http://www.childsoft.com/childsoft`

Email
`info@childsoft.com`

Prices
From $16.95 to $49.99.

Shipping Fees (in the U.S.)
A $5 flat fee for two-day delivery.

International orders are accepted.

"How-To" Video Extravaganza

The InfoVid Outlet online catalog is "your complete guide to the best educational, instructional, and informative videos from around the world, with over 3,500 hard-to-find titles on a wide variety of subjects."

So many "how-to" and educational videos are of extremely poor quality (home-use video cameras, poor sound, etc.). The InfoVid Outlet takes the guesswork out of buying. According to them, "only videos with the highest production values and best information content are included" in their catalog.

The catalog lives up to its claim that it contains "videos for every man, woman, and child." There are over 30 categories to choose from. When you click on a subject of interest, you'll be transported to a denser list of choices.

The pages listing the videos are laid out well and are easy to navigate. You get the name of the video and a brief description, along with the tape's length and price. The prices seem fair to me, especially for such niche topics.

Although I'm a prolific reader, I do acknowledge that some concepts are communicated better through pictures and sound. So if you want to improve your golf game, plant a more robust garden, dazzle your friends with magic, or dance the rhumba at your next Christmas party, InfoVid's "educational and how-to video warehouse" will probably have the tape you want.

Shopping on the Internet and Beyond

Exclusive Deal

InfoVid Outlet

10 percent off your first order
of $25 or more.

Exclusive deal for readers of this book only!
You must mention this offer when you place your order.

Company
InfoVid Outlet (Tampa, FL)

Where
World Wide Web

Web Address
`http://branch.com:1080/infovid/c100.html`

Email
`digitali@renoir.cftnet.com`

Prices
From $9.95 to $79.95.

Shipping Fees
$3.50 for the first video, 75 cents for each additional video. International orders have higher shipping fees.

International orders are accepted.

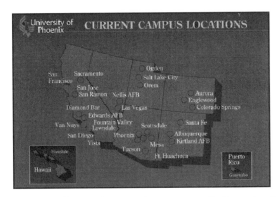

You don't need to go to Phoenix to go to the University of Phoenix. All you need is a computer, a modem, and a hankerin' to learn.

College Degrees Online

Imagine this: No matter where you are or how tight your schedule, you can earn a college degree—all you need is a computer and a modem to attend online classes at the University of Phoenix.

Founded in 1976, the University of Phoenix is a fully accredited school that enrolls over 14,000 students per year, of which a growing percentage are online. The school offers Masters programs in Business Administration and Arts in Management, as well as a Bachelor of Science degree in Business Administration and a Bachelor of Arts degree in Management.

Here's how it works: Using customized computer technology, students and instructors work together in a collaborative environment. You become an active member of a learning group of about 10 to 15 working adults. Online study groups work on assigned projects together.

Students take one course at a time, with each course lasting 5 to 6 weeks in length. The typical University of Phoenix program requires about 2 to 2 1/2 years, 12 to 15 hours per week, and about

$15,000 to $16,000 (an average of $360 per credit hour). Add to these costs textbooks and online phone time (about one hour per week).

The average student age is 38; 32 percent are female and 68 percent are male. Most are either middle managers, licensed professionals, or executive/small business owners.

As part of your admission requirements—which are relatively noncompetitive—you are required to complete a University of Phoenix Comprehensive Cognitive Assessment. Other admission requirements are reasonable, and include at least two to three years of full-time, post high school work experience.

Company
University of Phoenix (Phoenix, AZ)

Where
CompuServe, Prodigy, World Wide Web

Shortcut (CompuServe)
Go *up*

Shortcut (Prodigy)
Jump *univ phoenix*

Web Address
http://www.uophx.edu/

Email
webmaster@apollo1.uophx.edu

Prices
Dependent on course curriculum.

International orders are accepted.

For More...

See the next page for additional sites for more great shopping opportunities related to education.

Honorable Mentions
in the category of
Education

Educational Videos

Instructional videos on Business, Law, Engineering, and Women's Leadership by well-known speakers.

Company
International Communications Corporation

Web Address
http://www.ip.net/ICC

Events, Seminars, and Conferences

Private party ads, on America Online, for events, seminars, and conferences.

America Online
Keyword *classifieds* then select *general merchandise boards*

Experiments in a Box

Technical and science products and kits.

Company
Wacky Web Pages

Web Address
http://scitech.lm.com/index.html

Financial Aid

Educational funding options beyond what's normally offered by the government and colleges.

Company
Chinook College Funding Service

Web Address
http://www.chinook.com/user/chinook2/

Email
info@chinook.com

Full Color Family Trees

Full color, suitable for framing, family trees—up to 72 family members can be included.

Company
Vitarbor Graphics

Web Address
http://www.teleport.com/~jcrunch/
vitarbor.html

Email
jcrunch@teleport.com

Genealogy Research

Full service geneology research firm using worldwide databases.

Company
Lineages Inc.

Web Address
http://cybermart.com/lineages/

Genealogy Resources

Outstanding selection of genealogy books, software, magazines and resources (birth, death and marriage records).

Company
Everton Publishers

Web Address
http://www.xmission.com/~jayhall/evcat.html

Learning-to-Read Aids

"Reading with Phonics is Fun" multimedia software, books, and videos.

Company
Arrow Publishing Company

Web Address
http://www2.interpath.net:/spadion/arrow

Mental Fitness

Products to help people enter states of deep relaxation on demand.

Company
Mind Gear, Inc.

Web Address
http://www.gate.net./~mind/

NPR Materials

Transcripts and cassettes of NPR programming.

Company
National Public Radio

America Online
Keyword *npr*

Personal Growth

Catalog of trainings, books, and tapes in Neuro Linguistic Programming, Time Line Therapy, hypnosis, and Ancient Hawaiian Huna.

Company
Advanced Neuro Dynamics

Web Address
http://www.aloha.com/~mind

Science of the Mind

Books and video on the psychology and physics of consciousness.

Company
Unarius Academy of Science

Web Address
http://www.cts.com/~unarius

Email
unarius@cts.com

Science Kits

Kits for safe, responsible home experimentation. Simple instructions and a parent/teacher guide included with each kit.

Company
SciTech, Inc.

Web Address
http://www.scitechsoft.com

ShareViews Video Tutor

Learn about the functions of tools of the Internet via video.

Company
ShareViews Video Tutor

Web Address
http://www.cyberzine.org/html/Video/
video2.html

Stephen Covey Merchandise

Leadership training products from the author of the *Seven Habits of Highly Effective People*.

Company
Covey Leadership Center

Web Address
http://www2.pcy.mci.net/marketplace/
covey/

World Book Products

Encyclopedias and the rest of their educational line of toys and books.

Company
World Book

Web Address
http://www.shopping2000.com/shopping2000/
worldbook/

Flowers, Plants, & Gardening

Invest just a few ounces of effort and get a pond of beauty.

Country Garden Supplies

No matter what state your garden is in—lifeless and piled high with brown leaves or perfectly sheared and shrubbed—Jan's Country Garden has something for you. The company specializes in "everything garden" from flowers to greenhouses, garden ponds to landscape lighting.

In the floral department, look for unbelievable quality and prices for Jackson & Perkins Roses, as well as perennials. Once you get your flower garden growing, you might want to consider an arbor "as a focal point for dazzling displays of climbing flowers such as roses, clematis, and ornamental vines." Jan's offers three types: metal, cedar (premium quality—non shifting) and polyvinyl (durable—will never chip, crack, rot, or peel).

If you'd like to add some pizzazz to your garden, how about installing a pond? "Jan's pond kits include everything you need from start to finish. Just follow the easy step-by-step instructions to a beautiful showcase your friend's will be envious of. These kits include top grade rubber (45 mil versus the 22 to 32 found in most other kits), aquatic plant stimulant, even a pump complete with fountain."

Everything in the Jan Country Garden online catalog is discounted and sent direct to your door. For the best buys, look for their weekly specials. For gardening advice, check out "Jan's Garden Party," a question and answer forum for new and seasoned gardeners alike.

Shopping on the Internet and Beyond

Exclusive Deal

Jan's Country Garden

$250 off a Grand-Luxe Greenhouse
and/or $5 off your first order
of $40 or more.

Exclusive deal for readers of this book only!
You must mention this offer when you place your order.

Company
Jan's Country Garden (Albany, NY)

Where
World Wide Web

Web Address
http://www.globalone.net/jcg/

Garden Supplies (continued)

Email
jverba@globalone.net

Prices
From $9.80 to $2,900.

Shipping Fees (in the U.S.)
From $3.95 up to 10 percent of your order, based on size.

International orders are accepted.

Go ahead, splurge on love: Send your sweetheart a bouquet a day from 800-Flowers.

800-Flowers

Even before they went online, 800-Flowers made ordering floral arrangements, bouquets, and baskets as easy as picking a daisy. Customer representatives were available 24 hours a day, 365 days a year. Before the company went online, the only frustration was that you had to rely on the floral descriptions given to you over the phone by the reps. Those days are over—at least for those who have a modem. The company's online catalog lets you view a photo of every item they offer. (Their Web site has everything; their America Online area has plenty to look at, but it's still incomplete.)

Name an occasion and 800-Flowers will almost certainly have several different appropriate offerings, and in some cases, as many as eleven. Look for especially festive options for events like congratulations, anniversary, new baby, birthday, get well soon, thank you, and "just because."

In addition to such traditional floral combinations and arrangements as roses and spring flowers, you'll also find less common items such as "gardens in a basket," "mylar balloon bouquets," "plants-a-plenty," and "basket of autumn."

According to the company, 800-Flowers' products are "created from the freshest, most perfect flowers available, and individually prepared by hand-picked local florists."

Company
800-Flowers

Where
America Online, World Wide Web

America Online
Keyword *flowers*

Web Address
http://www.shopping2000.com/shopping2000/
teleway/

Prices
Small, medium, and large arrangements at reasonable prices.

Remember!

For periodic updates of this book, send email to *shop@easton.com*. See *Introduction* for more details.

Hey! Stop and smell the roses!

Online Fresh Flower Market

There's nothing quite like the Flower Stop anywhere online. Providing a combination grower direct-to-you rose and flower company, as well as FTD service, these folks handle virtually every type of floral order—much of which can be delivered worldwide.

The roots of The Flower Stop are at their Long Distance Roses division. Shipped from the company's greenhouses located "in the pure high-altitude air of Colorado," your order arrives overnight via FedEx Priority One delivery (included in the price) in a specially designed styrofoam gift box. The Flower Stop guarantees these roses as "the longest lasting, sweetest smelling, and highest quality you'll find anywhere. A "Year of Roses" (one dozen per month) at an extremely attractive price is also available.

If want to send bouquets instead of roses, the Flower Stop offers the same outstanding quality. The company contracts with growers specializing in specific flower varieties. Your order is shipped directly from the field for ultimate freshness.

International flower orders are tricky, but the Flower Stop handles them with panache, alacrity, and a little advice, if warranted. Planning to send white flowers to a Japanese business associate or friend? Don't be surprised if one of

the Flower Stop's well-trained sales associates asks you if you're sure the occasion is one of sympathy, because Japanese ritual dictates white flowers for funerals.

As an additional incentive, the Flower Stop rewards customers who plan ahead. Place your order at least one week in advance and you'll get a 10 percent discount.

Also, there is a *200 percent* guarantee. "You must be totally satisfied with the service, quality, and reliability or you do not pay for the order. The flowers will be resent, your money refunded, or both."

Company
Flower Stop Marketing Corp.
(Colorado Springs, CO)

Where
CompuServe, World Wide Web

CompuServe
Go *fs*

Web Address
http://www.flowerstop.com/fstop

Email
orders@1droses.com

Prices
Good pricing on everything they offer. FTD arrangement prices are on par with other outlets.

Shipping Fees

Shipping is included in the price for all continental U.S. deliveries. Reasonable fees added for other destinations.

International orders are accepted.

So how you doin? I'm vine, thanks.

Miniature Grapevines

If you've always wanted your own vineyard, but haven't had the money or the space, consider one of these miniature grapevines—available in Cabernet, Sauvignon Blanc, and Chardonnay varieties.

Developed by using "a secret miniaturization technique developed years ago in Bordeaux, France...these vines go through their regular life cycle of dormancy, budding, leafing out and producing fruit when properly cared for." Okay, so it's not that much fruit—maybe one raisin each for six of your closest friends.

As easy as it is to quantify your annual harvest, it's just as easy to care for your vine(s). "Just fertilize lightly, water, and keep your vines away from severe temperatures...If you snip the vines

back yearly, they'll keep their incredible size and become more dignified and robust with age."

Shipped from the heart of California's premium wine country, these vines are hand-picked for quality and state certified for shipment to all 50 states. Your vine(s) will arrive in an "authentic oriental bonsai ceramic pot" with complete care instructions.

It may be worth getting one of these just for the pun-of-it. Put one on your desk at work and the next time you spread a rumor or share information on the QT, mention that you "heard it through your grapevine."

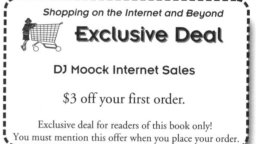

Shopping on the Internet and Beyond

Exclusive Deal

DJ Moock Internet Sales

$3 off your first order.

Exclusive deal for readers of this book only! You must mention this offer when you place your order.

Company
DJ Moock Internet Sales (Windsor, CA)

Where
World Wide Web

Web Address
http://branch.com/dutch/dutch.htm

Email
dutch@branch.com

Prices
From $59.95 to $149.95.

Shipping Fees
Single vines are $20. Double vines are $30.

For somebody super—a superbatch from Nature's Blooms.

Flowers in Superbatches

Nature's Blooms have set themselves apart from all other online florists by providing phenomenal value in their "Superbatches" of flowers. This is hardly a puny bouquet; it's "a giant field-of-flowers...a home decorator's dream come true. So many flowers you won't know where to start. It's the largest assortment of four different flower varieties available at a wholesale price."

What you get is four *huge* arrangements of flowers and one large arrangement of brilliant greenery. At the time of this writing, one Superbatch cost $42, with a retail value, according to the company, of over $100. Assortments are seasonal and can even include such luxurious varieties as lilies and tulips.

Superbatches are available one time only or as part of a six-month or twelve-month plan, in which you are billed monthly. For every six-month period that you purchase, the sixth month is free. That works out to only $33 per month for enough flowers to adorn your entire house.

If you want a more formal flower arrangement, Nature's Blooms have some stunning and unique selections, all of which you can see for yourself via the photos at the company's Web site. For example, you will not believe their *giant* gerbera daisies, which blossom to a hefty four inches in diameter, or the authentic Chinese carnations available in four varieties. The Alluring Alstroemeria live up to their name, with their "profusion of long stemmed, multi-colored tropical blossoms, so beautifully exotic they think you've sent orchids."

Nature's Blooms flowers are cut fresh to order from their private gardens. Within hours of the time of your order, the flowers are on their way to you or your special someone. Orders received by 3:00 PM Eastern time are generally delivered the following day.

Company
Nature's Blooms (Miami, FL)

Where
World Wide Web

Web Address
http://cybermart.com/nb/

Email
blooms@gate.net

Prices
From $23.00 to $95.00.

Shipping Fees (in the U.S.)
$6.95

BamBOO!! Did I scare you?

Bamboo Bonanza

"Wow! What an experience! Imagine standing in the center of a grove of giant moso bamboo. It's almost as if you were an ant amongst a regiment of soldiers, standing tall and silent."

The Bamboo Giant company expects their speciality products to be "the plants of the decade." They consider the bamboos in their collection as "fabulous as highlights in a garden or next to a hot tub or water garden." Homeowners who've wanted additional privacy barriers have found their solution here. Furthermore, "fast growing and hardy erosion-control dwarf bamboos can resolve embankment problems quickly and permanently with more success than any other plant. Many species of bamboo can bind the soil together so tightly that it can be almost impossible to tear it apart. For erosion control, there is not a plant on earth that can do a better job of holding the soil firmly in place. Bamboo, pound for pound, is stronger than steel."

From a decorative standpoint, bamboo is an elegant addition to any landscape, with such rare and unusual types as ebony black ebony, banana yellow, and even one shaped in square canes.

Some bamboos grow up to 120 feet (equivalent to a nine-story building) at a rate of four feet

every day. Some people claim you can actually see them flourish before you eyes. They are the fastest growing plant on earth.

The Bamboo Giant company is "the number one choice for rare select bamboos." They are cultivated on a 31-acre site that includes over 8 acres and 70 species of specialty bamboos. Considering that bamboo sellers are difficult to find, it's even more amazing to find one with the depth, selection, and knowledge of this company.

Company
Bamboo Giant (Apptos, CA)

Where
World Wide Web

Web Address
http://sensemedia.net/sprawl/bamboo

Email
bamboo@sensemedia.net

Prices
From $19 to $2,500.

Shipping Fees
Quoted based on order type and size.

International orders are accepted.

Vermi Culture

I bet you haven't given worm castings much thought. The folks at Green Hut are out to change that. In fact, they're evangelizing daily via their World Wide Web site, which offers "all the equipment and supplies needed to raise worms for vermi composting—the art of recycling garbage into castings, the world's best fertilizer."

Says the company, "these lively, hungry, insatiable creatures are what you want for recycling garbage, garden clippings, and other organics. They produce casting to be used as fertilizer, help you *and* the environment.

"Put these castings in your garden to aerate the soil, loosen the soil's texture, and increase the soil's water retention ability. The worms clean up the dead organics in the top layer of the soil and turn them into castings to feed your plants." The castings work for any kind of plant—from seedlings to mature trees.

First you start with one pound of nature's finest live earthworms (about $25, with a "live delivery guarantee") and a recycling bin, of which Green Hut offers three: the live worm recycling bin, the double bin recycler, and the aerobic composting bin.

Green Hut considers vermi composting to be a family affair (they offer a children's worm kit too) and one that requires such a small space even apartment dwellers can get in on the action.

While every order includes "easy to follow instructions," you can browse the company's Worm FAQ or Vermi Composting at Home sections. If you still don't find the answers you need, submit your question to Green Hut's "Wormeister" through the company's exclusive On-Line Worm Forum.

Perhaps this is *the perfect gift* for the person who has everything.

Shopping on the Internet and Beyond

Exclusive Deal

Green Hut

On your first order, buy one and get a second of the same item at 50 percent off. No limit.

Exclusive deal for readers of this book only! You must mention this offer when you place your order.

Company
Green Hut (San Diego, California)

Where
World Wide Web

Web Address
`http://www.cts.com/~netsales/greenhut`

Email
`tonys@cts.com`

Prices
From $8 to $125.

Shipping Fees
Included in prices.

International orders are accepted.

Remember!

If you have full Internet access, you also have access to the World Wide Web. All you need is a Web browser, such as Mosaic or Netscape.

Here's the perfect gift for someone who's rare and exotic, or at least for someone who'd like to feel that way.

Flowers from Kauai

On over twelve acres of tropical farmland on the Hawaiian island of Kaua'i grow some of the most beautiful flowers in the world. Since this is also the wettest place on earth (over 500 inches of rainfall a year at 80 plus degrees), the flora on Kaua'i really thrive in a steamy, jungle-like climate.

The only company that offers these lush and breath-taking blossoms online is Kaua'i Exotix—lovingly run by three women farmers.

This is not your run of the mill Hawaiian floral collection. Kaua'i Exotix "produces tropical plants and flowers usually found in the endangered rainforests of the world...and the rich, volcanic Kaua'ian soil produces varieties that are long-lasting and rich in color and shapes."

Kaua'i Exotix offers gift boxes of these "rare and exotic flowers and lush tropical foliage in boxes of 14 stems (The Aloha) and 25 stems (The Ali'i)."

These flowers are so sturdy you can make all sorts of interesting arrangements or simply put them in a vase alone.

"Each combination of flowers and foliage is different and there is no single right way to arrange them. The old time Hawaiian style favors a mass of vivid color that dazzles the eye, and the more you have, the better. You can intermingle tropicals with locally grown flowers. The bold upright look of heliconias and gingers is compatible with all varieties of flowers and foliage."

Shopping on the Internet and Beyond

Exclusive Deal

Kaua'i Exotix

10 percent off your first order.

Exclusive deal for readers of this book only! You must mention this offer when you place your order.

Company
Kaua'i Exotix (Kauai, HI)

Where
World Wide Web

Web Address
http://planet-hawaii.com/~exotix

Email
kexotix@aloha.net

Prices
From $39 to $65.

Shipping Fees
Included in the price for most destinations.

Bonsai Trees

If you want to send a message "forever," consider a Bonsai gift, since these little guys last for years.

Bonsai dwarf trees are easy to maintain and quite interesting to look at. Properly pruned, the plants are kept small and in true proportion to their

Bonsai Trees (continued)

full-scale, natural counterparts. This miniaturization is achieved by growing them in small containers, and feeding and watering them just enough for healthy growth.

Bonsai Boy of New York offers three varieties:

- The Juniper Bonsai are about five years old and are the most popular evergreen in the United States—basically what we think a traditional Bonsai looks like.

- The Snow Rose Serissa type is perfect for the beginner. Six years old and about nine inches tall, "this subtropical evergreen, imported from Japan, blooms profusely throughout the year with white or double-white flowers."

- Attracted to blue foliage? Try the Blue Moss Cypress, which "develops a nice trunk and forms a natural broom style." It can even be shaped into pom poms and is resilient in cold weather areas.

"Each bonsai tree is potted in a glazed, ceramic container and includes naturally collected mosses, multi-colored textured rock accessories, humidity tray with pebbles, and hand printed tree ID tag." It doesn't get its own Social Security number, though.

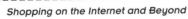

Shopping on the Internet and Beyond

Exclusive Deal

Bonsai Boy of New York

$5 off any order
of $49.95 or more.

Exclusive deal for readers of this book only!
You must mention this offer when you place your order.

Company
Bonsai Boy of New York
(Long Island, NY)

Where
World Wide Web

Web Address
`http://branch.com/bonsai`

Email
`bonsai@branch.com`

Prices
From $35.95 to $49.95.

Shipping Fees
$7.95 via two-day UPS.

For More...

See the next page for additional sites for more great shopping opportunities related to flowers.

Honorable Mentions
in the category of
Flowers, Plants, & Gardening

24k Gold Flowers

24k gold-plated roses and orchids, Disney-themed arrangements. Teleflora flowers and gifts are also available.

Company
A White Dove On-Line Flower and Gift Shop

Web Address
http://branch.com/flower-shop/

Email
whitedove@branch.com

All Occasion Flowers

Dried and fresh flowers for all occassions. Worldwide delivery.

Company
Intercontinental Florist

Web Address
http://www2.pcy.mci.net/marketplace/icf/

Bouquets

Worldwide delivery of bouqets for every occasion.

Company
Flower Basket

Web Address
http://usa.net/flower/basket.html

Exotic Flowers

Long lasting Hawaiian bouquets shipped directly from Hawaii.

Company
Exotic Flowers of Hawaii

Web Address
http://branch.com/hawaii/

Email
hawaii@branch.com

Floral Arrangement

Flowers for CompuServe members from the "Florist of the Year," named by the St. Louis Hospitality Industry Council.

Company
Walter Knoll Florist

CompuServe
Go *gk*

Flowers & Balloons

FTD flowers and balloons for Prodigy members. Holiday specials.

Company
PC Flowers

Prodigy
Jump *pc flowers*

Flowers and Plants

Flower baskets, roses, and blooming plants.

Company
Flowers On Lexington

Web Address
http://branch.com/lexington/

FTD Flowers

Easy FTD flower ordering for CompuServe members.

Company
FTD Online

CompuServe
Go *ftd*

Gourmet Seeds

"The seed source for the best-tasting varieties of herbs, vegetables, and edible flowers."

Company
Gourment Gardner

Web Address
http://metroux.metrobbs.com/tgg/index.htm

Hawaiian Head Leis

Made-to-order head leis. Freezable for multiple wearings. Dried Haku hats are also available.

Company
Maile's Leis

Web Address
http://www.maui.net/~reman/leis.html

Indoor Oasis

"A backlit mini-indoor water featured desert oasis...with a variety of succulents. No two alike."

Company
Whimsical Waterfalls

Web Address
http://www.dgsys.com/~rthonen/ording.html

Natural Repellent

Nature's insect repellent for shrubs and crops.

Company
Garlic Barrier

Web Address
http://www.primenet.com/commercial/
bcbmark/garlic.html

Email
bcbmark@primenet.com

Orchids

Fresh flowering orchid and bromeliad plants direct from the grower. These high-quality plants bloom for weeks and are guaranteed to arrive in top condition.

Company
Blue Ribbon Orchids

Web Address
http://www.cts.com/~netsales/bro

Official FTD

The Internet's official FTD Storefront. Pictures of virtually every item in the entire FTD flower, plant, and bouquet line.

Company
FTD Internet

Web Address
http://www.novator.com/FTD-Catalog/FTD-
Internet.html

Special Floral Goods

Award winning dried flower designs, lavender sachets, leaf balls, aromatic herb wreaths, and swags.

Company
Floreal

Web Address
http://www.eca.com/Floreal.html

Teleflora

Bouquet selections from the worlds largest privately owned floral wire service.

Company
Teleflora

Web Address
http://www.shopping2000.com/shopping2000/
teleflora/

Food

Mammoth Pecan Halves ready for gift giving (but not until the October harvest).

A Real "Nut House"

Sometimes you feel like a nut. Sometimes you don't. When you do, Sunnyland Farms is your one-stop nut shop. For over 45 years, they've been shipping nuts across the nation from their office in the middle of a Georgia pecan grove. "You'll get the brightest, freshest nuts you ever tasted at direct-from-the-grove-to-you prices."

These guys are totally nuts: pecans, cashews, pistachios, macadamias, almonds, and walnuts. They sell them halved, whole, slivered, in pieces, in gift boxes, in tins, and in bulk. Get 'em raw or toasted, salted or unsalted, ground into meal, dipped in chocolate—even orange-frosted.

Sunnyland Farms is most famous for their pecans—especially their Extra-Fancy Natural Mammoth Pecan halves—so big they might as well be whole.

Do-it yourselfers will love Sunnyland's Schley pecans. These thin-shelled pecans are "unusually firm-textured crisp meats, highest in those unsaturated oils that give pecans their unique flavor, with shells so thin you can easily crack one nut against another in your hand."

The home boxes, delivered in a "plain poly bag inside a stout shipping box," contain the same products as their gift pack counterparts, sans the pricey container. These home boxes are quite a deal. Purchase an economy pack of 10 pounds of their best pecans and your net cost will average a mere $6.90 per pound, and that *includes* shipping.

Other eye-catchers in the Sunnyland nut arsenal are their California-grown, easy-to-open Colossal Pistachios (in home boxes for as little as $4.50 per pound *including* shipping) and their Royal Mix (one of their biggest sellers)—a combination of cashews, pecans, almonds, brazils, and hazelnuts, "toasted separately, then blended, but not salted."

To fully appreciate Sunnyland's mind-boggling inventory, you'll have to pay a visit to their Web site—the nuttiest this side of Bellevue.

Company
Sunnyland Farms (Albany, GA)

Where
World Wide Web

Web Address
http://www.shopping2000.com/shopping2000/sunnyland/

Email
sunnylandf@aol.com

Prices
$14.40 and up. Extremely reasonable.

Shipping Fees
Included in all prices.

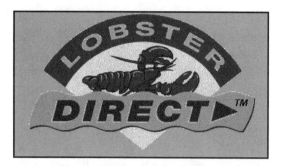

"Canadian Crayfish" fresh from Lobster Direct.

Nova Scotia Lobster

Nova Scotia is often considered to be home to some of the world's best-tasting salmon, but the same could be said of everyone's favorite crustacean—lobster. What's this province's mouthwatering secret for harvesting some of the best of the "King of Seafood"? Water, of course. It's the cold, clear waters of the Canadian Atlantic, with icy temperatures that are perfect for encouraging development of a full, hard shell and signature large claws.

Lobster Direct ships lobsters to your door via FedEx next-day delivery, in a specially designed Styrofoam packing box. Orders must be a minimum of 2.5 pounds (about 2 lobsters) up to as many as your credit card limit will allow. For special occasions, consider the "Talk of the Town Special," which includes 12 hard-shell lobsters weighing in at 15 pounds total.

You receive the lobsters live, of course, and despite the infamous scene you might remember from "Annie Hall," they are easily wrangled into the pot. Actually, cracking and consuming are perhaps the bigger challenges. You'll find terrific graphics detailing tried and true cracking, meat removal, and serving suggestions on the Lobster Direct Web site.

When you go online, you'll also find lobster recipes and an option to subscribe to Lobster Direct's free monthly newsletter (sent via email), which contains favorite seafood recipes, current market prices, and product information. In fact, once each month, one of the newsletter's subscribers, picked at random, wins a Seafood Lover's Special (four lobsters, five pounds total) and a pound of Lobster Direct's Seabright Nova Scotia lox.

With the advent of such new technologies as dryland lobster holding systems and a carefully managed year-round supply, Lobster Direct is your best source for buying from the 3-million-pound harvest of the region's annual catch.

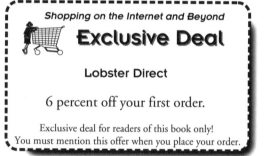

Shopping on the Internet and Beyond

Exclusive Deal

Lobster Direct

6 percent off your first order.

Exclusive deal for readers of this book only!
You must mention this offer when you place your order.

Company
Lobster Direct (Halifax, Canada)

Where
World Wide Web

Web Address
http://novaweb.com/lobster

Email
lobster@fox.nstn.ca

Prices
Seasonal.

Shipping Fees
Included in price.

Monterey Jack meets the Baby Muenster to duke it out at this cheesy Web site.

Amish Country Cheese

"From the hollows of the Appalachian Hills to the homesteads of the Midwest, the Plain People—Amish, Mennonites, and Hutterites—maintain their communities and hard-working traditional way of life. Their commitment to quality and time-honored ways contribute to the old-fashioned taste found in Amish Country Cheese."

The varieties of cheese made by the Amish include medium colby, sharp colby, aged cheddar, Monterey jack, baby swiss, baby muenster, tasty gouda, a cheddar and almond cheese log, and a horseradish cheese spread.

Perhaps based on the Lay's potato chip philosophy that no one can eat just one, Amish Country Cheese sells products in assortments—from a snacktime pack containing three varieties to their Mr. Big collection, which contains a healthy sampling of most of their catalog.

Though the Amish live a life based on times long past, they've certainly kept pace with the food fashions of the modern world. Forthcoming to their Web site will be a line of cheeses that are 50 percent lower in fat than their counterparts. Perhaps this is evidence that the Amish have found a way to participate in the trends of modern society without compromising their traditional world view.

Shopping on the Internet and Beyond

Exclusive Deal

Amish Country Cheese

Get two free cheese samples with your first order of $15 or more.

Exclusive deal for readers of this book only!
You must mention this offer when you place your order.

Company
Amish Country Cheese
(Linwood, MI)

Where
World Wide Web

Web Address
`http://webcom.com/~cheese/welcome.html`

Email
`cheese@webcom.com`

Prices
From $5.00 to $40.00.

Shipping Fees
Included in their prices.

Remember!

For periodic updates of this book and additional discounts, send email to *shop@easton.com*. See *Introduction* for more details.

Delicious products direct from the Orient to your Wokway.

Ethnic Spices and Sauces

Although many supermarkets in major cities stock an expanding array of ethnic condiments and seasonings, you'll be hard pressed to find a selection that compares to the variety available at Spice Merchant's Online shop. Here you'll find authentic Asian and oriental seasonings, sauces, oils, and more for preparing your favorite Chinese, Japanese, Thai, Indonesian, and Indian dishes.

Even if you can locate some of these "flavor secrets" locally, the quality and prices are still rivaled by Spice Merchant.

The highlights in the Chinese section include oyster, lemon, and bean sauces, along with four different types of soy—including light (lower in salt), dark (mushroom base), black (for Hunan-style braising), and thin (a light soy for colorful dishes like Moo Goo Gai Pan).

If you want to learn Chinese cooking and don't know exactly where to start—although the kitchen is a good place—Spice Merchant offers a "Shelf Stocker" package that groups all the essentials for preparing most Chinese dishes. A similar kit is available for beginning Thai cooks.

If you really want to stretch your culinary expertise and are a Japanese food lover, consider home-made sushi (a tasty alternative for your next trout catch). Spice Merchant has all the ingredients you'll need, and you can purchase them separately or as a kit. The company even sells a video called "I Love Sushi," which provides step-by-step instructions.

The selections in the Indonesian and Indian sections are equally as impressive as those that I've already mentioned. Each item in their extensive inventory is clearly described, and explains not only the product but how it is used.

Company
Spice Merchant (Jackson Hole, WY)

Where
World Wide Web

Web Address
`http://eMall.com/Spice/Spice1.html`

Reminder! This Web address is case sensitive. Make sure you enter it *exactly* as shown.

Email
`71553.436@compuserve.com`

Prices
From 75 cents to $7.

Shipping Fees (in the U.S.)
$6.95 per order.

International orders are accepted.

Capsaicine got your tongue? Sweat it out at this site.

"Hot" Pursuits

The folks at Hot Hot Hot like to refer to their online retail outlet as "The Internet's First Culinary *Headshop*." While it's certainly difficult to summarize their inventory in one sentence, Hot Hot Hot absolutely is one of the best stores on the Internet and for that reason also one of the most popular.

Hot Hot Hot's success can partially be attributed to their outstanding products and the public's new-found interest in fiery foods. "Among culinary adventures, there's an ultimate in thrillseeking: hot sauces," they note. "Like bungie jumping over a volcano, hot sauces are unique experiences that skirt the edge of danger. These sauces we carry can be mild enough to just tickle your tongue or wild enough to make you salivate, sweat, sniffle, cry—and still ask for more."

But hot sauces, they point out, are not just about heat. "We have a wide range of flavors from fruity and sweet to mustardy to smoky, vinegary, nutty— the list is as boundless as the imaginations of the alchemists who brew these incendiary potions."

The Hot Hot Hot online shop carries well over 100 sauces. To make navigating their site super easy, they've organized their sauces into four categories: by heat, by origin, by ingredients, and by name—and the names are as entertaining as their sauces are flaming.

There's Capital Punishment ("For those who treat every meal as if it were their last"), Jump

Up and Kiss Me ("Guaranteed to take you places you've never been"), and Gib's Nuclear Hell ("You may have to call the Hazardous Materials Squad for this one.")

Then, of course, there's Hot Hot Hot's biggest seller: Dave's Insanity Sauce, considered the hottest sauce in the universe, which is sold in eyedropper vials. If you're an experienced chilihead, there's always Dave's Insanity *Private Reserve*, "hand signed and numbered by the Madman himself...this makes even Dave sweat. Twice as hot as his original, it comes in its own wood box with yellow caution tape wrapped around it" with instructions to use only a half-drop at a time.

When you visit the Hot Hot Hot site, keep in mind this helpful hint from the owners: "Hot sauce is just about the only food that openly brags about how much it's going to hurt you, but don't take it seriously. At worst, the burn only lasts six or seven minutes. Hot sauce labels are notoriously flamboyant, competing with each other for who can scare their customers more."

Hot Hot Hot's vivid sauce descriptions are so good you can almost taste them. Combined with playful "heat" icons and colorful quick-loading graphics, the purveyors at Hot Hot Hot have certainly earned their cyber *non de plume* as the "Coolest Hot Spot on the Net."

"Hot" Pursuits (continued)

Company
Hot Hot Hot (Pasadena, CA)

Where
World Wide Web

Web Address
http://www.hot.presence.com/hot

Email
hothothot@hothothot.com

Prices
From $3.50 to $8.50.

Shipping Fees
Reasonable and based on order total.

International orders are accepted.

The Fusano family's roots trace back to Bari, Italy, but their product roots are firmly planted in California soil.

Hand-Stuffed Olives

Hand-picked and hand-stuffed, California-grown Fusano olives will make you forget about anything you might have tried from the Mediterranean.

Since 1909, the Fusano Company has grown these green wonders in the San Joaquin and Sacramento valleys. Not only are the olives special, but so are their stuffings. Fusano has ventured well past the solitary puny pimiento routine.

Now, mind you, they do have a pimiento-stuffed olive, but theirs is cured in a brine with vermouth. Instead of putting the olive in the martini, they've put the martini in the olive. This olive is the per-

fect complement to their onion edition, which has a tiny pearl cocktail onion packed inside.

Other olive combinations include almond (with a whole almond substituting for the pit), jumbo garlic (the brine cure expunges the garlic linger) and Cantina style, which are cured in a paprika/chili-pepper brine bath.

Fusano's olives have a six-month shelf life if left unopened and will hold up indefinitely when refrigerated. "Indefinitely" in this context is certainly relative. These olives are so tasty they'll be off the shelf and in your mouth before you have a chance to say "Why not take olive me?"

Shopping on the Internet and Beyond

Exclusive Deal

Fusano California Valley Specialty Olive Company

Choose one free *large* bottle of any of their olives with an order of $30 or more.

Exclusive deal for readers of this book only!
You must mention this offer when you place your order.

Company
Fusano California Valley Specialty Olive Company (Cambria, California)

Where
World Wide Web

Web Address
http://www.callamer.com/~mwinfo/fusano.html

Prices
From $3 to $6.

Shipping Fees
Included in the price.

International orders are accepted.

When is an olive oil not an olive oil? When it's better than olive oil—such as the Castalia flavored oils.

Infused Olive Oils

While flavored vinegar has been popular for some time, only recently have we begun to see the proliferation of their logical counterpart: flavored oil.

Central Coast Gourmet has risen to the gourmet challenge by creating a line of six oils, flavored with the herbs and natural essence of basil, garlic, lemon, mushroom, red pepper, and rosemary.

The company uses only the best ingredients available—this is not mass-produced vegetable oil loaded with artificial flavorings. The flavors are actually *infused* into extra virgin olive oil—the highest quality, derived from the first pressing of the olives.

While no oil is actually good for you in terms of fat content, olive oil has a healthful reputation because it contains the highest percentage of monounsaturated fat compared to most other oils.

These creations are "very versatile oils, which can be substituted for almost any oil in any recipe." The basil gives extra zing to pesto sauces, the lemon adds the better half in salad dressing, the mushroom is a natural for gravies and marinades, the red pepper is perfect for pasta, and the rosemary is a great baste for lamb and duck.

Of course you can always combine a few together for the ultimate taste sensation.

Shopping on the Internet and Beyond

Exclusive Deal

Central Coast Gourmet

10 percent off your first order of $25 or more.

Exclusive deal for readers of this book only! You must mention this offer when you place your order.

Company
Central Coast Gourmet
(Paso Robles, California)

Where
World Wide Web

Web Address
`http://www.callamer.com/~mwinfo/ccgour.html`

Email
`mgwinfo@magicwindows.com`

Prices
From $6.95 per 8.33-ounce bottle

Shipping Fees
Actual shipping charges. No handling fees.

International orders are accepted.

Remember!

For 100 percent subjective reviews and opinions of popular consumer products, take a look at the Usenet Group *misc.comsumers* and *alt.consumer.experiences*.

If you pass up this site, well, you're not berry bright.

Maine Berries

You wouldn't know by its name that Whistling Wings is a berry farm—a real berry farm, Knott like some others. It's in Maine, which means you get berry products without pesticides, chemicals, or too much sugar. In fact, their berry products use so little sugar that they lost their account with the renowned L.L. Bean Company over that "little" fact.

As the story goes, Whistling Wings provided Bean's private-label jams and jellies. When someone told the Bean company that there wasn't enough sugar in the jam for it to be labeled "jam," the L.L. Bean company asked Whistling Wings to sweeten it up.

But the Farm said "no, that they weren't willing to comprise their recipes or the health factor of their products" and forfeited the contract.

Despite the demise of the Bean contract, Whistling Wings' spreadable fruit lives on in eight varieties, including wild blueberry, blueberry-cranberry, royal purple raspberry, and raspberry-cranberry. In addition, you can find raspberry honey, blueberry, strawberry, and raspberry syrups as well as delightful berry vinegars.

Sales are brisk at Whistling Wings, and some of their most famous customers include George and Barbara Bush, the King of Norway, Chicken-King Frank Perdue, and Sam Donaldson.

If you're in a berry state of mind, you'll especially appreciate the care given to the Whistling Wings Web site. While the company has plenty of goods to sell, they have equally as much to teach you about berries—*if* you're interested. There are raspberry and blueberry answers to frequently asked questions (FAQs), raspberry research areas, and loads of information on berry farming. There you'll find more berry puns per byte here than at any other Web site.

Shopping on the Internet and Beyond

Exclusive Deal

Whistling Wings Farms

10 percent off your first order.

Exclusive deal for readers of this book only!
You must mention this offer when you place your order.

Company
Whistling Wings Farm (Biddeford, ME)

Where
World Wide Web

Web Address
`http://www.biddeford.com/~dtaylor/ww/ww1.html`

Email
`dharper@wwfarm.com`

Prices
From $4.50 to $8.35.

Shipping Fees
Shipping and insurance included in price.

International orders are accepted.

Hey! Who spilled the beans—er, nuts?

Peanut Paradise

Nothing compares to the Virginia Diner—known as the "Peanut Capital of the World"—first famous for serving peanuts from their local fields to the diner guests instead of after-dinner mints. What was once a quirky dessert substitute has since spiraled into—using your best Robin Leach intonation—an "international gourmet peanut extravaganza!"

The secret behind their out-of-this-world product is in the cooking, which is done by hand. Actually, it's done by the hand of Melvin, who's been cooking the Virginia Diner peanuts for over 20 years—from the time he was "tall enough to see into the peanut fryer with the help of a crate," timing his batches to perfection without the aid of a clock. The only peanut product in the Virginia Diner lineup that gives Melvin a break are the *raw* shelled redskin crop.

Starting with their specialty—the basic roasted peanut in a shell—you can choose from salted, unsalted, and cajun flavors sold by the peck, tin, one-pound bag, or wooden bushel.

Year-round peanut addicts can join one of the Virginia Diner's Perpetual Peanut Clubs. As a member, you automatically receive one 2.5 lb. can of salted, unsalted, butter toasted, or salt-substitute flavors every month ("The Totally Nuts Club") or six times per year ("The Half Nuts Club") for well-under $20 per month.

The company also offers other special monthly shipment deals, such as the VIP (Very Important Peanut-Lover) Club, which ships a special assortment of peanut goodies thematically tied into the month in which they're being delivered, such as November's "in-the-shell for football" pack or February's peanut-packed heart shaped box.

After 60 years in the peanut business, there isn't a peanut-related product you could think of that you won't find at the Virginia Diner's Web site, including peanut brittle, chocolate-covered peanuts, chocolate-covered peanut brittle, peanut butter taffy, peanut butter cocoa, peanut pie tarts, PeaNuggets (peanut-shaped milk chocolate wrapped around peanut butter), boiled peanuts, and even peanut soup.

Every item in the Virginia Diner lineup is unconditionally guaranteed. If you are unhappy with anything you've ordered, they'll "cheerfully 'shell-out' a complete refund or replacement."

Shopping on the Internet and Beyond

Exclusive Deal

Virginia Diner

5 percent off your
first order of $50 or more.

Exclusive deal for readers of this book only!
You must mention this offer when you place your order.

Company
Virginia Diner (Wakefield, VA)

Where
World Wide Web

Web Address
http://www.infi.net/vadiner/index.html

Email
vadiner@infi.net

Prices
From $5 to $75.

When you order the Amana Sampler, the company will toss in a 120-page cookbook—free.

Midwestern Pork and Beef

If it stands on four legs and is native to the Midwest, chances are Amana Steaks & Chops is selling it in the form of a tenderloin, crown roast, or other premium cut.

Their corn-fed beef selections include "fork-tender" filet mignons, ribeye roasts, ribeye steaks, 16-ounce T-bones, 85-percent lean steakburgers, and boneless strip sirloins. If you can't decide which side of the beef is best, Amana offers a Homecoming Assortment of their four most popular cuts, which they highly recommend for cookouts.

On the pork front of Amana's online catalog are their world famous Iowa chops. They're available in a variety of cuts, styles, and flavors, including a 12-ounce, hand-carved loin, a German smoked and cured loin center, as well as a butterfly cut, which is perfect for stuffing.

Amana also offers boneless, pork loin roasts, crown roasts, and a variety of pork tenderloins available breaded or bacon-wrapped.

To be absolutely sure that your meat arrives as fresh as when they sent it, Amana has engineered a reuseable "deep freeze cooler," which surrounds your order in a plethora of dry ice. "No matter how hot the weather, your meat will arrive in Premium condition." In fact, Amana's meat is so fresh it's almost like going direct from pasture to plate.

Shopping on the Internet and Beyond

Exclusive Deal

Amana Steaks & Chops

$5.00 off your first order of $49.95 or more.

Exclusive deal for readers of this book only! You must mention this offer when you place your order.

Company
Amana Steaks & Chops (Ankeny, IA)

Where
World Wide Web

Web Address
http://www.ioweb.com/amana

Email
iowa800242@aol.com

Prices
From $16.95 to $99.95.

Shipping Fees (in the U.S.)
$6.50

International orders are accepted.

Healthy, Gourmet Sausage

Healthy sausage may seem like an oxymoron, but the folks at the San Luis Sausage Company have made it happen—almost by accident. They set out to prepare the best gourmet links avail-

Gourmet Sausage (continued)

able by using solid cuts of prime meat. These choice cuts happen to be naturally lower in fat and hence produce a significantly healthier sausage. By way of example, their pork sausage is ground from the roast instead of some high-fat, unidentifiable appendage (which the USDA actually allows).

The fat analysis in one chicken sausage link ranks the leanest at three grams (chicken-apple) and the fattiest at (a still very respectable) six grams (the culprit here is the coconut that they add to their Jamaican Jerk style). Each link weighs in at a generous quarter pound, which only makes these fat gram figures more impressive.

Furthermore, most commercial-brands are laden with chemicals and preservatives—including the dreaded sodium brothers, nitrate and phosphate. All of San Luis Sausages are free of such toxins because they are vacuum packed and flash frozen immediately after they're made.

Now that you know you can enjoy San Luis' edible sensations guilt-free, let's get to the "gourmet" part.

The flavor choices are amazing. In the chicken category, choose from Southwestern Thai, Italian, Apple, Fiesta, Jamaican Jerk , and Andouille (which has a spicy Louisiana/Cajun flair to it).

The turkey sausages, which fat-gram-wise are almost as low as the chicken links, are available in Country-style, Sweet Italian, and Hot Italian.

The San Luis company also offers pork and lamb links. While not nearly as low-fat as their fowl competition, they sound equally as delicious, with over six flavors to choose from.

The San Luis company has clearly achieved their goal to produce the highest-quality sausage anywhere. In fact I wouldn't be surprised to learn that Jimmy Dean has sneaked a link or two on the side.

Shopping on the Internet and Beyond

Exclusive Deal

San Luis Sausage

With your first order, select two quarter-pound sample sausages of your choice.

Exclusive deal for readers of this book only! You must mention this offer when you place your order.

Company
San Luis Sausage (Los Osos, CA)

Where
World Wide Web

Web Address
http://www.callamer.com/~mwinfo/slosaug.html

Email
slsausage@aol.com

Prices
From $3 to $4.50 per pound.

Shipping Fees
Vary on method and order size.

Hams Protected by Law

Olde Smithfield Farms' peanut-fed hogs make for a virtual ham-o-rama. Their Genuine and Country styles are pepper coated, hickory smoked and hung for six months or longer (something I'd like to do to a particular radio talk show host). If you're not up for country ham, or for baking one, but want something fine-trimmed, try their Honey Glazed style, which is slow cooked—for over 30 hours.

Legend has it that in the 1700s these distinctive hams from Smithfield, Virginia were served at the tables of European royalty. In fact, Queen

Hams Protected By Law (continued)

Victoria apparently always had a Smithfield served for State functions. Today, the Smithfield curing and aging method is so precise it is literally protected by law. Each ham must meet the county's rigorous requirements before it can be labeled as a genuine Smithfield and "only hams cured within the Smithfield town limits can bear the prestigious name."

In addition to whole and half-hams, the company also sells ham sausage with a flavor so distinct they suggest you can even serve it at dinner or as an hors d'oeuvre.

If you prefer fowl to pork, this colonial hamlet also offers smoked turkeys, whole or breast-only. A complete bird weighs between 9 and 11 pounds, while the smoked breasts weigh in at about 5 to 7 pounds each. All of these turkey choices are described by the company as "buffet favorites."

Ol' Queen Victoria might not have been much fun at parties, but at least her hams were a hit.

Shopping on the Internet and Beyond
Exclusive Deal

Olde Smithfield Farms

$5 off your first order of $30 or more.

Exclusive deal for readers of this book only!
You must mention this offer when you place your order.

Company
Olde Smithfield Farms (Smithfield, VA)

Where
World Wide Web

Web Address
http://www.ip.net/smithfield/home.html

Email
smithfield@shopkeeper.com

Prices
From $34.95 to $79.95.

Shipping Fees (in the U.S.)
$7.50 (ground) or $17.50 2nd Day Air

Y'all come down to the swamp for some serious good cookin' sauces.

Carolina Swamp Stuff

Carolina Swamp Stuff? Whoa! Now doesn't *that* sound appetizing. Well, just wait until you read the following list of names used to describe this unique brand of cooking sauces and salad dressings geared "for the little bit of redneck in us all!"

The Swamp Stuff line is packaged in three kits and sold in rustic hand-crafted wooden boxes that "can be used and enjoyed long after the sauces are gone."

The Chest pack contains Swamp Sauce, a spicy Caribbean-style marinade; Blue Tick Dressing, a cholesterol-free, salt free salad dressing made with raspberries and poppy seeds; and Tadpole Tea, "a rich, low-calorie balsamic vinaigrette seasoned with Italian herbs, so versatile you get to decide exactly what it is."

In addition to the Chest pack, you can choose from The Shed and The Shed Too (I guess they were all named-out by the time they needed a moniker for the latter.)

Swamp Stuff (continued)

Seaweed Splash, a low-calorie pesto and Cedar Spray, a lime, curry and cilantro sauce/dressing make up The Shed. The Shed Too contains Pine Tar, a soy/sesame/ginger stir-fry sauce and Red Tide, a very Mediterranean low-cal sauce/dressing full of sweet red peppers, cumin, garlic, and balsamic vinegar.

The company suggests that you not "let the quirky names and humorous packaging fool you—this is serious good stuff."

Heck, I think that if these sauces and dressings are half as good as their names, we've stumbled onto an epicurean motherlode.

Shopping on the Internet and Beyond

Exclusive Deal

Carolina Swamp Stuff

10 percent off your first order.

Exclusive deal for readers of this book only!
You must mention this offer when you place your order.

Company
Reedy Creek (Four Oaks, NC)

Where
World Wide Web

Web Address
http://www.nando.net/prof/reedy/css.html

Email
ndavis@nando.net

Prices
From $22 to $28.

Shipping Fees (in the U.S.)
Based on order size

International orders are accepted.

Go dive into this site. But be warned—you might never want to come back out.

Godiva Chocolates

Even though Godiva Chocolates is named in honor of Lady Godiva of Conventry, some people think it's a play on the phrase "Go die for"—which is what many people would do for these confections.

Developed in 1926 by Joseph Draps in Belgium, the same recipes are used today. "All Godiva creations have a sublimely delicious taste," cites the company, "along with an intense aroma and delicate appearance of chocolates created from only the finest ingredients, packaged in wonderfully creative presentations."

Their online catalog has a "Feature Presentation" that, at the time of this writing, focused on the "Flavors of Brazil" with a collection of exotic desserts from the South American country.

You'll also find seasonal treats. During warmer weather, keep your eye out for their Summer Truffles—"cool as a summer breeze and just as welcome" with such flavors as "Lemon Chiffon, Key Lime, Jasmine (a whisper of jasmine covered in ivory), Strawberry, and Coconut.

Godiva Chocolates (continued)

Of course, no matter what the season or the weather, you can always find traditional Godiva favorites, such as their Ballotin box ("Godiva's golden collection...classic milk, dark, and ivory pieces in a spectrum of sizes, an array of flavors"), truffle assortments, Caramel Nut Bouchees, and the Cocoa Godiva Tin.

Godiva is also offering a "Cafe Collection" of coffees with "six two-ounce bags of Cinnamon Praline Regular and Decaf, Godiva Special Roast Regular and Decaf, and Vanilla Hazelnut and Toasted."

Chocoholics will especially love this Web site: Godiva teamed with *Chocolatier Magazine* for some special surprises—"A chocolate lover's playground" as they call it. Here you'll find "a sprinkling of trivia and heaps of facts and folklore all about chocolate and a batch of exclusive recipes," which are divided into several sections, including "Godiva Liqueur Recipes for the Utterly Indulgent," "Recipes to be Approached with Reckless Abandon," and a chronology of chocolate history starting 4,000 years ago.

Before you place your order, keep in mind that Godiva will only ship to addresses in the United States to preserve freshness.

Company
Godiva Chocolatier (Clinton, CT)

Where
World Wide Web

Web Address
`http://www.godiva.com/`

Prices
From $8 to 120.00.

Shipping Fees
Based on order total.

This is easily one of the sappiest sites on the Web.

Canadian Maple Marvels

When I read at the Reidridge Farm Web site that 40 gallons of maple sap are required to make *one* gallon of maple syrup, I was amazed. I now also understand why maple has such an intense, albeit delightful, flavor.

Canada is renown for making what is considered by many to be the best maple syrup in the world—though I'm sure a few Vermonters would beg to differ—producing almost 75 percent of the world's output. Reidridge Farms, in the Quebec province, is one of these esteemed manufacturers, supplying a stunning array of maple products through their online catalog.

Needless to say, they offer plenty of maple syrup, but they also sell some interesting variations, including maple candy, hard maple sugar, maple butter, maple taffy, maple lollipops, and maple jelly. Since everything they make is obtained exclusively from maple sap, the words 'Pure Maple' can be used on their labels.

You can buy Reidridge's syrups by the liters or in pints for much less than what you would pay at the supermarket for a frankly inferior product. Note that at the time of this writing Reidridge was listing their prices in *Canadian* dollars; therefore, you will want to deduct 25 percent for an approximate American price.

You can get their syrups by the can or by the case. If you want to sample a variety of maple wonders, consider one of their many gift packs, each of which contains a number of their quality maple products.

Know that you can safely buy Reidridge selections in quantity since pure maple products freeze extremely well. Of course this makes sense—Canada is not exactly the warmest spot in North America.

Shopping on the Internet and Beyond

Exclusive Deal

Reidridge Maple Products

A free 11-ounce jar of maple jelly with your first order of $25 (U.S. dollars) or more.

Exclusive deal for readers of this book only! You must mention this offer when you place your order.

Company
Reidridge Maple Products
(Huntington, Quebec, Canada)

Where
World Wide Web

Web Address
http://www.cam.org/~sailor/maple.htm

Email
sailor@cam.org

Prices
From $1.00 to $28.00 (Canadian).

Shipping Fees
Varied, based on destination.

International orders are accepted.

Foodware— where food is everywhere.

Foodware

"Foodware is a software program developed by food lovers for food lovers to make meal planning, food shopping, and entertaining more enjoyable."

The Foodware software is actually a system. There is a master program with over 300 recipes "drawn from a library of over 40 best-selling cookbooks and food magazines." The company also offers a library of add-on modules that they refer to as "Cookbooks-On-Disk"—from which there are over 20 to choose. From French cooking to Chinese, just soups or special recipes for diabetics, you're bound to find more than a few Cookbooks-On-Disk" to enhance your Foodware program. For the little bit of Julia Child in all of us, Foodware also lets you add your own recipes.

Because the software functions like a database, you can search by "ingredient, recipe, cooking method, ethnic origin, cookbook title, budget item, nutritional value, or by such unique criteria as dinner-for-one, make-ahead dishes, or preparation time.

This software also has some very convenient features. You can plan one meal or a week's worth and the program will print all the recipes and an *organized* shopping list based on the recipes you've selected.

There are a lot of meal-planning cookbook programs on the market, but none I have heard of

Foodware (continued)

come close to the care, quality, or customization features of this one.

Note that the prices on their Web site are in Canadian dollars. To get a ballpark figure of the U.S. dollar cost, subtract 25 percent from the figures listed.

Shopping on the Internet and Beyond

Exclusive Deal

Foodware

Get $5 off (in the U.S.) of your first order of the Starter Edition.

Exclusive deal for readers of this book only! You must mention this offer when you place your order.

Company
Foodware (Toronto, Canada)

Where
World Wide Web

Reminder! Most Web addresses are case sensitive. Make sure you enter the address exactly as shown.

Web Address
`http://www.novator.com/FOODWARE/`

Email
`pending`

Prices
From $19.95 to $69.95 (Canadian).

Shipping Fees
Based on size and method.

International orders are accepted.

For More...

See the next page for additional sites for more great shopping opportunities related to food.

Honorable Mentions

in the category of

Food

Arctic Salmon

From the cold waters of Iceland, choose from cured salmon, smoked salmon and peppered salmon.

Company
Icefood

Web Address
http://www.arctic.is/Business/Salmon/
Icefood/

Avocado Products

Guacamole spice blend and Avocado/Italian salad dressing.

Company
Old San Luis Avocado Products

Web Address
http://www.callamer.com/~mwinfo/jax.html

Burgers, Veggie Style

100-percent vegetable protein burgers. 75-percent less fat than the carnivorous equivalent.

Company
Miland Harvest

Web Address
http://eMall.com/Harvest/Harvest1.html

Email
springs@emall.com

Canadian Smoked Salmon

Red Spring Lox, cold-smoked and cured using a special recipe. Only wild caught salmon are used.

Company
Imperial Salmon House

Web Address
http://www.worldtel.com/salmon/
Imperial_salmon_home.html

Cheese

Every variety of cheese: hard, soft, bleu, low-fat, low-salt, goat, even sheep—on Prodigy.

Company
Cheeseboard

Prodigy
Jump *cheeseboard*

Chinese Cooking Videos

Videocassettes teaching the secrets of "mysterious Oriental secret recipes."

Company
Cook Video

Web Address
http://www.supermall.com/pacific/
oriental.html

Country Cured Hams and Turkeys

Award-winning uncooked and cooked hams and honey-baked turkey from the acclaimed Johnston County Company.

Company
Johnston County Hams (Reedy)

Web Address
http://www.nando.net/prof/reedy/jham.html

Dried Fruits and Vegetables

Preservative-free dried strawberries, cherries, blueberries, cranberries, yellow tomatoes, red tomatoes, and a wide varitey of mushrooms.

Company
Aardvarks Unlimited

Web Address
http://www.shore.net:/~adfx/7.html

Egg Substitute

One 16-ounce package is equivalent to five-dozen eggs. Great for low-fat cooks.

Company
Springs of Life

Web Address
http://emall.com/springs/cupboard/
egg.html

Ethnic and Healthy Food

Specializing in homestyle salsa and Mexican food.

Company
Desert Rose Foods, Inc.

Web Address
http://biz.rtd.com/desert_rose/

Fine Citrus Fruits

Variety of Indian River citrus, fresh-picked, hand-packed, and shipped to all of North America and selected European countries.

Company
Florida's Finest Fruit Company

Web Address
`http://www.gate.net/~flfruit/`

Florida Fruit

Premium oranges, tangelos, tangerines and grapefruit picked at their flavor peak—on CompuServe.

Company
Florida Fruit Shippers

CompuServe
Go *ffs*

Gourmet Cooking Oils

Unique grapeseed oils infused with chardonnay, citrus-cilantro, roasted garlic, and chili.

Company
Orfila Vineyards

Web Address
`http://www.branch.com:80/orfila/`

Gourmet Food

Full-service gourmet shop on CompuServe.

Company
Adventures in Food

CompuServe
Go *aif*

Gourmet Mustard

Specializing in unusual mustards like basil-garlic, California blend, and Hot 'n Honey, plus mustard gift baskets.

Company
Holly's Harvest

Web Address
`http://www.callamer.com/~mwinfo/`
`holly.html`

Email
`mwinfo@magicwindows.com`

Ham

Hams from the renown HoneyBaked brand, probably most famous for introducing the worldto the joys of spiral slicing—on CompuServe.

Company
HoneyBaked Foods

CompuServe
Go *ham*

Ham

Whole and half honey-cooked hams, shipped anywhere in the U.S.

Company
Honey Bee Hams

Web Address
`http://mail.eskimo.com/~jeffpolo/`

Health Food and Health Products

Sellers of grain mills, organic grains and berries, sprout houes, sprout bags, sprout cookbooks and natural herbs.

Company
Naturally Yours

Web Address
http://www.america.com/mall/store/
naturally.html

Email
cris@america.com

Hot Sauces

Chile of the Month Club and Hot Sauce of the Month Club.

Company
Chile Today

Web Address
http://eMall.com/Chile/Chile1.html

Email
chile@emall.com

Irish Smoked Salmon

Atlantic salmon smoked over oak chips shipped from the Emerald Isle in vacuum packages.

Company
Burren Fish Products Ltd.

Web Address
http://www.iol.ie/resource/produce/
burren/burrenfish.html

Italian Pretzels

Low-fat pretzels made with wine and olive oil. Flavors include pizza, garlic, onion, anise, fennel, and rosemary.

Company
Allocco's

Web Address
http://www.callamer.com/~mwinfo/
allocco.html

Maine Lobster

Hard shell lobsters. Whole, tails, or meat only. Bibs and claw crackers included.

Company
Coastal Maine Enterprises

Web Address
http://www.xmission.com:80/~wwwads/
maine.html

Maine Lobster

Shipped live from Maine, hand selected and shipped in a foam-insulated cooler. Overnight shipping.

Company
Lobsternet

Web Address
http://branch.com/lobster/lobster.htm

Email
lobsternet@delphi.com

New England Country Cupboard

Cranberries—dried, dried and chocolate covered, jelly, marmalade, chutney, preserves and honey.

Company
Everything Cranberry

Web Address
http://www.xmission.com/~arts/necc/
neccmain.html

Email
necc@snow.tiac.net

North Carolina Sauces

Barbeque sauces, dressings, and marinades from rural Northern Carolina recipes.

Company
Thomas Sauce (Reedy)

Web Address
http://www.nando.net/prof/reedy/
thomas.html

Peanut Butter Bonanza

Fabulous peanut butter and related products from the oldest peanut butter maker in America.

Company
Krema Nut Company

Web Address
http://www.infinet.com/~schapman/
mwow.cmh/krema/homepage.html

Pineapple Guava Products

Exotic fruit, originally from South America. A tart and palate-pleasing variety. Fresh marmalades and preserves.

Company
Summerset Ranch

Web Address
http://www.callamer.com/~mwinfo/
summer.html

Email
mwinfo@magicwindoes.com

Popcorn-on-the-Cob

Fabulous selection of popcorn and related gift packs, including popcorn-on-the-cob—the kernels literally pop on the cob when microwaved.

Company
Shallowford Farms Popcorn

Web Address
http://www.nando.net/prof/reedy/shal.html

Email
ndavis@nando.net

Reserve Food Supplies

Emergency and survival foods from America's leading reserve food system. "Peace of mind for emergency situations."

Company
Sam Andy

Web Address
http://www.supermall.com/samandy/
samandy.html

Email
survival@supermall.com

Salmon Jerky

Salmon jerky made from smoked salmon caught off the western coast of Canada. Salmon fillets also available.

Company
West Coast Select

Web Address
http://www.helix.net/bcss/bcss.html

Salsa

Salsas, hot sauces, and spicy dips.

Company
Salsa Express

Web Address
http://www.stw.com/se/se.htm

Sauces

Specializing in international sauces and toppings: sweet, spicy, and burning hot.

Company
Taste Unlimited

Web Address
http://www.ip.net/tu/

Scottish Smoked Salmon

From the Scottish Highlands, Scottish sweet-cured smoked salmon or Glen Moray Whiskey Cure. Kippers and herring also available.

Company
Summer Isles Food

Web Address
http://www.highlandtrail.co.uk/
highlandtrail/fish.html

Southern Sauces

Bubba Brand Southern salsas, Bubba-Q-Sauce, Back Bay Marinade, Steak Shake, Fish Zing, and Peppa Ketchup.

Company
Atlantis Coastal Foods

Web Address
http://www.sims.net/organizations/bubba/
bubba.html

Email
mzemke@sc.net

Spicy Foods

"Hot Stuff from the valleys of Thailand to the hills of Belize...from mild to wild."

Company
International Hot Foods

Web Address
http://www.xnet.com:80/~hotfoods/

Steaks (Corn-fed Beef)

Corn-fed beef serving "beef lovers from coast to coast" since 1917—on CompuServe.

Company
Omaha Steaks

CompuServe
Go *os*

Gifts & Jewelry

Lava lamps would've been really far out if they'd been on the Enterprise.

Spencer Gifts

Lava lamps are back and Spencer Gifts online has them—in addition to other eclectic and equally appealing gift ideas.

According to Spencer Gifts, "the lava lamp is the most popular mood light of all time. After more than 30 years, it continues to make a statement. Perpetually in motion, creating patterns that soothe and fascinate. It's a nostalgic look from the 1960s and a futuristic look for the 21st century. No home, apartment, or dorm room is complete without one."

In case you have some excuse not to own one ("it won't match my decor"), Spencer offers lava lamps in *eighteen* color combinations, which mix and match the bases, liquid, and lava. The lava colors choices are white, black, purple, green,

yellow, red, and blue with liquid colors of orange, pink, red, blue, and clear.

If you prefer mood lighting emanating from neon instead, Spencer has an entire neon shop on their Web site—featuring everything from Budweiser and Coca-Cola signs to a neon phone that flashes when it rings.

And for Trekkies, here's something for even the hardest core fan: the *exclusive* Limited Edition Star Trek Phone—a replica of the Enterprise. When it rings, "an authentic red alert is sounded as the engine pods light up. Each unit displays Leonard Nimoy's signature and the phone's limited edition number, with a matching numbered certificate of authenticity."

With over 500 retails store offline, Spencer Gifts continues to be the leader in stocking a diverse selection of trendy and amusing merchandise. If you need a gift for "the person who has everything," you can bet Spencer gifts offers something "the person who has everything" *doesn't* have.

Spencer Gifts (continued)

Company
Spencer Gifts (Pleasantville, NJ)

Where
World Wide Web

Web Address
http://www.btg.com/spencer

Email
spencer@btg.com

Prices
From $3.95 to 399.95.

Shipping Fees
Based on order total.

International orders are accepted.

I wonder if you could put these two together and have them play "Someone to Watch Over Me"?

Musical Keepsakes

The San Francisco Music Box company has taken the concept of tunes in a box and extended it into keepsakes for every occasion.

Mind you, they carry plenty of traditional music boxes, some of which are limited editions and quite beautiful. But you'll also find musical keepsakes for nursery knicknacks or general home decor.

These gifts are both personal and personalized. For a large percentage of the items, *you* get to pick the tune from a hefty list of over 100 selections. The inventory has something for everyone, from such music box standards as "Claire de Lune" and "Pachabel's Canon in D" to contemporary hits like "I Will Always Love You" and "You've Got a Friend."

Of course, the fun begins when you start matching tune choices with their keepsakes. For the Ivy-Trimmed White Bird Cage, consider "Wind Beneath My Wings," or for their Puppy Dog Figurines, try "Memory" from the hit play *Cats*.

Other out-of-the-ordinary musical keepsakes include picture frame boxes, paper weights, stuffed animals, and alabaster carillons.

This Web site is truly multimedia, too. By clicking on a sound icon, you can hear a few bars from each tune, plus you'll find photos of everything featured at the site.

To keep you coming back for more, the San Francisco Music Box company has a special Collector's Club. "Each time your total purchases exceed $100, even if the purchases are months apart, you're awarded a $10 Collector's Certificate, which can be used like cash on future purchases."

Company
San Francisco Music Box
(San Francisco, CA)

Where
World Wide Web

Web Address
http://www.shopping2000.com/shopping2000/music_box/

Romance won't go stale when you order from Take the Cake.

Tasty Cakes

Take The Cake is taking the Internet by storm, offering an exclusive line of handmade cakes that are so good the company refers to them as "tradition inspiring."

While this line is a natural for birthday occasions, Take The Cake considers their products equally fitting for Valentine's Day, Christmas, or as a special "thank you."

You can choose from four flavors:

- Chocolate Grand Marnier: "A moist, deep chocolate cake topped with walnuts and drenched in a signature glaze."
- Rum Pecan: "A meltingly delicious pound cake, rich with butter and dark rum, topped off with pecans. A tempting alternative to holiday fruitcake."
- Lemon Almond: "Baked with dark rum and topped with lemon glaze and an avalanche of almonds."
- Apple Walnut: "A buttery yellow cake with sweet apples and cinnamon and topped with glazed walnuts."

Each cake weighs three pounds and serves from 12 to 20, depending on how you slice it. If you tend to be somewhat forgetful, Take The Cake offers a free reminder service. Simply send them your gift list of important dates throughout the year and they will automatically send the cake of your choice to the recipient, with a reminder note to *you* to call that person on his or her special day. Since it's the thought that counts, if you forget to think, nothing counts!

Shopping on the Internet and Beyond

Exclusive Deal

Take The Cake

$3 off your first order.

Exclusive deal for readers of this book only! You must mention this offer when you place your order.

Company
Take The Cake (Baltimore, MD)

Where
World Wide Web

Web Address
`http://www.iis.com/cakes`

Email
`cake-info@cakes.com`

Prices
$26.00

Shipping Fees
Actual costs based on order destination. No handling fees.

International orders are accepted.

Remember!

The World Wide Web is available from all the major online servies including America Online, CompuServe, and Prodigy.

Whether you want to scare the bejeebers out of your co-workers or signal an incoming UFO, Lakeside Novelty has just the product for you.

Gag Gifts Galore

Gag gifts are always fun, but sometimes hard to find. Lakeside Novelty Products has been in business for over 35 years and they've got 'em: "funky, fun, downright useful, and cheap." They suggest using them not only as gifts but as party favors or stocking stuffers.

Yes they have the world-famous whoopie cushion as well as the ever-popular handshake buzzer, but one of their biggest sellers is The Sex Card. "If you're in the mood for sex, keep this card and smile," it reads. "If you're *not* in the mood, tear this card up." The catch is that the card cannot, under any circumstance, be torn—no matter how hard a person tries. "It's an outstanding conversation starter and door opener," the company declares.

Some more playful and far less suggestive items include the laughing bag, waving hand, glass-breaking sonic hammer (which sounds like glass shattering when it hits an object), and switchblade comb to name just a few of the dozens and dozens of items in their playful inventory.

Now, if you want the gag to be literally *on you*, check out the blinking bow tie, a festive accessory for the next office party, or the matching blinking hat, which attracts attention when you want it most—when jogging at night or camping in a secluded area.

One of my favorite items is the Simulated Electronic Beeper—the perfect business accessory for the 90s. The beeper "looks and sounds exactly like an expensive pager. It clips on to a shirt pocket or belt buckle and comes with a numeric display and flashing signal light. You activate the button on the side of the unit and five seconds later it will begin to beep as if you are being paged. A great excuse to get away from meetings or boring conversations. Great for home, office, and parties."

Despite the extensive inventory, the site is easy to maneuver, with no prank links, which you might suspect from this company.

Shopping on the Internet and Beyond

Exclusive Deal

Lakeside Novelty Products

10 percent off first order of $50 or more.

Exclusive deal for readers of this book only!
You must mention this offer when you place your order.

Company
Lakeside Novelty Products (Chicago, IL)

Where
World Wide Web

Web Address
`http://www.virtumall.com/Lakeside/Lakeside.html`

Prices
From $1 to $20.

Shipping Fees (in the U.S.)
10 percent of your order total. $3 minimum shipping charge.

International orders are accepted.

The Ultimate Relaxation basket is filled with champagne bottle bubble bath, anti-stress foaming bath crystals, nail care kit, loofa sponge, decorator soaps and potpourri.

Gift Basket Bonanza

Basket Mania is the gift *solution* you've been looking for. For every occasion, holiday, or theme, this company offers a stunning selection of gift baskets. Even if you have a specific arrangement in mind but don't have time to gather the components, Basket Mania will be happy to put it together for you.

A sampling of their more unusual pre-designed baskets include "Welcome to Your New Home," "Bridesmaid's Thank You," "Parent of the Bride or Groom," "College Relief," "Ultimate Relaxation," "Movie," "Pasta," and even "Fitness" (perfect as a New Year's gift). Every basket is available in three versions, each offered at a price you're bound to like.

While stuffing baskets is their mainstay, this company also loves to use creative containers like bags, ice buckets, hampers, hardwood crates, doctor's bags (Get Well Soon), or anything else you specify.

The site is divided into four areas: Corporate, Holidays (where *every* holiday is listed, unless you count Groundhog Day and Flag Day), All Occasions, and Theme Baskets.

If you want to super-customize your gift, Basket Mania offers personalized fortunes tucked into a chocolate-dipped cookie, as well as a giant seven-inch cookie personalized with a company logo.

Every item sent is topped with a handmade bow and a personalized enclosure card.

Next time you're stuck with a gift-giving dilemma, point your browser to the pros at Basket Mania for a quick resolution. Guaranteed.

Shopping on the Internet and Beyond

Exclusive Deal

Basket Mania

$5 off your first order of $50 or more

Exclusive deal for readers of this book only!
You must mention this offer when you place your order.

Company
Basket Mania (New York, NY)

Where
World Wide Web

Web Address
http://www.basket.com/basket/

Email
stacey@basket.com

Prices
From $30 to $175.

Shipping Fees (in the U.S.)
UPS ground rates.

International orders are accepted.

Computer acting buggy again? Don't get mad. Eat this one in its presence and say "you're next if you don't shape up."

Custom Chocolate Novelties

Since 1984, the Chocolate Factory has been amazing the public with their outstanding array of chocolate novelties. Using only the finest ingredients available, the company has been whipping up every chocolate creation that customers request.

One of their wackiest orders came from Columbia Records, who asked the Chocolate Factory to cook and carve up a 25-pound chunk of chocolate (the size of a basketball) into a replica of a Golden Globe statue for Bruce Springsteen in honor of his prestigious award for the ballad "Philadelphia."

As a Christmas gift, one romantic gentleman asked the company to stuff an elaborate diamond necklace into a miniature, chocolate-shaped golf bag. The wife's reaction at first was "Honey, why would I want to eat chocolate this early in the morning?" Bet she was glad she did!

One of the Chocolate Factory's biggest sellers on the World Wide Web is "Edible Hardware." For this novelty, they use a 15-ounce slab of solid chocolate and shape it into a computer complete with "a white chocolate mouse (the kind with a tail), a milk chocolate 5-1/2" floppy, a milk chocolate integrated circuit board, and finally, a two-ounce PC (to travel with)." A 25-character personalized screen message is available.

In addition to their novelties and custom and contract molding, the Chocolate Factory offers a plethora of themed chocolate-filled gift baskets, as well as hand-rolled chocolates with creme centers—including peppermint patties that are double-dipped (once in dark chocolate and a second dunk in milk chocolate) and filled with a soft, white creme center that has "incited people to riot. This bears no resemblance to anything from York."

If your order is destined for a climate above 70 degrees, the Chocolate Factory uses an insulated carton with a reusable gel ice pack for shipping, virtually guaranteeing that your shipment will arrive in pristine shape.

According to a Usenet news group dedicated to chocolate, the Chocolate Factory's actual chocolate is considered to be among the best anywhere. And if that's not enough of an incentive, the Factory also offers free gift wrapping.

Chocolate Novelties (continued)

Company
The Chocolate Factory (Trumbauersville, PA)

Where
World Wide Web

Web Address
http://mmink.cts.com/mmink/dossiers/choco.html

Email
chocfactry@aol.com

Prices
From $10 to $54.

Shipping Fees
Actual charges. No handling fees. Varies on method and destination.

International orders are accepted.

These chocolates look sooo at home in their beautiful glass box. It wouldn't be wrong to take them out and eat them, would it? Of course it would—everybody knows that chocolate is immoral.

Elegantly Boxed Chocolates

"Pink Moment Sweets cannot be responsible for the level of enjoyment our delicious confections will produce" warns their home page. Not only do the chocolates and other sweets sound incredible, their packaging is literally art.

The company offers a leaded glass bonboniere—"capturing the mission style of Frank Lloyd Wright with transparent irridescent art glass—which they consider "the most elegant way in the world to serve fine chocolates. A perfect accompaniment to handmade Pink Moment Sweets truffles, creams, and nougats. The bonboniere is designed to sit on a coffee table, desk, or bar and specially made to accommodate the lift-out liner of a Pink Moment's 12-piece giftbox." The consumable selections are seasonal. For instance, in the summer you can enjoy their famous fruit patés, which are fat free and come in such flavors as plum and lemon.

These bonboniere boxes are limited editions. In fact, each one is numbered and signed by the artist. David Schwinner, who plays "Ross" on the television series *Friends*, bought one as a birthday gift for a friend. Talk-show host Jerry Springer also purchased one.

Working with a master chocolatier who trained in Italy and Switzerland, Pink Moment Sweets uses the best American ingredients for their European line of confections. The online catalog is updated seasonally and for major gift-giving holidays.

The highlights of their collection include California Wine Truffles, Oregon Fruit Pates, Kentucky Bourbon Fudge, Kentucky Derby Bourbon Balls, New Jersey Boardwalk Salt Water Taffy, Austrian MozatKuglen, Almond Toffee, Lemon Drop Cookies, even Pink Chocolate.

Pink Moment Sweets named themselves after "the pink moment" when the setting sun's rays bounce off mountain tops into a valley, radiating a stunning purple glow for about 10 minutes each day. They consider their confections such a sensation it made sense to them to name the company after this "unique, natural phenomenon."

Company
Pink Moment Sweets (Ojai, CA)

Where
World Wide Web

Web Address
`http://www.systemv.com/pink/`

Prices
From $13 to $165.

Shipping Fees
Based on method. Actual charges. No handling fees.

International orders are accepted.

Reluctant to pay high prices for jewelry? Let Associate Jeweler's Tradeshop dangle their low-priced carats around your neck, fingers, wrist, and on your lapel.

Fine Jewelry and Gems at Bargain Prices

Associate Jeweler's Tradeshop might be one of the best commercial sites on the Web. There isn't

a jewelry desire or need that this company cannot fulfill. They offer everything from fine jewelry to diamonds (rock only or set), custom pieces, special orders, remounts, and stone setting—all at an enormous savings—plus plenty of information on jewelry buying, manufacturing, grading and other useful facts. And there's something for anyone's budget.

"Most fine jewelry sold in traditional stores averages a 200 to 300 percent markup" according to Ray Elsey, one of the Associate Jeweler's Tradeshop presidents. "On the average, we only mark up 10 percent, which means that a $3,000 engagement ring you would find in a mall can cost as little as $1,000 from us. I tell the customer upfront *exactly* what the markup is. I'm honest. And I haven't raised my wholesale prices in four years."

These huge discounts for such fine quality may make you wonder if this is for real. It is. Associate Jeweler's is the biggest wholesale union shops in Portland, Oregon. They use "only highly skilled benchworkers, career union professionals." On their Web site, they even list the phone numbers for the Portland Better Business Bureau and the head of the Jeweler's Union Local 41, inviting you to verify for yourself that they have been satisfying customers for over 20 years, without one compliant. In fact, Associate Jewelers is even listed with Dun & Bradstreet.

How have they accomplished this reputation? "We treat everyone with courtesy and deference" says Elsey.

The same care has been taken with respect to their inventory. Associate Jewelers has over 2 million dollars in diamonds and over 200 in-stock items. They happily provide custom work as well. You can design your own piece (fax them a sketch) or for extra savings, take a look at their wax catalog of fine patterns, which features over

Bargain-Priced Jewelry (continued)

10,000 designs. Ordering from a pattern rather than from your own, original "blueprint" is much less expensive. Everything you buy from Associate Jewelers is guaranteed for one year, including custom orders.

Whether you're looking for a simple band, a fancy pair of earrings, the perfect diamond (even without a setting), or any other fine jewelry, I highly recommend you shop elsewhere first and then come to the Associate Jeweler's Web site. You'll quickly realize that the bargains here are real gems.

Shopping on the Internet and Beyond

Exclusive Deal

Associate Jewelers Tradeshop

2 percent off your
first order of $990 or more.

Exclusive deal for readers of this book only!
You must mention this offer when you place your order.

Company
Associate Jewelers (Portland, OR)

Where
World Wide Web

Web Address
http://www.teleport.com/~raylc/

Email
raylc@teleport.com

Prices
From $124 to 300,000.

Shipping Fees
Actual charges. No handling fees.

International orders are accepted.

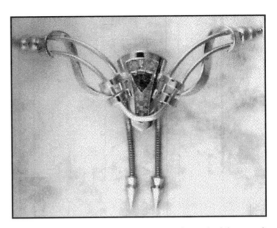

Buy her a rhodolite tonight.

Neo-Classic Women's Jewelry

The Gold Moon Precious Metal & Gem Works have carved two niches for themselves on the Internet and offer pieces you simply cannot find anywhere else.

Their neo-classic line provides a slight *deja vu* experience. because they've developed a contemporary line of jewelry inspired by deco, nouveau, and antique styles that have long since past.

Using the finest quality metal and gemstones, they handcraft each of their originals. One example is the Rhodolite necklace (pictured above), which they describe as "flowing ribbons of yellow gold surrounding a backdrop of white gold filigree, highlighted by a 5mm triangle rhodolite. Solid pendulums of gold dangle freely from the main frame. This large necklace wraps itself just below the hollow of the neck."

Their Tanzanite Showbox Pendant, a three-dimensional piece, is equally as exquisite. Photos

Neo-Classic Jewelry (continued)

of everything in their catalog can be found at their Web site.

Gold Moon also offers a service they call Scrap Value. They'll "rework discarded, possibly damaged pieces of once-sentimental jewelry into sparkling new trinkets, the design of which is tailored just for you." This custom concept strikes me as a great way to refashion old, worn, or bent engagement or wedding rings.

Gold Moon points out that they buy all their stones from accredited dealers and gemologists using only "precision cut diamonds and colored gemstones of the highest caliber."

The company updates their online catalog often. If you are buying for a jewelry lover who seems to have a bit of everything, chances are astronomically good that anything you buy from Gold Moon will add to and complement even the most extensive collection.

Shopping on the Internet and Beyond

Exclusive Deal

Gold Moon Precious Metal & Gem Works

5 percent off your first order.

Exclusive deal for readers of this book only!
You must mention this offer when you place your order.

Company
Gold Moon Precious Metal & Gem Works (Lathrup Village, MI)

Where
World Wide Web

Web Address
http://shops.net/shops/GOLD_MOON_JEWELRY/

Reminder! This Web address is case sensitive. Make sure you enter it *exactly* as shown.

Email
goldmoon@ic.net

Prices
Vary based on rotating catalog. Starting prices as low as $70.

Shipping Fees
Actual charges based on delivery method.

International orders are accepted.

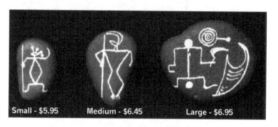

Small - $5.95   Medium - $6.45   Large - $6.95

According to legend, the rough translation for these is, "Hey, who threw my lava lamp down the volcano?"

Hawaiian Jewelry

The moment you land at the Things Hawaiian home page, you'll know you're going to find jewelry that is so unique—so Hawaiian—that nobody on the mainland United States could offer anything comparable.

All of the pieces in the Things Hawaiian online catalog are indigenous to the islands and fashioned based on ancient Hawaiian traditions and heritage. Every ornament is made by hand using materials native to the fiftieth state and are perfect reproductions of utilitarian objects.

For example, their Fish Hooks can actually be used for fishing if you so desire. However, the company advises that you instead consider string-

Hawaiian Jewelry (continued)

ing yours on the waxed cotton necklace that is included with your order. From a cultural standpoint, these hooks represent the "prized possession of the ancient Hawaiians, which used to be made from the bones of birds, humans, and dogs as well as whale ivory and turtle shells. Yours, however, will be made from boar bones and wood.

The most unique items that Things Hawaiian offers are ancient Hawaiian petroglphys (called "Ki'ipohaku" meaning "picture on the rock" in Hawaiian). In the early Hawaiian civilizations, these were the only form of communications and "even recorded events, births, marriages, death, conquests and trials." Available in three sizes ranging from small to large, these pieces are perfect for earrings or as a pendent on a necklace.

Scaled down replicas of canoe paddles, gourd masks, and Lei Niho Palaoa (a hook-like neckpiece worn by royalty) round out their roster, which is expanding as quickly as they can procure the pieces. Since these works are handmade, no two are exactly alike, which makes them that much more authentic.

Shopping on the Internet and Beyond

Exclusive Deal

Things Hawaiian

10 percent off your first order.

Exclusive deal for readers of this book only!
You must mention this offer when you place your order.

Company
Things Hawaiian
(Kihei, Maui, HI)

Where
World Wide Web

Web Address
```
http://planet-hawaii.com/~hawnexp/
the.things.html
```

Email
```
hawnexp@aloha.net
```

Prices
From $5 to $160.

Shipping Fees
Included in their prices.

International orders are accepted.

The Noah's Ark bracelet is breathtaking in its beauty and detail, but you do have to buy 'em two at a time. Just kidding!

Traditional Fine Jewelry

For a generous selection of more common jewelry styles, Ross-Simons is hard to beat. From simple, classic polished bangle to tender freshwater pearl necklace with heart pendant, their online catalog offers a wide range of choices, with enough to satisfy your desire for a good selection without being too overwhelming.

Offline, Ross-Simons has six stores scattered throughout the country. Everything they offer is top quality and, because they buy in quantity, their prices are quite competitive with what you'd find at a mall. A large percentage of their jewelry is imported from Italy, renowned for their superior quality and quiet elegance.

Fine Jewelry (continued)

In contrast to the Italian pieces is an American concept: cubic zirconia. My next statement might seem like a contradiction in terms; but this is some of the finest cubic zirconia available, so authentic looking that the Ross-Simons company loves to tell the story of the burglar who stole the jewelry made with the diamond impostors leaving the "real stuff," thinking it must be fake.

The online catalog is divided into seven sections including Glorious Gold, Bangles & Bracelets, Great Ear Looks, Precious Pearls, and Our Favorite Things. There are super-high-quality photographs of their offerings, which give you an excellent idea of what you are buying. The company will gladly refund your money within 30 days if you are not completely satisfied with your purchase. Personalized items are an exception, of course.

Company
Ross-Simons
(Cranston, RI)

Where
World Wide Web

Web Address
http://www.shopping2000.com/shopping2000/ross_simon/

Prices
From $25 to $15,000.

Shipping Fees (in the U.S.)
Based on order total. Includes insurance. Maximum of $40.

International orders are accepted.

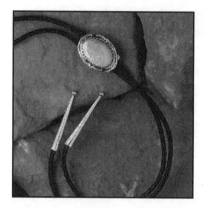

The Navaho bolo tie, made of the earth, wind, sea, and blessed by the spirit of the Gods.

Southwestern Jewelry

Some of the most distinctive jewelry in the world comes from the American Southwest. In fact, the Southwestern mystique combined with the uniqueness of the jewelry here is so far-reaching that 50 percent of the Milne Jewelry Company's orders originate from outside the U.S., most notably from Japan.

As one of our country's largest *wholesalers*, Milne Jewelry sells primarily to gift shops throughout the United States. Thanks to the Internet, they now sell directly you at substantial savings. Their online catalog includes Southwestern bolo ties, pendants, watch tips, and earrings, primarily from three tribes: Navajo, Zuni, and the Santo Domingo.

Their Navajo pieces are characteristic of this tribe—the largest in the Southwest. "With an excellence in silver working, Navajo jewelry is noted for its massive quality and simplicity of design. Turquoise and coral stones are used to enhance the beauty of the silver." Turquoise has its "roots deep in mythology and folklore, including the belief that one who sees a turquoise early in the morning will pass a fortunate day."

Southwestern Jewelry (continued)

Some of the best examples of the Zuni style on the Milne site are their Zuni fetishes (you could loosely think of a fetish as a charm), which are "handcarved from a variety of stones and sea shells, strung with ultra-fine shell heshi featuring a traditional thunderbird carved from turquoise in center."

Symbolism is also an integral part of Native American jewelry. For the mystical side of you, consider these symbols: the thunderbird, the highlight of the Zuni fetish described above, is "the sacred bearer of unlimited happiness;" the butterfly stands for everlasting life, the Sun for happiness, arrowheads for alertness, birds for carefree and light-hearted qualities, and bear claws for good luck, good omen, and protection from the Gods.

The Web site ensures us that this jewelry is "made of the earth, wind, sea, and blessed by the spirits of the Gods." Wow. You can't say *that* about your garden-variety bangles and beads, now can you?

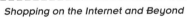

Shopping on the Internet and Beyond

Exclusive Deal

Milne Jewelry Company

10 percent off your
first order of $50 or more.

Exclusive deal for readers of this book only!
You must mention this offer when you place your order.

Company
Milne Jewelry Company (St. George, UT)

Where
World Wide Web

Web Address
http://www.xmission.com/~turq

Email
turq@xmission.com

Prices
From $16 and up.

Shipping Fees
Based on order total and destination.

International orders are accepted.

Make someone feel like royalty with Harry and David's Royal Riviera pears.

Fruit Boxes from Harry and David

Brothers Harry and David are considered by many to not only be the fathers of the mail order fruit business (which evolved into the Fruit-Of-The-Month Club) but gift baskets by mail in general.

It started with pears in the 1930s, a special Royal Riviera variety that they describe as "scarce, highly prized, truly distinctive...so big and juicy you can eat'em with a spoon." In fulfilling the orders, the brothers would "wrap each pear as carefully as you would a hen's egg and put the gift boxes on the next outbound train." (Gives you an added appreciation for FedEx, doesn't it? Imagine having to depend on Amtrak?)

Fruit Boxes (continued)

While the company has grown and their catalog continues to accommodate changes in food and gift trends, the pears live on and the only place you can get them is from Harry and David. You can choose from three gift packs, the most extravagant of which is their Cream of the Crop box—only the largest, most impressive pears make the cut. A six-pound box of five to eight pears (size dependent) runs about $27 (an average of $4 per pear).

Their infamous Fruit-Of-The-Month Club offers several options, from a 3-box plan to a 12-box year-round carnival featuring the pears and other first-rate fruit, such as mountain crisp apples, royal oranges, plums, peaches, and nectarines.

In addition to the club, you will find numerous one-time-only fruit baskets in several configurations—many of which are offered year round.

Capitalizing on the culinary treats trend, Harry and David also offer raspberry cheesecakes, bing cherry chocolates, and another exclusive, The Tower of Treats: *individual* gift boxes of "gourmet fruits and treats (cheeses, chocolates, whole cashews) wrapped, *stacked*, and topped with a bright bow." The standard size is a five-box tower but the product line continues up to their Ultimate Tower of Treats teetering with over 11 items.

On the non-food front, Harry and David have some unique gift ideas. Their exclusive complete, miniature rose garden is quite a delight. Three four-inch rose bushes (two red and one white) are pre-planted in a "handsome basket that's designed to go near any bright window." They ship about the time the plants are ready to bloom. After you've enjoyed the foliage, you can transplant them outdoors when the weather warms up the following spring.

While Harry and David have become one of the most successful businesses of its kind, the spirit of the brothers lives on. They continue to be the source for their products, not just the distributor, growing their own fruit, baking their own cakes, even weaving most of the gift baskets. In fact, "some of the ladies who hand-tie the satin ribbons bow and pack the gift baskets every Christmas have been with the company for the past 30 years."

The Harry and David company believe so strongly in their products and your satisfaction that they offer "the strongest guarantee in the business," backing not just your satisfaction, but the condition of the package and on-time arrival as well.

Company
Harry and David (Medford, OR)

Where
World Wide Web

Web Address
http://www.shopping2000.com/shopping2000/harry+david/

Prices
From $14.95 to 306.95.

Shipping Fees
$6.95 and up depending on destination and expediency requested.

International orders are accepted.

Hot Tip!

Be sure to check out CompuServe's Consumers' Forum, which is chock full of fabulous freebie info and great shopping resources. Go *conforum*.

Hawaiian Gift Baskets

If you want a gift basket that says "Aloha" in a big way, Hawaiian Treasures is your ticket to paradise. They've put together some of the best baskets around and at extraordinarily reasonable prices. In fact, their prices are so good that, if you tried to duplicate some of their packages on your own, it would cost you *more* money than buying from them. How do they do it? Volume purchasing from local suppliers.

These Hawaiian baskets are crammed with "an exciting array of tropical exotic favorites." Translation: This is *not* the stuff you find at the Honolulu airport. In fact, the company points out that these packs make great gifts to yourself because they let you sample a variety of Hawaiian culinary treasures you won't find elsewhere.

There are four baskets to choose from, starting with a basic four-item basket up to the Mauna Loa special that's loaded with everything from Hawaiian Korn Krunch to an ocean scene refrigerator magnet.

If you like some parts of one baskets as well goodies that are normally packed into another, the company will be happy to mix and match so that you receive exactly what you want.

In addition to baskets, Hawaiian Treasures features selections from the Maui Jelly Factory—all shipped in mailable gift boxes. The prices here are equally as good as the baskets. For example, a six-flavor pack of 1.5 ounce jellies, jams, and mustards costs only $7.25 at the time of this writing. Ditto for the three, ten-ounce bottles of Hawaiian syrups in the regional flavors of coconut, Maui strawberry, and Maui guava.

If you've ever wanted to try the *real* Hawaiian potato chips now made famous by corporate knock-offs, Hawaiian Treasures is one of the only companies in the world that ships the original Kitch'n Cook'd brand—available in five-quart buckets or four-gallon drums.

Around the holidays and during other national gift-giving occasions, be sure to check out Hawaiian Treasures for a rotating inventory of seasonal specials for specific holidays.

Company
Hawaiian Treasures (Honaunau, HI)

Where
World Wide Web

Web Address
http://www.kona-coffee.com/

Email
prim@interpac.net

Prices
From $30 to $35.

Shipping Fees (in the U.S.)
Based on order dollar amount. Ranges from $4 to $10.

International orders are accepted.

For More...

For more great gift shopping opportunities, see the next page.

Honorable Mentions

in the category of

Gifts & Jewelry

800-Gifthouse

Web surfers and AOL members have access to a wide assortment of gift baskets, keepsakes, balloons. Arranged by occasion.

Company
800 Gifthouse

Web Address
http://www.shopping2000.com/shopping2000/
teleway/

America Online
Keyword *flowers*

Arts, Crafts, and Gifts

Private party ads, on Prodigy, for arts, crafts and gifts.

Prodigy
Jump *classifieds* then select *browse ads*

Balloons

Balloon arrangements—standard or create-your-own bouquets.

Company
PC Balloons

Prodigy
Jump *pc balloons*

Bargain Earrings

Inexpensive stone and silver earrings using genuine stones and 14K precious metals.

Company
Earrings by Lisa

Web Address
http://mmink.com/mmink/kiosks/earrings/
earrings.html

Email
rdegel@cts.com

Bath Products

Fine bath products featuring "Treat Your Feet" gift sets and "MilBath Ginger" jars.

Company
Palo Verde

Web Address
```
http://www.olworld.com/olworld/mall/
mall_us/c_gifts/m_palove/index.html
```

Beaded Jewelry

Colorado-inspired hand-crafted jewelry emphasizing bead webbing and bead weaving designs.

Company
Earth Spirit Designs

Web Address
```
http://envirolink.org/espirit/
```

Email
```
craig@kentek.com
```

Candy Baskets

Hand-dipped candy and homestyle fudge from New England. Look for their Kosher Danish Mint Lentils.

Company
Barbra Jean's Famous Candies

Web Address
```
http://www.bjcandy.com/bjcandy/
```

Care Packages

Chocolate and candy, student care packages, and Halloween licorice hands.

Company
Sweet Enchantment

Web Address
```
http://www.wilder.com/sweet.html
```

Email
```
sweete@wilder.com
```

Clothing and Jewelry

Private party ads, on America Online, for clothing and jewelry.

America Online
Keyword *classifieds* then select *general merchandise boards*

Clothing, Cosmetics, and Jewelry

Private party ads, on America Online, for clothing, cosmetics, and jewelry.

America Online
Keyword *classifieds* then select *general merchandise boards*

Cookie Gifts

Now CompuServe members can have cookies shipped the day they are baked for every occasion.

Company
Gimmee Jimmy's Cookies

CompuServe
Go *gim*

Crystal & Zirconia Jewelry

European crystal and cubic zirconia jewelry laid in bracelets, earrings, pendants, pins, and rings.

Company
JewelQuest

Web Address
http://jewelquest.wwa.com

Culinary Gift Options

Wide selection of gourmet foods and gifts for Prodigy members.

Company
Gift Sender

Prodigy
Jump *gift sender*

Custom Jewelry

"Collectable but wearable" fine jewelry "from a distinctive collection."

Company
Steve Quick Jeweler

Web Address
http://www.Echi.com/SQJ.html

Diamonds Wholesale

Certified and uncertified stones.

Company
Wholesale Diamonds

Web Address
http://www.icw.com/diamonds/index.html

Email
diamond@icw.com

Fashion Jewelry

A variety of jewelry options for men and women.

Company
DJO Jewelers, Inc.

Web Address
http://www.digimark.net/DJO/

Fashion Rings

Diamond, sweetheart, sapphire, and ruby fashion rings.

Company
Out of Solitude Jewelry

Web Address
`http://www.ip.net/shops/`
`OUT_OF_SOLITUDE_JEWELRY/`

Free Gift Reminders

Prodigy members can set up a personal list of events for reminders via email.

Company
Gift Reminder

Prodigy
Jump *gift reminder*

General Gift Items

Gift shopping made easy. Shop by category with well-known companies via Prodigy.

Company
Find a Gift

Prodigy
Jump *find a gift*

General Gift Items

Distinctive and delicious gift selections available to Prodigy members.

Company
PC Gifts & Gourmet

Prodigy
Jump *pc gifts & gourmet*

General Gift Items

Wide assortment of out-of-the-ordinary gifts.

Company
Gift Connection

Web Address
`http://branch.com/frames/`

Email
`framenet@cnj.digex.net`

Gifts and Collectibles

Private party ads on Prodigy for gifts and collectibles.

Prodigy
Jump *classifieds* then select *browse ads*

Gift Baskets

Cookies, fudge, chocolate, and a chips and salsa basket round out the selections.

Company
Goodies from Goodman

Web Address
`http://branch.com/goodies/`

Gifts of Canadian Consumables

Something Special in British Columbia offers Saskatoon Berry chocolates, along with other unusual Canadian products.

Company
Something Special

Web Address
`http://www.wimsey.com/Magnet/shop/`
`index130.html`

Gifts Galore

CompuServe members can look here for a broad selection of gifts, plush animals, gourmet food, and gift baskets for all occassions.

Company
Breton Harbor Baskets & Gifts

CompuServe
Go *bh*

High-End Gifts

America Online members can choose gifts from small artisans and craftspeople located all over the world.

Company
The Celebration Fantastic

America Online
Keyword *2market* then select *collections* then select *the celebration fantastic*

Historic Newspapers

Original newspapers as published on the date you request.

Company
Historic Newspaper Archives

Web Address
http://www.infopost.com/histnews/
index.html

Liquor by Wire

CompuServe members can be sure to send a gift with "spirit," including wine, champagne, hard alcohol, and beer. Delivery to more than 30 countries.

Company
Liquor By Wire

CompuServe
Go *lbw*

Maple Gift Baskets

Gifts baskets featuring maple products. Other themes available.

Company
Maples Fruit Farm

Web Address
http://virtumall.com/MaplesFruitFarm/
greeting.html

Microchip Gifts

Computer cable bracelets, chokers, and eye glass straps, as well as microchip paperweights, magnets, and jewelry.

Company
Computer Jewelry

Web Address
http://branch.com/zimcom/index.html

Muffin Baskets

"Over 200 varieties of freshly baked gourmet muffins. Custom gift baskets shipped to any Web Address within the continental U.S."

Company
My Favorite Muffin

Web Address
http://www.satelnet.org/muffins/

Email
mfmuffin@satelnet.org

Niobium Jewelry

Eye-dazzling handcrafted from this refractory metal.

Company
Colorburst Studios

Web Address
http://www.teleport.com/~paulec/catalog.html

Email
paulec@teleport.com

Notecards

Notecards with photos of animals, flora, water scenes, and more.

Company
Nature's Notecards

Web Address
http://amsquare.com/america/nature.html

Oak Notepaper Holders

Kansas solid-oak notepaper holders with personalized refills available.

Company
Rob's Office

Web Address
http://amsquare.com/america/amerway/oakbox/oakbox.html

Personalized Jewelry

Diamond name rings, diamond nameplates, and gold name plates.

Company
Jewelry Mall

Web Address
http://www.ip.net/shops/JEWELRY-MALL/

Pins

Gorgeous matisse-like sterling silver dancer pins.

Company
Celebration of the Heart Pin

Web Address
http://www.webstore.com/tm01.htm

Puzzle Rings

Puzzled about your relationship? How about His and Hers puzzle rings. Eighteen styles available.

Company
Nuray & Co.

Web Address
http://www.olworld.com/olworld/mall/mall_us/c_gifts/m_nuray/index.html

Rainforest Assorted Candy

"Fine chocolates with tropical nuts that support rain forest causes."

Company
Toucan Chocolates

Web Address
`http://branch.com/toucan/toucan.html`

Email
`toucan@branch.com`

Rose Jewelry

"Rose jewelry packaged in deluxe, velvet presentation boxes."

Company
Rose Collection

Web Address
`http://www.webstore.com/rn01.htm`

Russian Watches

Quality, Moscow-made watches at wholesale prices.

Company
Dimas Trading Company

Web Address
`http://www.olworld.com/olworld/mall/`
`mall_us/c_gifts/m_dimas/index.html`

Email
`75357.174@compuserve.com`

Send a Song

Prodigy members choose from over 150 popular tunes played via telephone to the recipient.

Company
Send a Song

Prodigy
Jump *send a song*

Soap Boxes

Boxes with all natural, handmade, soap infused with Southwestern fragrances.

Company
Angel Mesa Soap of Taos

Web Address
`http://www.rt66.com/swest/`

Email
`swest@rt66.com`

Specialized Gift Baskets

Theme baskets including snacking, southern specialties, and Olympic themes.

Company
Signature Baskets

Web Address
`http://www.ip.net/shops/Signature_Baskets_Ltd/`

Turquoise Jewelry

Charms, earrings, bracelets, and rings made with genuine turquoise and precious metals.

Company
Talon Export Jewelry Company

Web Address
`http://www.swcp.com/~bwilkins/talon.html`

Health & Medicine

Dr. Foster Carr is re-shaping the doctor-patient relationship: It's now the doctor-be-patient-while-the-home-page-loads relationship.

Cyber-Doc

Foster P. Carr. M.D. is on a mission "to increase worldwide access to health information and services, reduce the cost of healthcare, and improve the quality of life for all human beings."

Combining his principles, the Hippocratic oath, and a modem, Dr. Carr has taken his vision to the Web, offering online services and healthcare for people with non-life threatening acute needs, those far from medical facilities, or those who require the general guidance of a well-trained physician. Dr. Carr's undergraduate degree is from Harvard and his medical degree is from Stanford, so you'd be hard-pressed to find a physician locally who has such distinguished credentials.

Under the umbrella of The Cyberspace TeleMedical Offices patients become members of the online clinic ($30 for 6 months, $50 for one year), which provides them with access to a plethora of services and products.

TeleMedical's primary services include "the creation of a personal medical history, and appoint-ments for computer-based medical conferences. If you have the right equipment and an appropriate medical problem, you will be able to receive remote diagnosis, have studies such as lab tests and X-rays ordered, receive prescriptions, and get referrals to other medical providers."

Members also have access to an impressive library of information, including a self-service medical database and a clearinghouse of worldwide clinical research information along with an online librarian.

Dr. Carr not only writes prescriptions, he can fill them too via his online drug store. Whether it's an over-the-counter remedy or a Valium refill, TeleMedical's Health and Wellness Center has everything you would find at your neighborhood pharmacy (including home healthcare products and diagnostic equipment), and even health software for consumers as well as for healthcare professionals.

To fulfill his vision of a *worldwide* service, Dr . Carr and TeleMedical will soon care for people who speak any of 22 languages—from Mandarin Chinese to French, Hebrew to Bengalese. Dr. Carr himself is proficient in English, German, and Spanish.

If you don't have a primary care physician, or you simply want access to medical information and assistance, or you travel frequently and a doctor online makes sense, TeleMedical is the perfect treatment for the modem-abled.

Cyber-Doc (continued)

Company
Cyberspace TeleMedical Offices
(San Diego, CA)

Where
World Wide Web

Web Address
`http://telemedical.com/~drcarr/`

Email
`drcarr@telemedical.com`

Prices
Varies by services rendered. Very reasonable.

With products from Health & Vitamin Express, you'll feel so good it hurts.

Vitamins & Health Products

Members of America Online, CompuServe, and Prodigy all have access to an impressive catalog of health and vitamin products via a company appropriately called Health & Vitamin Express (HVE).

Just about every health-related item is available here. Their motto: "Whatever your lifestyle, from a high-stressed business executive to a meditative vegetarian, our products will meet your daily needs."

Depending on which online service you use, you'll find approximately twenty product categories, including antioxidants, cold and flu remedies, Cybergenic products, health accessories, health "candy," herbs, homeopathic, Men's Needs (but no Women's), over-the-counter products, and more.

I'll use the over-the-counter products category as an example: HVE shows a "their" price and an "our price." HVE never explicitly says who "they" are, but the prices were comparable to the "theys" in my neighborhood, which means HVE's prices provide discounts of 30 percent and more. Excedrin Extra Strength (100 caps) are $8.49, 33 percent less than the $12.65 you might pay elsewhere. HVE lists over 29 name brands, and although not all prices are as low as the Excedrin offer, they're all noteworthy.

In fact, you'll find even deeper discounts on HVE's vitamins, supplements, and alternative health products. 400 IU tablets of Natural Vitamin E are easy to swallow at a slim $19.99, a 40-percent savings over "their" $33.98 counterpart.

If you don't have easy access to a health food store or other alternative health outlet, you'll be in heaven at HVE; they carry an extremely impressive selection of non-traditional well-being products. Feel good, look great, and spend less at Health & Vitamin Express.

Company
Health & Vitamin Express

Where
America Online, CompuServe, and Prodigy

America Online
Keyword *vitamin exp*

CompuServe
Go *rx*

Prodigy
Jump *vitamin express*

Prices
Everything is discounted.

Shipping Fees
Dependent on order size.

International orders are accepted.

The Monroe Institute looks inviting enough to be a vacation resort.

Audio Tapes for Well Being

Many people believe that healing and health happen first in the mind, then in the body. Some people take this belief a step-further, asserting that mental reprogramming can actually induce a physical cure.

The late Robert Monroe supported both theories and, as part of a much bigger picture, developed a set of audiotapes and CDs to hasten the process.

Based on a theory he named Hemi-Sync, "a patented auditory technology based on the natural functioning of the brain...these auditory guidance programs employ multiplexed binaural beats to induce a frequency-following response in the brain, verbal suggestion, relaxation exercises, guided imagery, autohypnosis, and placebo effect all carefully crafted to engender desired mental states of conscious.... It can be compared to a powerful software program that facilitates extraordinary levels of performance and productivity. There are no hidden messages. The listener is in control at all time with Hemi-Sync."

In total, over 200 tapes, CDs, and books are available here. You choose tapes based on the results you want. The groups are divided into thirty-one sections, with several choices for each section. Most of the single tapes cost about $15, and cassette "albums" (multiple tapes) are as high as $70.

For instance, in the Weight Control area, you'll find three tapes: "Eat/No Eat" for learning to reduce your desire for food; "Nutricia," which conditions the "control processing of what is eaten by either maximizing or minimizing the caloric value retained;" and "De-Hab," for learning to override the influence of old eating habits.

The Pregnancy and Childbirth group is loaded with goodies, including Hemi-Sync products to "help reduce the perception of pain during labor, another for easing the physical stress of labor and, my favorite, "Catnapper," to make up for missed sleep due to night feedings. (Although it'll probably also work following triggered car alarms at 2:00 AM in the city.)

Another category, Addictive Behavior, has products for quitting smoking, redirecting negativity, "off-loading" (for flexibility in attitudes and behaviors), and eliminating compulsive thinking.

There are tons of audio programs on the market that claim to be the ultimate mental reprogramming mechanisms. I approach them with a balance of hope and skepticism. However, after reading through some of the Monroe Institute background material, I was impressed with the philosophy and execution of these programs, and I strongly suggest that, if you're seeking this therapeutic approach, you owe it to yourself to consider the Hemi-Sync programs.

Tapes for Well-Being (continued)

Company
Monroe Institute (Lovingston, VA)

Where
World Wide Web

Web Address
http://www.monroe-inst.com/

Email
monroeinst@aol.com

Prices
From $12 to $365.

Shipping Fees
Based on order total.

International orders are accepted.

For More...

For more great health shopping opportunities, see the next page.

Honorable Mentions

in the category of

Health & Medicine

A Day's Fruit and Veggies

Get the vitamins of five servings of fruits or vegetables in eight small coated caplets.

Company
MR Health Products

Web Address
http://www.supermall.com/juicing/
juicing.html

Allergy-Proof Products

Allergy-free products, including mattresses, pillows, cleaners, filters, vacuums, carpet cleaners, mildew and mold inhibitors, and much more.

Company
Allergy Clean Environments

Web Address
http://www.w2.com/allergy.html

Alternative Health Store

Vitamins, personal care, bulk items all geared for people who prefer alternative health care.

Company
Liberty Natural Products

Web Address
http://www.teleport.com/~liberty/

Contact Lenses

Lynda Carter's favorite vision care system is now available to CompuServe members.

Company
Lens Express

CompuServe
Go *lens*

Contact Lens Supplies

CompuServe and Prodigy members can save up to 65 percent on over 120,000 lenses in inventory. All purchases come with a 30-day guarantee.

Company
Contact Lens Supply

CompuServe
Go *cl*

Prodigy
Jump *contact lens*

Ginseng Products

A wide variety of ginseng capsules and herb teas.

Company
Ginseng Select Products Inc.

Web Address
http://tpa.cent.com/ginseng.html

Email
ginseng@tpa.cent.com

Health and Fitness

Private party ads, on Prodigy, for health and fitness.

Prodigy
Jump *classifieds* then select *browse ads*

Health and Personal Items

Private party ads, on America Online, for health and personal items.

America Online
Keyword *classifieds* then select *general merchandise boards*

Health Products

Bee pollen, propolis, green barley, aloe drinks, antioxidants, and more.

Company
Formulas for Health

Web Address
http://branch.com/health/health.html

Email
vitamin@branch.com

Health Topics

Private party ads, on CompuServe, offering health-related information.

CompuServe
Go *classifieds* then select *miscellaneous info* then select *merchandise*

Lead Testing Kits

Household lead testing kits.

Company
Lead Tester

Web Address
http://www.branch.com/epa/epa.html

Email
leadtest@interramp.com

Mobility Scooter

Indoor/outdoor PaceSaver Excel mobility scooter. Latest design. Quieter ride.

Company
ABC Mobility

Web Address
http://branch.com/abc/

Email
abc@branch.com

Sears Home Healthcare

Products for bath safety, personal care, and fitness.

Company
Sears Home Healthcare

Web Address
http://www.shopping2000.com/shopping2000/
sears-healthcare/

Self-Improvement

Private party ads, on CompuServe, offering self-improvement information.

CompuServe
Go *classifieds* then select *miscellaneous info* then select *merchandise*

Supplements

Thousands of supplements discounted. All top brands.

Company
DFH Discount Supplements

Web Address
http://branch.com:1080/vitamin/
vitamin.html

Email
martinhead@aol.com

Vitamins

CompuServe members can get the official vitamins of the Miami Dolphins and the Swimming Hall of Fame. Guaranteed full satisfaction or your money back.

Company
SDV Vitamins

CompuServe
Go *sdv*

Email
70007.1533@compuserve.com

World's Most Natural Vitamins

Family manufactured vitamins since 1928 and praised as some of the highest-quality vitamins available in the world. Over 250 vitamins and supplements in stock.

Company
Freeda Vitamins

Web Address
```
http://virtumall.com/Freeda/
FREEDAhome.html
```

Home Furnishings

Y'all take off yer shoes and sit a spell.

Adirondack Chairs

Chairs Inc., best known in their home city of Portland, Oregon, is *the place* to go for chair refinishing, glueing, caning, weaving, and any other restoration need you may have. On the Internet, Chairs Inc. is known as *the place* for the ever-popular Adirondack chair.

"The angular lawn classic with slatted seat and back has only its name to connect it to the region. Its provenance remains a mystery, meaning that it is still confused with the older Westport chair, to which it bears a resemblance. The Westport chair is certified Adirondack, but the Adirondack chair has not yet been proven to have originated in the Adirondacks.

"The Adirondack chair is constructed of slats, making it very light in weight but amply proportioned. The chair may date from the 1920s, and was certainly commonplace by World War II.

"There is the thought that the Adirondack chair was designed as convalescent furniture to accommodate the hundreds of tubercular patients flocking to the Adirondack Mountains for the 'wilderness cure'—weeks of quiet rest and fresh air spent on the porches and gardens of resorts and cottages."

Even though it's made of wood, the chair is extremely comfortable. You can sit in it all day without experiencing any physical fatigue.

The company sells these comfy wooden wonders in easy-to-assemble kits made of western red cedar. If you have any questions about how to put yours together, Chairs Inc. encourages you to call any of their "chairmen."

Shopping on the Internet and Beyond

Exclusive Deal

Chairs, Inc.

10 percent off every order.

Exclusive deal for readers of this book only!
You must mention this offer when you place your order.

Company
Chairs, Inc. (Portland, OR)

Where
World Wide Web

Web Address
http://www.xmission.com/~wwwads/chairs/company.html

Adirondack Chairs (continued)

Email
chairs@europa.com

Prices
$99.95

Shipping Fees
Included in price.

Can't decide on one design? Try the Sampler quilt for a little patch of everything.

Handmade Quilts

It's nice to see one of the lowest-tech businesses in the world taking full advantage of current technology to encourage the world to "warm up" to their products.

The Quiltery makes handmade quilts by custom order. And they do mean *handmade*. "All quilts are made in people's homes. The quilting and appliquéing are done exclusively by hand using tiny stitches. The fabric is 100-percent cotton; the batting inside is a synthetic or cotton-poly blend, for durability and ease in laundering."

It's also important to note that, for each quilt, only one woman, picked from among the dozens the quiltery represents, does all the stitching from start to finish to ensure the highest quality and continuity. All the quilters are extremely skilled. Some have been working with The Quiltery since the company opened its doors in 1972.

On The Quiltery Web site, you'll find photographs of their most popular quilt styles, along with prices for each quilt (based on size—from crib/wall hangings to king-size bed). Their big sellers are the Double Wedding Ring, Bridal Wreath, and Log Cabin styles, but you can think of these "stock" samples as merely suggestions.

Since The Quiltery quilts can be custom-made, if you've seen a quilt somewhere and you'd like it duplicated, submit a photo or a magazine picture and The Quiltery will give you an estimate based on their already extremely competitive prices. After you place your order, expect your quilt to arrive in approximately 90 days (or 60 days if you purchase a wall hanging). What a short wait for an "heirloom of tomorrow!"

Shopping on the Internet and Beyond

Exclusive Deal

The Quiltery

Free shipping on your first order (or an $8 shipping credit for international orders).

Exclusive deal for readers of this book only! You must mention this offer when you place your order.

Company
The Quiltery (Allentown, PA)

Where
World Wide Web

Web Address
http://mmink.com/mmink/dossiers/quilt/quilt.html

Handmade Quilts (continued)

Email
mnje65a@prodigy.com

Prices
From $200 to $900.

Shipping Fees (in the U.S.)
$8 via UPS Ground.

International orders are accepted

This colorful piece has two interesting faces. Each chevron on the front contains a variation of a diamond design—white, orange, and purple predominate. The back has stripes of purple, two oranges, and a little dark blue and green.

Moroccan Rugs and Pillows

Susan Schaefer Davis is an anthropologist who, for the past 29 years, has lived and worked on and off in Morocco. During these three decades she's been on a shopping spree, toting back one-of-a-kind Moroccan textiles for herself, her family, and friends. Susan felt it was time to debut her collection and has done so via her company, Marrakesh Express. Some of her finds are shown on her Web site in a Gallery section, with other pieces for sale via the site's Shop.

"All the pieces you will see are one-of-a-kind and handwoven (and a few embroidered) by Moroccan women and girls, usually for their own use." Morocco, located on the northwest corner of Africa, is populated by Berbers and Arabs, and is about the size of California. Moroccan weavers produce a large number of rug styles. Rabat rugs are commonly found in the United States. Other popular styles include a central medallion and deep pile, which often contain a predominance of red and blue threads.

This collection focuses on the lesser-known and more varied flatweaves (often called kilims) from the Middle Atlas mountains, with a few Glawa pieces from the High Atlas mountains, south of Marrakesh. Nearly all are woven from wool, with white designs (usually in cotton) for contrast.

If you see something in the Gallery for which there is no counterpart in the Shop, let Ms. Davis know and she will happily do some "custom shopping" for you on her next trip.

Davis buys directly from families, so these textiles are not made specifically for export; rather, they are part of a heritage. "Most people don't know about these rugs and pillows," says Davis. "They are a well-kept secret."

Davis grants all customers a reasonable evaluation period. If you find that a rug you've purchased doesn't work for you, simply return it for a full refund.

The prices are unbelievable—with bargains beginning at the $35 mark. It's like cruising a Moroccan bazaar without having to do any price haggling.

Moroccan Rugs, Pillows (continued)

Company
Marrakesh Express (Haverford, PA)

Where
World Wide Web

Web Address
http://uslink.net/ddavis

Email
sdavis@uslink.net

Prices
From $35 to $400 and up.

Shipping Fees
Included in all prices for UPS Ground.

International orders are accepted.

Better to light an energy-saving lamp than to curse your power bill.

10,000 Light Bulbs

How many people does it take to screw in every one of Lamp Technology's light bulbs? Try 10,000. That's how many bulbs this company carries in their 12,000-square-foot warehouse. Whatever your bulb replacement needs happen to be, Lamp Technology can bring the light back into your life.

Check out their low prices on halogens, projection, medical, and energy-saving lamps. By purchasing their stock in quantity from over 200 vendors, the company can offer a multitude of specialty light bulbs for the entire spectrum of lighting applications—often at heavily discounted prices. Serving the replacement light bulb market worldwide for more than 15 years, they are an authorized distributor for G.E., Phillips, and Osram/Sylvania.

As lighting specialists, Lamp Technology, Inc. loves a challenge and can identify virtually any bulb made. To make the process much easier, the company has a set of images on their Web site to help you identify the bulb you want. With over eight graphics, each a grouping of up to 20 or more lamps, you can easily find what you need based on its category—such as miniature bulbs, halogens, even European bulbs.

Lamp Technology also offers super-high-quality flashlights at fabulous prices. Their Revolution Revolving Head Flashlight is only $16.95. Their Streamlight Jr. (with push-button power) is *2,000 percent* brighter than most other flashlights, but it's practically a giveaway at $9.95.

To power your flashlights, Lamp Technology, Inc. also sells alkaline batteries, at prices that rival what I pay at a warehouse discount store. Nine-volt batteries sell for $1.75 (I realized what a bargain this is when I bought the same battery elsewhere for $3.19) and AAs go for a mere 50 cents apiece when bought in 2-packs.

Whether it's a 60-watt softlight or a 1972 bulb for your slide projector, you can "lighten up because Lamp Technology's got it!"

Remember!

For periodic updates of this book, send email to *shop@easton.com*. See *Introduction* for more details.

10,000 Light Bulbs (continued)

Company
Lamp Technology, Inc. (Bohemia, NY)

Where
World Wide Web

Web Address
http://www.webscope.com/lamptech/info.html

E-mail
lamptech@panix.com

Prices
From $2 to $40.

Shipping Fees (in the U.S.)
Actual UPS Ground charges.

International orders are accepted.

Southwestern Trail Blankets

In many Native American nations, the use of blankets is a sacred part of many rituals. Blankets are used in key ceremonies and many Native Americans consider it an honor to give and receive them. In fact, it is common among Native Americans to request that they be buried in a blanket that has special meaning.

Blankets so beautiful they're a fashion accessory.

The Dewey Trading Company, with its profound respect for Native American culture, approached the world-renown Pendleton Woolen Mills and asked them to be the exclusive manufacturer of a line of limited edition Southwestern trail blankets to commemorate the "myths and traditions of the American West."

The result is an elite line of six stunning blankets, each honoring trails named after a particular tribe. For pristine authenticity, the company hired prominent Hopi artist Ramona Sakiestewa, which makes her the first Native American to design Pendleton blankets.

Ms. Sakiestewa's weavings and tapestries have been honored by many museums. In fact, the blankets she's designed for Pendleton are now included in such prestigious collections as the Gene Autry Western Heritage Museum in Los Angeles and the National Museum of the American Indian in New York (part of the Smithsonian Institute).

Even though these blankets hang in museums, they still have utilitarian value as a covering for most beds (at 64" by 80" they cover the top of a queen with only an inch to spare). Since these blankets are a blend of 82-percent wool and 12-percent cotton, they'll keep you nice and toasty in winter, but without the irritating scratchiness generally associated with wool. Most people,

Southwestern Blankets (continued)

however, choose to use them as decorations, especially as wall hangings.

Because Ms. Sakiestewa's designs are so beautiful, they pop up from time to time as backgrounds in the popular media—one was even featured on the soap opera "Days of Our Lives" as the only "clothing" a female character wore for several scenes.

Even though the blankets are manufactured by Pendleton, they are made exclusively for the Dewey Trading Company and hence can only be purchased from them.

Shopping on the Internet and Beyond

Exclusive Deal

Dewey Trading Company

$25 off your first blanket purchase.

Exclusive deal for readers of this book only!
You must mention this offer when you place your order.

Company
Dewey Trading Company
(Santa Fe, NM)

Where
World Wide Web

Web Address
http://www.nets.com/dewey

Email
deweytrading@nets.com

Prices
From $250 to $355.

Shipping Fees
$10 per blanket.

International orders are accepted.

Now you see it...

now you don't.

Two Rooms in One

"In the evening, you entertain a friend in your elegant dining room. Later, you stretch out in your well-appointed bedroom to read a good book before a night of restful sleep. What's unusual? Each of these rooms occupies the same space, which is transformed at the touch of a button."

The Mezzanine is a space wonder and blessing. Its Oriental influence and French concept and design accomplish no small feat: doubling the function of one room.

The platform is raised and lowered at the touch of a button and can "easily accommodate a king-size mattress, reading lights, a clock-radio, a small TV, books, and magazines...everything that you would keep at your bedside. (Larger, custom models are available.) Equipped with telephone jacks, electrical outlets, and halogen lights, the Mezzanine is easily like adding a second floor. "This is not Star Wars, but a space revolution," cites company literature.

All that's required is an eight-foot ceiling. "When raised, the Mezzanine fits snugly against the ceiling, occupying a mere 16", and providing an ample 6' 8" of headroom below. The lower limit may be set to any level, depending on the height of the underlying furniture, and is easily adjusted by repositioning platform stops."

It works perfectly as a playroom or as a large work area for hobbyists. If necessary, you can raise the platform out of view and away from kids. One customer purchased the Mezzazine as a bedroom, and put a home gym underneath.

As a LAMA executive so succinctly put it, "with the Mezzazine you aren't buying an elevating floor, you're buying the space underneath it."

Shopping on the Internet and Beyond

Exclusive Deal

LAMA

10 percent off all orders.

Exclusive deal for readers of this book only!
You must mention this offer when you place your order.

Company
LAMA (New York, NY)

Where
World Wide Web

Web Address
http://branch.com:1080/lama/lama.html

Prices
From $5,310 to $8,510.

Shipping Fees
Actual costs. Based on destination.

International orders are accepted.

Oh give me a home, with a roof like a dome, where the walls and the plumbing rotate....

The Remarkable Dome Home

Although I've titled this chapter "Home Furnishings," one Web site can actually furnish you with your own home.

You have to see it to believe it. The Domespace home is an architectural masterpiece—a spectacular structure oozing with serenity from both the interior and exterior. In a word, it's DaVincian.

Over 100 Domespaces have been built already, mostly in Europe, with a few in the Far East and a few more are headed for the United States. Most are bought either as private homes or as weekend retreats—a dome away from home. However, they are also great for businesses, with a few already functioning as restaurants, schools, and storefronts. The potential uses are really limitless.

A Domespace can be as little as 400 square feet (as an auxiliary office or guest house) or as big as 2,900 square feet, which is equivalent to a five-bedroom home. In fact, even larger sizes are also available. But no matter how big you'd like your residential orb, the shape will remain the same.

The Dome Home (continued)

The spherical aspect is even more practical than you might realize. The Domespace is virtually earthquake-resistant, cyclone-proof, and a challenge to unwanted intruders, since it's nearly impossible to break into the house via one of the windows.

The dome home is so "perfectly balanced you can rotate it yourself." You can purchase an optional motor that you can start either manually or on a timer so that your home rotates with the sun, maximizing the flow of natural light. Since all the plumbing and electrical connections are installed using flexible tubing and conduits, you don't need to worry about disconnecting any internal connections.

The Domespace is a "pro-environment" structure, made *entirely* of wood—including the insulation, the roof, and the frame. The wood also works as a barrier by not allowing humidity or moisture to penetrate the structure. "The roof is perfectly adapted to any solar energy device."

To get your Domespace in place, you need to supply the plot of land. After the cement is poured, your Domespace can be erected within only a few weeks. Every aspect of the home is customizable: You decide how many rooms you want and how large they will be. After you place your order, you work closely with the company, citing your wishlist of features. You can build it yourself or have the company build it for you. Everything is included in the price, including the key to the front door.

Company
Domespace (New York, NY)

Where
World Wide Web

Web Address
http://branch.com/dome/dome.html

Email
svencat@pipeline.com

Instant Information
dome@branch.com

Prices
$110 per square foot, which includes materials and labor.

International orders are accepted.

With Books That Work's 3D Landscape software, you can take Mother Nature a few steps further.

Home Project Books & Software

Tool timers unite—Books That Work is your "home project resource" on the Internet. This Web site is a fabulous resource for any "do-it-yourselfer."

While the company has plenty to sell, they also give you plenty for free. For instance, their *Complete Guide to Garden Stuff* "contains information on more than 500 items, covering

Home Projects (continued)

everything from tools and pesticides to gargoyles and bonsai. Use it to find the right item for your job or to learn more about something you already own." You can perform full text searches or simply browse the table of contents. If mulches have *you* mulching or your pests are out of control, you'll find a simple solution via this free online text.

Other fabulous freebies include a database of "mostly toll-free numbers for over 800 companies and organizations that provide information or products related to the home and garden," clearly organized by topic. They even provide a directory of related Web sites that the company feels would be useful for a budding Bob Vila or Vita Sackville-West.

The company sells Windows software that will "help you save money, time, and hassle on projects around your yard and garden....using multimedia how-to-instructions, complete with sound, color photographs, and animated videos." The titles in this series include the popular Garden Encyclopedia, 3D Lanscape, and 3D Deck.

If your interests are more toward the interior of the house, Books That Work has plenty to offer, including a paint calculator (for determining how much paint is required to paint a room) and a span calculator (which figures the maximum distance between floor joists—ever notice how you never have one of these when you need one?).

For "a high-tech solution to home repair," consider their Home Repair Encyclopedia software, which will tell you as well as *show* you how to do a job. If you plan do some electrical work, the Get Wired software will "guide you through

home wiring repairs and improvements. Its Circuit Simulator enables you to lay out and test new circuitry for your home and practice wiring it *on screen* before you ever lift a cable in real life."

Company
Books That Work (Palo Alto, CA)

Where
World Wide Web

Web Address
http://www.btw.com/

Email
sales@btw.com

Prices
From $14.49 to $49.99.

Shipping Fees
$5.95 via UPS Ground.

 A database of numbers of companies and organizations providing information or products related to home and garden.

For More...

For more great home furnishing shopping opportunities, see the next page.

Honorable Mentions

in the category of

Home Furnishings

Appliances and Electronics

Private party ads, on Prodigy, for appliances and electronics.

Prodigy
Jump *classifieds* then select *browse ads*

Ceramic Art Tile

Hand-painted tiles for hanging as art or for use as a trivet.

Company
Sun Tile

Web Address
http://www.olworld.com/olworld/mall/
mall_us/c_gifts/m_suntil/

Email
suntile@aol.com

Discount Mattresses

CompuServe members can get Sealy, Serta, Simmons, and more for much less than department store prices.

Company
Dial-A-Mattress

CompuServe
Go *beds*

Ergonomic Chairs

Special computer chairs to improve posture and reduce back problems.

Company
JDI Group

Web Address
http://www.awa.com/jdi/index.html

Email
jdi@branch.com

Furniture

Classical, solid furniture for the bedroom, dining room, and more is available to CompuServe members.

Company
Bassett Furniture Co.

CompuServe
Go *bfc*

Home Automation

CompuServe members can automate their home on a small scale with starter kits or on a larger scale with expanded control units.

Company
Hybrid Tech. Systems, Inc.

CompuServe
Go *hts*

Home Improvement

Building and home-improvement supplies for CompuServe members.

Company
Sutherland's HouseMart

CompuServe
Go *hm*

Household Items and Goods

Private party ads, on Prodigy, for household items and goods.

Prodigy
Jump *classifieds* then select *browse ads*

Housewares and Furniture

Private party ads, on America Online, for housewares and furniture.

America Online
Keyword *classifieds* then select *general merchandise boards*

Kitchen Accessories

Top-notch cookware and kitchen accessories from around the world available to America Online and CompuServe members.

Company
Chef's Catalog

America Online
Keyword *collections* then select *chef's data*

CompuServe
Go *cc*

Mary Ellen's Picks

Helpful, time-saving products for America Online members from Mary Ellen of "Helpful Hints" fame.

Company
Mary Ellen's Marketplace

America Online
Keyword *women's day* then select *wd departments* then select *mary ellen*

Mugs

Quality 11-ounce mugs that humorously display your connection to the Internet, with such sayings as "alt.internet.mug" and "You can find me on the Internet."

Company
Cybermugs - Stelcom Inc.

Web Address
http://www.webscope.com:80/cybermugs/

Email
cybermugs@webscope.com

Native American Blankets

Good selection of the bright, beautiful, and culturally important Star Blankets.

Company
Internet Solutions, Inc.

Web Address
http://www.AbInfoHwy.CA/abinfohwy/abobus/kermode/starblkt.html

Pie Plates

"Wheel-thrown pie plates from the heart of the Adirondacks."

Company
New Moon Pottery

Web Address
http://www.icw.com/america/newmoon.html

Raised Flooring

Specializing in raised computer flooring, anti-static carpets, and floor panel matching.

Company
Access Floor Systems Inc.

Web Address
http://www.neosoft.com/citylink/afshome/

Email
blake@neosoft.com

Redwood Patio Furniture

Featuring Convert-A-Table, which transforms from a bench to a table in seconds.

Company
Premiere Unlimited

Web Address
http://www.imall.com/imall/Housewares/premiere/premiere.html

Solar Products

Resources for solar living.

Company
Real Goods Trading Corporation

Web Address
http://www.well.com/www/realgood/

Email
realgood@well.sf.ca.us

Stoneware

Award winning stoneware from a renown potter.

Company
Young's Studio and Gallery

Web Address
http://www.icw.com/america/young.html

Super Snow Shovel

"More than a shovel, it's a snow plow on a stick." Self-sharpening edge. No bending. No lifting.

Company
Snow Plow Shovel, Inc.

Web Address
http://www.imall.com/imall/Housewares/
shovel/shovel.html

Supplies for Woodworking

Hand and power woodworking tools and supplies available to CompuServe members.

Company
Garrett Wade

CompuServe
Go *gw*

Tableware

A great selection of china, crystal, and flatware for Prodigy members.

Company
Placesettings

Prodigy
Jump *placesettings*

Tools

Home improvement fans rejoice...it's a craftsman extravaganza! Available to Web surfers and Prodigy members.

Company
Sears Power & HandTools

Web Address
http://www.shopping2000.com/shopping2000/
sears-tools/

Prodigy
Jump *sears*

Vacuums

Online retailer of Miele vacuums, famous for their power, durability, and performance.

Company
Sweeps Vacuum & Repair Center

Web Address
http://branch.com/sweeps/miele.htm

Email
sweeps@vacuums.com

Windows

"America's #1 choice in windows" for every room in your house; available to Prodigy members.

Company
Andersen Windows

Prodigy
Jump *andersen windows*

Inventive Notions

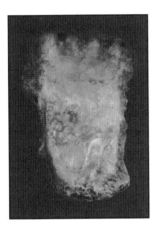

No, it's not a moon rock or some other cheap imitation. It's a totally down-to-earth and authentic Sasquatch footprint cast.

Sasquatch Tracks

"Whether you believe Sasquatch (a.k.a. Bigfoot) is a real animal or a longstanding hoax, these copies of original Sasquatch tracks are an excellent conversation piece." Use them as a decorative ashtray, house-warming gift, or trivet.

"All the casts are exact duplicates of tracks found in the wilderness of the Pacific Northwest and their authenticity has been verified by a Dr. Krantz, university professor, the foremost scientific authority on Sasquatch. All casts are made of hydrocal white plaster, coated with a sealer with a string embedded in the back for hanging." Both hand and foot tracks are available, which means you could create your own Sasquatch Chinese Theater.

You have a large selection to choose from, including some unusual casts like the track from Southern Indiana, circa 1990, one of the few discovered outside the Pacific Northwest.

You can also find a "Crippled Foot," considered "one of the most important Sasquatch track finds, because the crippled foot of this individual has allowed Dr. Krantz to reconstruct the internal anatomy of the foot, providing very strong evidence for the existence of Sasquatch."

There are pictures of most of the available items in the online catalog, along with links to the Bigfoot Research Project and the Western Bigfoot Society. So *you* decide: Is Sasquatch the "missing link," or was he left stranded by visiting space aliens? I vote for space aliens.

Shopping on the Internet and Beyond

Exclusive Deal

Ira Walters Company

$5 off your first order of $25 or more.

Exclusive deal for readers of this book only! You must mention this offer when you place your order.

Company
Ira Walters (Pullman, WA)

Where
World Wide Web

Sasquatch Tracks (continued)

Web Address
http://www.wsu.edu:8000/~walters/tracks.html

Email
walters@mail.wsu.edu

Prices
From $12 to $580.

Shipping Fees (in the U.S.)
$5

International orders are accepted.

Although you can't actually get free books on tape or free contact lenses, these companies will send you free catalogs and samples from the Free Offer Forum.

Oodles of Free Stuff

The Free Offer Forum is a bonanza of freebies that cater to every interest, every lifestyle, every age.

You begin by choosing one of the 17 categories: Apparel/Gift, Books/Music, Business, Business Opportunity, Computers, Entertainment, Free Catalogs, Home Office, Home Study, Insurance, Magazines, Money, Night Life/Adult Entertainment, Potpourri, Science/Technology, Sports, and Wellness.

Most of the freebies are in the form of brochures or other written materials, but there are still plenty of tangible freebies to make your trip worthwhile.

Some of the best stuff available at the time of this writing include a video demonstrating the "Strong Arm Pitching Machine," a free copy of the *National Review* (William Buckley's rebuttal magazine to what he considers a "sick and liberal media bias"), an audiocassette and 44-page report on Ken Robert's commodities training program, a free issue of *Special Situations*, "meticulously researched stock recommendation reports," and a free laminated first aid guide courtesy of FastMark.

The ordering is as easy as the receiving. Just fill in your vital statistics online and the goods will be sent directly to you via snail mail.

You can browse the offerings by category, or browse them all in a row. One visit here will probably be enough to lure you back time and again, and the Free Offer Forum has the perpetual grazer in mind, with a special "newest offers" section so that you can skip right to the new loot.

Company
Free Offer Forum/Venture Communications (New York, NY)

Where
CompuServe, Prodigy, World Wide Web

CompuServe
Go *freeoutlet*

Prodigy
Jump *free offer store*

Web Address
http://shopping2000.com/freeforum

Email
venture@pipeline.com

Let George Roman tell you when it's safe to fall in love or to sign that megabucks business deal.

Beverly Hills Love Psychic

Confused? Angry? Alone? Want the advice of a top-rated psychic, but don't want to plunk down four bucks a minute for one of Dionne Warwick's flunkies at the Psychic Friends Network? Well, thanks to "George Roman's Online Resource for Personal and Relationship Transformation," you can cut out the middle-psychic, and go right to the source!

This Web site is a one stop shop for all things metaphysical. For example, in the "Personal Explorations" section you can get a 50-page, in-depth analysis of your personal astrological profile using what Roman considers the very reliable Vedic astrology approach or a 45-page personal numerological analysis.

In the Love and Romance section, you can compare horoscopes, numerological compatibility and biorythms with your partner, get a well-rounded picture of your compatibility along with notes as to which are potential "bad days" (thus letting you determine the best time to plan that four-day business trip). You can also order a "Sex-O-Scope," which sounds like some kind of sick binocular, but is actually described as a "revealing look into your love and sex life. Find out what really turns you or your partner on. A great conversation starter," Roman states.

These reports are intended to be guides for helping you along "desirable paths and warning you of the pitfalls in life, in yourself, and in your relationships."

When compared to a private reading that can cost as much as $150 an hour, these are a good value. Think of it: Six months worth of lotto readings for only $24.95. If you win, who cares about cost? Besides, the wide variety of options on this site make it a worthy stop, if only for the entertainment value (if you don't happen to be a believer in the methods used).

It should be noted that George Roman is a very respected psychic/astrologer who's been in private practice since 1981 and has been featured in prestigious publications such as the *Boston Globe* and has made several nationwide television appearances.

This helps explain why this site has none of the feel of a 900-number (and, of course, you don't have to deal with those messy per-minute charges). Besides, if Dionne Warwick's Psychic Friends are such good buddies, you'd think they would at least tell here to stop the fashion *faux pas* of constantly wearing sunglasses on top of her head when she's indoors.

Shopping on the Internet and Beyond

Exclusive Deal

George Roman

20 percent off your first report purchase of $24.95 or more and 20 percent off your first private reading.

Exclusive deal for readers of this book only!
You must mention this offer when you place your order.

Beverly Hills Love Psychic (continued)

Company
George Roman (Beverly Hills, CA)

Where
World Wide Web

Web Address
http://www.cyberzine.org/html/Psychic/
loveguru.html

Reminder! This Web address is case sensitive. Make sure you enter it *exactly* as shown.

Email
loveguru@netcom.com

Prices
From $3 to $39.95.

Shipping Fees (in the U.S.)
$3

International orders are accepted.

Online Credit Bureau

Scenario 1: You're about to sign a business deal with a company you've known for only a short time. You feel good about the arrangement but want to cover all your bases.

Scenario 2: You need to get in touch with a former employee, but when you dial her old phone number, it's been disconnected and your snail mail has been returned. All you have is a Social Security number. Now what?

Scenario #3: It has been 17 years since you've touched base with an old flame. You're divorced now and would love to know if there's still a spark. What do you do?

The solution to all of these scenarios? The Internet Credit Bureau (ICB), a full-service credit reporting agency and information source that offers its services exclusively online. They offer more than five services, including:

- *Credit Reports.* For only $35 you can get a complete payment history on any company in the United States or Canada. (Businesses only; no personal reports.)

- *Social Security Number checks.* This will identify the owner of a Social Security number and will give you their current address. Handy for collection purposes.

- *Finder's Report.* Using credit bureau information, ICB will attempt to locate an individual with as little information as just a name. A great deal for only $45.

- *Telephone Number Identification Search.* Give ICB a phone number and they will tell you who it belongs to. Handy for that number you jotted in a matchbook cover for reasons that have become lost in last night's inebriated fog.

- *Address Verification Search.* This one is kind of sneaky. Give ICB an address and they will tell you the name of the current occupant, plus information about their neighbors.

It's frightening how easy it is to get information on someone—personal, tangible data. The fault, however, is our own—not ICB's—since much of this is information we supply when filing out credit forms. In fact, you might consider using the service to determine what information is publicly available about *you* , so that you can take steps to limit what you want the world to know.

Company
Internet Credit Bureau, Inc.
(Fort Lauderdale, FL)

Where
World Wide Web

Web Address
http://www.satelnet.org/credit

Online Credit Bureau (continued)

Email
icb@icb.com

Prices
From $4.50 to $45.

International orders are accepted.

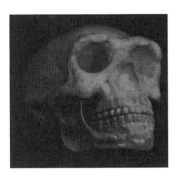

Ira Walters has skulls for all your party needs.

Thick Skulls

You won't see these on the Home Shopping Club, but they make nifty decorations: skulls. Not just any skulls, but those of prehistoric ancestors from millennia long past.

Although these artifacts look like the real thing, they're actually "quality plaster reconstructions of skulls of human ancestors. They are perfect for educational use, unique decor, or the perfect gift." The casts are original reconstructions by famed Washington State University professor Dr. Grover Krantz and feature elements cast from original hominid fossils. "They are handmade from silicon rubber molds using hydrocal white plaster and animal collagen added as hardener. Casts can be left in their original white color or stained with coffee." (In other words, you get to specify which color you want.)

You don't have to buy the whole magilla, either. Skull parts are available. Need just a jaw, brain-case, or cranium? No prob. Just indicate which pieces you need and every effort will be made for a perfect match.

These prehistoric reconstructions have long and frightening names—many of which are so challenging I'm scared to type them. But a full list is available on the company's Web site and it's worth a look if only to challenge a friend to a pronunciation game. (I've read flu remedy labels with shorter ingredient names.)

Since these are accurate reproductions, their size is about that of a human skull and as such would make a great cactus planter, halloween gag, or theater prop for your next production of "Hamlet."

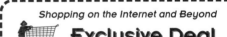

Shopping on the Internet and Beyond

Exclusive Deal

Ira Walters Company

10 percent off your first order.

Exclusive deal for readers of this book only!
You must mention this offer when you place your order.

Company
Ira Walters Company (Pullman, WA)

Where
World Wide Web

Web Address
http://www.wsu.edu:8000/~walters/skull.html

Email
walters@mail.wsu.edu

Prices
From $40 to $150.

Shipping Fees (in the U.S.)
$5

International orders areaccepted.

Barbie and Ken were made for each other, literally. But their friend Jen is kinda plastic.

The Barbie Trading Post

Did you or other family members go nuts with Barbies when you were a kid? Do you still own fifteen Malibu Barbies, but not a single Very Violent Barbie? Do you have absolutely no idea what I'm talking about? Well, then. Perhaps you need to make a stop at The Barbie Trading Post.

Here, you'll learn all about the obsessive and complex world of Barbie trading, and maybe you'll even be inspired to trade those Malibus and start building your own more esoteric collection.

The dolls are rated from NRFB (which is not a new rock band, it just stands for "Never Removed From Box") down to Very Good (which means it was played with a lot, but still looks good—no missing limbs or chew marks) and Poor (played with a lot, and has cut hair and dented boobs).

Individual collectors email their list of what they have available to the Barbie Trading Post, and the fun begins. Looking for a Sears Silver Sweetheart Barbie, never out of the box? Done, for 45 bucks. A 1980 Oriental Barbie? For $140, its yours.

The Barbies listed during my visit ranged in price from cheap up to $1800—and for that kind of money you can get an actual live Barbie—maybe even Barbie Benton; she's not doing much these days.

Barbie, Ken, Midge, and the gang can all be found here, as well as the occasional non-Barbie doll. Vanilla Ice, last seen on a milk carton over the heading "Have you seen this rapper?" has a doll listed as well as a "'90s Official New Kids On The Block" doll, described as "The smiling blond—haven't found out which he is yet." Neither has the rest of America. But if it lights things on fire, you know it's Donny Wahlberg.

Pushing aside the peripheral dolls, The Barbie Trading Post is *the* one-stop shop for finding that elusive plastic princess for which you've been searching at garage sales, in classified ads, and friends', relatives' and even strangers' attics. You might not get as good of a deal as you would by convincing some old farmer that the "worthless doll" you want him to sell you for fifty cents just has sentimental value, but the convenience alone makes up for the prices you'll pay.

Company
Barbie Trading Post

Where
World Wide Web

Web Address
http://www.deeptht.armory.com/~zenugirl/barbie.html

Email
zoliyan@sco.com

Prices
From $5 to $1,800 and up.

Shipping Fees
Vary based on sellers.

International orders are accepted.

When you feel the earth move under your feet, you'll be glad to know you've already purchased your Safe-Pak.

Survival Paks

Safe-Pak asks one simple question: Are you ready for "The Big One?"

Considering I live in Los Angeles, I liked to believe I've lived through my share of earthquakes and other natural disasters that seem to plague my beloved city at least once a year, but Safe-Pak less-than-subtly reminds us that emergencies can strike at any time and it's best to be prepared.

What they feature are kits with 72 hours worth of emergency supplies. There are one-person and two-person packs, another specifically for hikers, and two more that serve as general first aid kits.

The basic survival pack's contents include garbage bags with ties (to provide shelter), a food bar that supplies enough calories for 9 meals (at 1,200 calories per day), but doesn't require water the way a Power Bar would, twelve four-ounce packs of water, two 12-hour lightsticks (a quick snap starts the illumination), emergency blankets, bandages, pressure dressing for cuts, alcohol prep pads, Kleenex, and a whistle.

Now, you could probably put the same kit together for less than this company charges, but Safe-Pak has a five-year shelf life and is neatly assembled in a special sack that you can keep by your door, in your car truck, or under a bed for easy access.

The bag itself is a "durable weather-resistant nylon carry-all pack with non-corrosive zippers and large carry handles for easy portability."

Similar contents are contained in the Hiker's survival pak, except this one includes weatherproof matches. The Marine/Auto and Home First Aid Packs include basic supplies for any minor medical emergency.

No matter where you live, some type of natural disaster poses a threat to you, so keeping Survial Paks on hand makes sense for just about everybody. Besides, this is probably the only site on the Web that hopes you only have to visit once.

Shopping on the Internet and Beyond

Exclusive Deal

SafePak Earthquake Survival Kits

$3 off your first order of a survival kit.

Exclusive deal for readers of this book only!
You must mention this offer when you place your order.

Company
Safe Pak Earthquake Survival Kits (Seattle, WA)

Where
World Wide Web

Web Address
http://giant.mindlink.net/survival/

Email
safe_pak@mindlink.bc.ca

Prices
From $21.95 to 47.95.

Shipping Fees
Included in price.

International orders are accepted.

So you think you're weird? Well, you've never visited Archie McPhee. Now they're weird—but fun.

Outfitters of Popular Culture

The Archie McPhee company refers to itself as "the outfitter of popular culture—the great lost dime store." They offer rubber chickens, lawn flamingos, and tiki-god patio lights "and other detritus of the Plastic Age."

"Archie McPhee is your link to the best and weirdest treasures in the world—from classic goofball oddities like rubber chickens to creepy anatomical items bordering dangerously on the practical," like their Van Gogh ear-shaped clips and alarm clocks "so bizarre they'll not only wake you up—they'll freak you out!

One of my favorites in their online catalog is the Tube of Gloom, which happens to be one of their biggest sellers. "Tilt it and it makes a mournful, forlorn, cow-like noise. The sound is so sad it will cheer you up! Lost your job? Your love? Your Net connection?"

Other highlights include brains in the form of a thinking cap, brain candles, and a rubber brain (when just one won't do), Deluxe Rubber Chick-ens—"over 20 inches of soft quality rubber, hand-painted yellow and orange," and last but not least, the most disgusting item I found at any of the thousands and thousands of sites I visited researching this book: Larvets.

Larvets are the Original Worm Snax. They've been approved for human consumption by the FDA, complete with regulation nutritional fact labeling, and are available in BBQ, cheddar cheese, and Mexican spice flavors. "You don't have to drink a whole bottle of mezcal to get the worm!" cites the folks at McPhee, "'Tastes just like chicken' will have a whole new meaning." The ingredient label says it all: insect larvae and seasoning. No calories. No fat. No sugar. But these are for real. I swear. "Your entymologist friends will think you've learned how to cook."

Company
Archie McPhee (Seattle, WA)

Where
World Wide Web

Web Address
http://www.halcyon.com/mcphee/

Email
mcphee@halcyon.com

Prices
From $2 to 32.

Shipping Fees (in the U.S.)
From $4.95 to 15.95 based on order total.

International orders are accepted.

Remember!
The World Wide Web is available from all the major online servies including America Online, CompuServe, and Prodigy.

Homesick and overseas? Let American Supply bring a little bit of home to you.

American Products Shipped Anywhere

Imagine living abroad for an extended period of time. While at first the change might be culturally refreshing, after awhile you may long for familiar things from home.

That's the concept behind American Supply International Inc., a company that specializes in shipping grocery products and general merchandise to people abroad.

Their customer list includes "American Foreign Service and military personnel, U.S. Embassy commisaries, recreation clubs, and individuals everywhere." Their services, however, are not confined to people residing in foreign lands. "These services are especially helpful for anyone living in remote or rural areas of the United States and for elderly or disabled individuals who find it difficult or impossible to go shopping."

The product line "includes virtually anything you would find in a U.S. supermarket and drug store, with the exception of frozen and refrigerated goods." This includes housewares, pet products, and office supplies.

You work from a catalog that can be quickly downloaded from the American Supply Web site. In it, you'll find over 4,000 products in over 70 categories. "It's like an entire supermarket and general store by mail."

Their biggest seller is Starkist chunk light tuna, followed by pet food, baby supplies, breakfast cereals, and diet foods. If it's not in their catalog, American Supply will be happy to find it for you. Be specific about what you want, and the item will shipped as soon as the company locates what you've requested. Don't believe me? Just ask the man who requested and received a Mercedes Benz hood ornament.

Orders enter the fulfillment process as soon as they are received, with an average of three to five days before your order goes out the door. Why the delay? American Supply does not stock inventory and they never ship product 'seconds'. Instead, they buy from suppliers when you place your order so that everything is "fresh, fresh, fresh."

Your purchases are unconditionally guaranteed, too. You'll receive your shipment in good condition or the company will provide a free replacement of goods lost or damaged in the transit.

Now a word about the lingering question of prices: American Supply's markup is 30 percent over what they pay. Since they buy in such large quantities at wholesale, it is often equal to what an average Joe Consumer would spend at a regular grocery store. They stock name brands and generics, so their prices are really fair.

Shipping fees are actual costs plus a fee for each of the high-strength cartons and packaging materials they use. American Supply says "we would rather not hide these costs in inflated merchandise prices; we charge separately for order packaging and postage, and only pass along our actual costs." The average packing fee for most medium- to large-size orders averages from $10 to $12.

So, if you're feeling homesick, order a little medicine from American Supply.

Company
American Supply International, Inc.
(Waldorf, MD)

Where
World Wide Web

Web Address
http://www.dgsys.com/~asii

Email
asii@dgsys.com

Prices
From 30 cents to $60.

Shipping Fees
Based on order, as explained above.

International orders are accepted.

Brownie-Grams

Brownie-Grams represent one of the most unique and delightful ways I've found to acknowledge an occasion—any occasion—even a reward to yourself.

You have a choice between a 28-ounce Brownie-Gram ($24.95) or a 56-ounce ($34.95) size, both of which *include* overnight shipping. You can order as late as 3:00 PM Eastern time on the day before you want your brownies to arrive. A personalized message is included, which is printed on a spiffy four-color note with outstanding graphics. Factor in Joan & Annie's perky box graphics, and it makes for an impressive presentation.

So if that's the sizzle, what about the steak? According to my team of taste-testers, these brownies were sensational. Overly-health-conscious staff members who normally don't go near sugar, chocolate, nor all the other things that make life worth living, were found sneaking seconds when they thought nobody was looking.

Choose from Cream Cheese Delight, Toffee Bar Chip, Double Chocolate Chips, Chunks and Hunks (A "Baywatch" episode?), Walnut Lover's Chocolate Chip Deluxe, Butterscotch & Chocolate Glories, and Pecan Carmel Chocolate Chip Rapture (soon to be a major motion picture).

The company uses only creamy Vermont butter, fresh Vermont eggs, and premium-grade chocolate. Immediately after baking, the brownies are frozen to enhance the flavor. The chocolate becomes more chocolately through cold storage, and the brownies are shipped only after the mandated freezing time for maximum flavor (which can be from a few days to a few months).

Since 1988, Joan & Annie's Brownies company has sold over 100,000 Brownie-Grams—at a price much lower than a generous bouquet of flowers. So, the next time you want to say Happy Birthday, Thank You, I Love You, Good Job, Miss You, Bon Voyage, Great Teamwork, Happy Chanukah, Merry Christmas, or Happy Flag Day, give a Brownie-Gram and wait for the phone call from your friend or relative, who's sure to offer squeals of delight from this unusual and tasteful gift.

Brownie-Grams (continued)

Shopping on the Internet and Beyond
Exclusive Deal

Joan & Annie's Brownies

5 percent off your
first order of $34.95 or more.

Exclusive deal for readers of this book only!
You must mention this offer when you place your order.

Company
Joan & Annie's Brownies (Williston, VT)

Where
World Wide Web

Web Address
`http://mmink.com/mmink/dossiers/jaa/brownies.html`

Email
`brownie@together.net`

Prices
From $24.95 to $34.95.

Shipping Fees
Overnight shipping is included in the price.

Genuine Dinosaur Relics

Lately, I was telling a friend how hard I had been searching for a complete Camarasaur skeleton, early Jurassic period, nothing less than 155 million years old, and *bang*, the next day I find one online at a bargain-basement price of $2.5 million dollars. What are the odds?

So, you own a Camaro. Big deal. If you don't have at least one camarasaur in your garage, you're just not living.

Well, the odds are in your favor when you visit the Artificats-R-Us Web page, a completely genuine and certified inventory of dinosaur parts, prehistoric collectibles, and other impossible-to-find relics, such as the Mars rock.

This site entered the media spotlight when it represented the seller of a dinosaur egg dug up in China. "A CAT scan shows an embryo inside. The egg is of the Sauropod species of dinosaur, 250 million years old." Cost: 1.5 million dollars, which includes free delivery anywhere in the world.

But you don't have to be Bill Gates to shop here. There are more than a few items in the several hundred to several thousand dollar range.

For instance, you can get a triceratops vertebrae and brow horns for $400 to $8,000. Various meteorites from various parts of the world start at $200 and go up to $3,600 depending on rarity, material content, color, and size.

Then there's the Prehistoric Bat in Matrix from the Early Eocene period. "Fifty-five million years old. Only five have been discovered. This is the second best quality in the group. In addition to being the oldest bat ever found, it has the best profile." At $77,000, this would make for a great Halloween decoration or gift to Adam West.

Dinosaur Relics (continued)

The inventory changes constantly and there is always plenty to choose from, regardless of your budget.

By special arrangement with the U.S. distributor, buyers of this book are entitled to a 10 percent discount on their first order on *any item* from Artifacts-R-Us. And I mean anything, including the $2.5 million dollar Camarasaur skeleton. This means the $19.99 you paid for this publication could save you as much as a quarter of a million dollars. Now admit it: Isn't this the best book deal you've ever found?

Shopping on the Internet and Beyond
Exclusive Deal

Artifacts-R-Us

10 percent off your first order, including the $2.5 million Camarasaur Skeleton (up to a $250,000.00 value!).

Exclusive deal for readers of this book only!
You must mention this offer when you place your order.

Company
Artifacts-R-Us (Ramsey, NJ)

Where
World Wide Web

Web Address
http://www.nis.net/artifacts

Email
egg@nis.net

Prices
From $110 to $2.5 million (and no, that's not a misprint).

International orders are accepted.

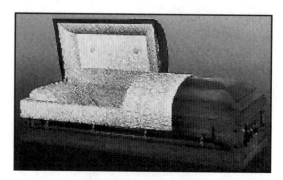
We all gotta go, so we might as well go in style.

Cyber Funeral Home

"The priority of people taking priority over profit." That's the philosophy of Carlos A. Howard, the owner of the first online funeral company. This man is dedicated to making the hardship of death as emotionally and financially painless as possible—a career decision he made at the tender age of five when his best friend was run over by a school bus.

This is a man of his word. During my interview with Carlos Howard, I was awestruck by the compassion and empathy he has for his clients and his company. Nobody goes into business with a 100-percent altruistic stance, but this man comes close.

The bottom line is this: Caskets bought via The Carlos A. Howard Funeral Web page are marked up only $200. That's it. For example, consider the Montrachet Mahogany casket with the Champagne Whitehall Velvet—the exact coffin Jacqueline Kennedy Onassis was buried in. Her family probably paid about $16,000 for the casket. Literally the *identical* coffin sells here for $4,100.

The Montrachet model is the most expensive on the site, but with its laundry list of features—

Cyber Funeral Home (continued)

including a fail-safe liner, safety bottom, adjustable bed and mattress and hand-crafted marquetry veneer—it's one of the nicest mass-produced coffins made. Carlos told me that this is the casket he would choose for himself.

There are over 10 models on the pages, priced from a low of $495 and up, complete with photos and detailed descriptions.

The Carlos A. Howard Funeral Home provides both pre-need and at-need services. You can buy a casket today, thus locking in a price, and it will then be shipped when necessary. Contrary to popular belief, Federal Trade Commission laws clearly state that a family has a legal right to provide their own casket. So, if you live across the country, you can still make local arrangements and have the casket put on the next plane to your location, packed in a special air tray ensuring its arrival in pristine condition.

Because of their Internet presence, the funeral home has a worldwide clientele and has shipped their goods all over the planet—including Finland, France, and Canada.

If you're not currently in the market for a casket, consider their Funeral Planning Package, which includes a will, statistical form, and a funeral instruction sheet. The time to educate yourself is now, when you are not under any emotional or time pressures and can better absorb the information provided.

"If you're like most people, you avoid thinking about death," Howard declares on the funeral home's home page. "However, it is just as real as other events that occur in our lives. And planning and budgeting for it is just as necessary as planning and budgeting for the other major

events in life." Unless you plan, your death will put a tremendous burden on your loved ones: emotionally and financially.

Shopping on the Internet and Beyond

Exclusive Deal

Carlos A. Howard Funeral Homes

$15 off your first purchase
of a Funeral Planning Package.

Exclusive deal for readers of this book only!
You must mention this offer when you place your order.

Company

Carlos A. Howard Funeral Homes
(Norfolk, VA)

Where

World Wide Web

Web Address

`http://www.melanet.com/shops/`
`Carlos_A_Howard_Funeral_Home/`

Reminder! This Web address is case sensitive. Make sure you enter it *exactly* as shown.

Email

`melanet@melanet.com`

Prices

From $495 to $4,100.

Shipping Fees

Overnight shipping runs about $236.

International orders are accepted.

Remember!

For periodic updates of this book, send email to *shop@easton.com*. See *Introduction* for more details.

You, too, can have your logo—or any personalized message—imprinted on a T-shirt from T-Shirts online.

Your Art on a T-Shirt

Imagine that your son (we'll call him Russell) has spent six hours electronically painting a masterpiece using his favorite draw program. Typically you might print it on your color printer and hang it on the family's refrigerator art gallery. But why not take this same image and for a few dollars have it put on a T-shirt?

This scenario is just one of the advantages of T-Shirts Online, a company that will take any graphics file (and I mean *any* graphics file — TIFF, GIF, PCX, BMP, PICT, and other formats) and put it on a T-shirt.

The ordering process is simple. Upload the graphics file to the company via any of their email accounts (America Online, CompuServe, or Internet) along with your credit card number. In a few days, you'll receive a T-shirt with your image in vivid glory.

I discovered T-Shirts Online shortly after my radio show, Log On U.S.A., began. We have a

nifty logo for the show and I wanted a small quantity of shirts. My research showed that just the setup fees for a custom order would eat half of my T-shirt budget.

Slightly incredulous, I decided to give T-Shirts Online a shot and was knocked to the floor when my tee arrived. Using only a basic 300 dpi color image, the T-Shirts Online wizards produced great results. And the quality of the shirt itself was nothing short of amazing—a 100-percent cotton Hanes Beefy-T of such durability and weight it could almost stand up by itself. The company carries sizes from newborn through XXXL, so no matter how big or small your group, everyone can get a shirt. And if you only want one, that's fine too.

I've since placed many orders with T-Shirts Online and recommend them to everyone I know, all of whom have been equally as delighted. They've submitted orders for one-time events or when they need just a few shirts with their company logo.

T-Shirts Online are as dedicated to customer service as they are to printing the finest tees online. Their quality standards are so high that I can even recall a case where they forfeited three shirts because the results didn't meet with their approval.

Shopping on the Internet and Beyond

Exclusive Deal

T-Shirts Online

$5 off your first T-shirt order.

Exclusive deal for readers of this book only!
You must mention this offer when you place your order.

T-Shirts Online (continued)

Company

T-Shirts Online (Huntsville, AL)

Where

World Wide Web

Email

tshirts@cici.com or
tshirtsol@aol.ccom or
72066.620@compuserve.com

Prices

$19.90 per shirt. Price breaks on quantities.

Shipping Fees

$3 for every two shirts.

International orders areaccepted.

For More...

For more great inventive shopping opportunities, see the next page.

Honorable Mentions
in the category of
Inventive Notions

Airplanes and Accessories

Private party ads on CompuServe selling airplanes and acessories.

CompuServe
Go *classifieds* then select *cars/boats/planes/rvs/cycles*

Aviation Galore

A plethora of aircraft for sale: new, pre-owned, manufacturers, dealers, brokers, and much, much more.

Company
Aircraft Shopper Online

Web Address
http://www.sonic.net/aso/

Binary Watch

For the techie. Thirteen triangles on three levels present you with the exact binary time. A natural for hardcore programmers.

Company
Kimberley Direct

Web Address
http://mmink.com/mmink/dossiers/
kimberely/binary.html

Email
dr_net@iglou.com

Braille Translations

Translation of text into English Grade II braille.

Company
Braille Translation Service

Web Address
http://www.trib.com/service/braille.html

Email
kearney@trib.com

Cosmic Self-Teching Aids

Learn how to use a crystall ball, Ouija board, candle lore, crystal wands, astrology, and more. Personalized tarot cards are available as well.

Company
Phyllis Givens

Web Address
http://www.sedona.net/sd/phyllis.html

Custom Banners

"Large, custom colorful banners in paper, plastic, and vinyl."

Company
Banner Graphics

Web Address
http://www.automatrix.com/banners/

Email
bannerz@aol.com

Custom Knit Products

Personalized, custom knit products. Especially baby blankets. Great stuff!

Company
Jan's Custom Knits

Web Address
http://www.puffin.com/puffin/index.html

Email
knits@puffin.com

Day-to-Day Forecasts and More

Outstanding astrological reports. Choose from natal chart interpretations to day-to-day forecasts—a zillion times more accurate and detailed than anything you'll find in your daily newspaper—all from the company considered one of the best in the business.

Company
Astrogram

Web Address
http://www.dol.com/astrogram

Email
astrogram@aol.com

Events, Seminars, and Conferences

Private party ads on America Online for announcements and information.

America Online
Keyword *classifieds* then select *general merchandise boards*

Grocery Coupons

"The Internet's largest coupon site." You select the coupons you want—$200 worth for $19.95.

Company
Coupon Connection

Web Address
http://www.pic.net/uniloc/coupon

Guitar and Piano Toilet Seats

Patent pending, "the comfort of a finely crafted bathroom accoutrement with the legendary looks of your favorite guitars (and piano). Six styles made from Appalachian oak.

Company
Jammin Johns

Web Address
http://iglou.com/Jammin-Johns/

Incense

Choose from over 25 fragrances in sticks, super-strength cones...natural oils too. Good prices.

Company
Net Scents

Web Address
http://artitude.com/incense.htm

Email
artitude@ix.netcom.com

Information and Merchandise

Private party ads on CompuServe offering a cornucopia of information and services.

CompuServe
Go *classifieds* then select *miscellaneous info/ merchandise*

International Cigar and Tobacco

Cigars from the Dominican Republic, Mexico, Honduras, Jamaica, Texas with discounts on multiple boxes.

Company
Ruta Maya Tobacco

Web Address
http://www.onr.com/maya/tobacco.html

Legal and Investigative Services

Private party ads on CompuServe.

CompuServe
Go *classifieds* then select *business services/investments*

Miscellaneous Items

Private party ads on Prodigy.

Prodigy
Jump *classifieds* then *select browse ads*

Miscellaneous Stuff

Private party ads on Prodigy for items for sale.

Prodigy
Jump *classifieds* then select *browse ads*

One Inch of Maui Land

"For the person who has everything and the person who has nothing." For $10 get one square inch of paradise. Authentic Certificate of Deed and map included.

Company
Maui "Buy" The Inch

Web Address
http://www.maui.net/shop/mauiinch.html

Newsletters and Reports

Private party ads on CompuServe offering newsletters and reports.

CompuServe
Go *classifieds* then select *miscellaneous info/merchandise*

Personalized Prints

Very personal messages, to express any sentiment. "Give your love in a frame."

Company
HeartPrints

Web Address
http://www.cts.com/~hrtprt

Email
hrtprt@heartprints.com

Personalized Stone Products

Personalized stone desk and house plates. Hand cut, crafted, polished, and engraved Natural Stone Products.

Company
StoneYard

Web Address
http://www.ip.net/shops/StoneYard/

Email
xjkx18a@prodigy.com

Personal Safety Devices

Protect yourself with one of these alarms, locks, and motion detectors.

Company
Safety Products International

Web Address
http://mainsail.com/safety/safety.htm

Photo Calendars

"Calenders featuring your photos. Great for birthdays, vacation memories, weddings, and family activities."

Company
Kalendarized Keepsakes

Web Address
http://www.onramp.net/imagemaker/calendar.html

Email
townsend@onramp.net

Shremagraphs

Three-dimensional, kinetic art. "Watch as two images disappear and reappear before your naked eye."

Company
Shremagraphs

Web Address
http://www.webscope.com/shremgraphs/info.html

Solar Powered "Batteries"

Personal panel to replace C and D battery operated devices.

Company
Solar Panel Power

Web Address
http://www.wilder.com/solar.html

Email
bdrogo@world.std.com

Spiritual, Religious, and New Age Products

Private pary ads on America Online.

America Online
Keyword *classifieds* then select *general merchandise boards*

Stock Quote Service

Stock quotes, business news, market analysis and commentary, charts, and historical data.

Company
QuoteCom

Web Address
http://www.quote.com

Email
info@quote.com

Sunglasses, Shavers, and More

The "more" consists of genuine Swiss Army knives and watches, cross pens, inline skates, and Cape Cod candles. Good prices.

Company
Sunglasses, Shavers and More!

CompuServe
Go *sun*

Email
sunglass@clark.net

Tiny Two-Way Radio

World's smallest two-way radio "with the power and feature of the larger portable. Fits in your shirt pocket."

Company
Micro Talk

Web Address
http://www.supermall.com/micro/micro.html

Translation Services

Translation and interpretation services for more than 50 language—from Arabic to Wolof.

Company
Translation Solutions

Web Address
`http://www.pacifier.com/market/latrans/`
`tranmain.html`

Email
`translat@pacifier.com`

Trophies

Manufacture all types of quality awards, including trophies, plaques, ribbons, and rosettes.

Company
Trophies by Edco, Inc.

Web Address
`http://edco.com/trophies/`

Tickets

Private part ads on America Online.

Americ Online
Keyword *classifieds* then select *general merchandise boards*

Kid's Stuff

White Rabbit Toys brings its famous Michigan store to your door via the Web.

International Toys

Playthings transcend language and culture, so White Rabbit Toys on the Web has selected the best from around the globe for your kids to enjoy at home.

Brio of Sweden, Ravensburg from Germany, and other major international brands are represented, as well as the best of the best of American toy manufacturers, including Gund, Primetime Playthings, and Creativity for Kids.

The online storefront is an extension of a premiere retail operation in Michigan. Considered one of the best toy stores in the Midwest, White Rabbit has selected their finest and favorite items from wooden railway cars that chug along natural beechwood tracks to Muttsy, "the softest, cuddliest stuffed dog you've ever seen or felt."

The selection rotates periodically. During the holidays "Net surfers can play Santa to conveniently order quality toys and have them shipped anywhere that reindeer fly." There's something for just about any age. Considering the international flavor here, you're bound to find unique playthings that you'd never find at a national chain.

You can order directly online. Within hours of recieving your request, the company sends an email confirmation, with an order number, itemization, total cost, and verification of shipping address. Most products are sent within 48 hours.

This site is well designed, too, with plenty of toys to choose from. The graphics are loaded only when you click to see a specific item. This can help you avoid over-shopping.

Admittedly, I have a habit of intending to buy one specific item for my nephew Russell, but somehow end up leaving a store with several full shopping bags. Since the White Rabbit's pages do not bombard you with more than what you want to see, you can slip in and out without flirting with your credit-line limit.

International Toys (continued)

Company
White Rabbit Toys (Ann Arbor, MI)

Where
World Wide Web

Web Address
http://www.toystore.com/~wrt

Email
bob@toystore.com

Prices
From $10 to $75.

Shipping Fees
10 percent of your total order.

International orders are accepted.

Park it here, kids.

Personalized Children's Gifts

In the ongoing baby boom of the 90s, there seems to be a kid's version of just about everything adult—baby Gap, baby Reeboks (called "Weeboks"), even baby Ralph Lauren. Delivered With Love leads the way in this regard by making great furniture and other childhood treasures for kids from toddler-hood and beyond. Nothing trendy here, and that's the point: This stuff that will be around for decades, the kind of gift that has true heirloom potential.

The Delivered With Love online catalog is segmented into a wide selection of childhood favorites. One of their biggest sellers is the personalized park bench, which also makes a great room decoration. The bench stands 1.5' high and 2' long. You can order a floral design (for girls, if you want to be traditional) or a stars pattern (for boys). You also can choose between pastel or primary colors. The seatback of the bench is personalized with the child's name.

Another favorite is the rocking chair, ideal for kids ages two through five. It starts its life as a room decoration for an infant but evolves into a piece of utilitarian furniture. "Kids love to read in rocking chairs" says the company "just like Mommy and Daddy." The chairs are economical as well.

Delivered With Love even has a section for sibling gifts—"an extra special touch" for the new big brother or sister when a newborn arrives. Each one is personalized and you can choose from water bottles to sunglasses to fanny packs.

The personalization is included in the price and is handled in a lightening-fast turnaround time of one to two days. If you have something in mind that you don't see on their Web site, Delivered With Love will be happy to fulfill your request. Years from now, when your kids have your grandkids, they're sure to remember that extra special touch you once Delivered With Love.

Children's Gifts (continued)

Company
Delivered With Love
(Lafayette Hill, PA)

Where
World Wide Web

Web Address
http://www.parentsplace.com/shopping/
delivered/index.cgi

Email
dlo64@aol.com

Prices
From $2.00 to $120.00.

Shipping Fees
From $3.85 to $20 based on order size.

International orders are accepted.

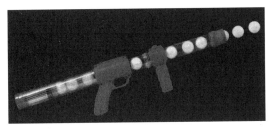

How Arnold Schwarzenegger got his start as a kid.

The Original Burp Gun

Uuuurp! Excuse *me!* All the rage in the 1950s, the original Burp Gun is back, but one of the few places you can find it is the World Wide Web.

"This is not a reproduction," the company assures, "this is *the* original Burp Gun, produced in Italy under license since the 1950s." The bazooka-looking toy earned its name based on the sound it makes when a ball is released.

The air-powered, pump-action shooter dispenses 15 ping-pong-type balls one at a time or in bursts, with an accuracy range of up to 20 feet. The ammunition, however, is not completely Nerf-like. It is possible for a human target to feel a *very slight* sting when hit.

Even so, the guns are designed for kids ages three and up and remain a favorite for head-to-head combat or more civilized competition using the included Burp Gun target—a piece of paper with different-sized holes—the smaller the hole, the greater the point value.

Burpco has sold over 60,000 units since they began importing the guns in 1989. The president of the company, who also happens to be a distinguished psychologist, notes that some therapists may use them as part of patient treatment and that they also function as a great "nonverbal communication device."

The guns are sold individually or in packs of 12 with a generous discount. These could make quite memorable party favors. Or you could simply bring a box to your next office party and fire off some aggression on those co-workers whom the boss should have fired *months* ago.

Company
Burpco (Portage, MI)

The Original Burp Gun (continued)

Where
World Wide Web

Web Address
http://branch.com/burpco/

Instant Information
burpco@branch.com

Prices
$19.95

Shipping Fees
$4.95

Love will steer the stars and hopefully your child, with the help of Kiddygrams.

Astrological Profiles for Children

Parenting is a tough job, but imagine if you had some insight into your child's emotional and physical chemistry? That's the idea behind Kiddygram, "an astrological portrait of your child intended to give you insight into his or her unique gifts and challenges."

Moira Collins, co-founder of Kiddygram, tells the story of a very athletic couple whose child showed little interest in anything physical. "When they saw the Kiddygram report and chart, it described a very mental child. It really put things in perspective for them."

"Much of a child's behavior, which can often puzzle or stymie parents, is quite normal...but in addition to these universal patterns, each child is an individual with particular qualities, potentials, and needs. An understanding of these can help you parent your child more wisely and effectively."

Kiddygram goes far beyond the type of astrology "chart" that you read in your daily newspaper. True astrology has its roots in science, but also relies on other variables that strengthen or weaken the traits in one's primary sign. "Kiddygrams also highlight the sign the moon is in when the child is born, and the sign rising on the horizon at the moment of birth, thus giving you a far more complete, more compelling astrological analysis."

Each Kiddygram report is completely personalized and is based on the precise time, date, year, and location your child was born. "Handsomely packaged and laser printed with glossy graphics, Kiddygrams make great gifts," cites the company.

In addition to Kiddygrams, the company offers a booklet called *Kidsigns*, which deals with both parents and children in various combinations. If you're a Pisces and your daughter is a Scorpio, it may help you understand your potential compatibilities and clashes.

Company
Kiddygram (Chicago, IL)

Where
World Wide Web

Web Address
http://www.dol.com/kiddygram/

Email
astrogram@aol.com

Prices
From $30 to $35.

Shipping Fees
$2.50

International orders are accepted.

I didn't do it. I swear I didn't do it!

Art for Infants

"Eclectic entertainment for 90s newborns" is how the Baby's Art Gallery defines itself. This is an art assembly unlike any you might have already seen—"a stimulating collection of high-contrast graphic designs to capture the attention of newborns and encourage parent-infant interaction."

It's universally accepted that infants—while their vision is developing—are quite drawn to black-and-white images. There are plenty of checkerboards and bullseyes available, but the Baby's Art Gallery's artist in residence, Amy Strycula, wanted to venture beyond these monotonous graphics to give infants something far more visually interesting.

You can view all of the images at the Gallery's Web site, but even the names alone do a good job describing the prints: Stare Squares, Round and Chubby, Scribbles, Starlight, and AhhGoo the Baby Whale are among the eight primary images available. There are actually a total of 15 because each piece, except the whale, is available in black on white or white on black (which they refer to as "negatives").

You purchase the images online, which lets you instantly download them to your computer to either print out, use as Windows wallpaper, or use as a screen saver to entertain your newborn when he or she is sitting with you at the machine.

The company also sells the series as a set of 4"× 5" flashcards, which contains the entire gallery of 15 images.

According to Strycula, "when infants are given the opportunity to experience high-contrast images through their early months, they show increased weight and height, as well as improved muscle coordination and self-esteem. "

Of course, it's also possible that infants exposed to Baby's Art Gallery might find themselves in their older years inexplicably drawn to the Cubist works of Braque, Leger, and Duchamp.

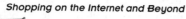

Art for Infants (continued)

Shopping on the Internet and Beyond

Exclusive Deal

Baby's Art Gallery

Free shipping on your first order of two or more flashcard sets (or a $2.25 shipping credit on international orders).

Exclusive deal for readers of this book only! You must mention this offer when you place your order.

Company
Baby's Art Gallery
(Ingomar, Pennsylvania)

Where
World Wide Web

Web Address
http://www.infohaus.com/access/by-seller/
Babys_Art_Gallery/

Reminder! This Web address is case sensitive. Make sure you enter it *exactly* as shown.

Email
babysart@infotique.lm.com

Prices
From $1.50 to $9.95.

Shipping Fees (in the U.S.)
Charged on flashcards only—$2.25.

International orders are accepted.

Talk about Kid Stuff

For comparing opinions on popular, child-related products, the Internet Usenet newsgroup "misc.kids.consumers" is *the* place to be.

Hmmm. Looks like rain. But only...on YOU!

The Ultimate Water Weapon

Technology is wonderful. When I was growing up, all we had for kiddie weaponry were plastic water pistols that held a couple ounces of water at best. They could only be used at close range and for a maximum of 10 good squirts. Next, the world was introduced to the Super Soaker, which according to several parents I know, didn't do much soaking before it was laid to rest in the trash. The "victim" was apparently dampened at best.

Enter Max Blaster, a patented feat of technology that will wow anyone, from any generation. This stroke of playful ingenuity is to a water pistol what a Harley Davidson is to a motorized scooter. There's simply no competition.

The specs are impressive. The unit requires no pumping (unlike a Super Soaker) because the pressure mechanism is built into the design. The water storage is contained in two two-liter bottles (which you supply using empty plastic soda containers) for over a gallon of water fun. The bottles refill in seconds from an ordinary hose or faucet, hence shortening precious downtime. The bottles rest in a backpack-type harness thus making your little water warrior look less like Rambo and more like a Ghostbuster.

Ultimate Water Weapon (continued)

But wait, there's more. The Max Blaster is equipped with a *dual-action* trigger. Press on the left side and you activate a stream of water that can reach as far as 30 feet, with precision accuracy. A squeeze of the right trigger lets out a close-range, high-volume blast for genuine drenching.

Parents of Max Blaster sharpshooters love the device as well and not just because it's so durable. Evidently, the apparatus is a great garden appliance because the water flow and capacity let you saturate hard-to-reach places (like your wife, trying to hide behind the rose trellis).

Shopping on the Internet and Beyond

Exclusive Deal

TPS

Max Blaster

Free shipping on your first order of two or more Max Blasters (or a $3.95 shipping credit on international orders).

Exclusive deal for readers of this book only! You must mention this offer when you place your order.

Company
TPS (Lynchburg, VA)

Where
World Wide Web

Web Address
http://www.inmind.com/max/

Email
maxblast@inmind.com

Prices
$18.95

International orders are accepted.

Science was never this much fun when I was a kid.

Science Toy Store

If you find it difficult to indulge your children's interest in science or if you just want to distract them from their Gameboy or CD-ROMs, Copernicus carries a galaxy of items to educate and entertain kids of all ages.

It's a rather varied catalog, with items so unique they don't even categorize well. Here are a few of the highlights:

- **The Pet Tornado:** "The fury of a real tornado safely trapped in a jar." (But don't drop that jar!)
- **Rattleback:** "A strange piece of plastic that will spin in only one direction. Try spinning it clockwise and it stops and reverses direction. Comes with a complete explanation."
- **Ant Farm:** The classic, pristine edition even *your parents* can remember.
- **Butterfly Garden:** Complete with caterpillars—watch the metamorphosis from larvae to pupa.
- **Triops:** "A kit that contains a tank, food, and eggs of a truly remarkable creature—freshwater shrimp that spring to life on contact with water. After a few days you can watch them double in size daily until they are over an inch long...the Sea Monkeys you always hoped for."

Science Toy Store (continued)

- **Motor Kits:** The best way to learn about motors. "This kit produces the world's simplest motor, just add a D battery, wind the coil, and watch it go."
- **Levitating Top:** "The top spins in the air in a magnetic field. No wires or hidden tricks, just pure physics."

When you visit this site, also look for the Bat House, Root Beer Making Kit, Glow-in-the-Dark Stars, Laser Spinner Top, and DaVinci's Tim Bird.

The Copernicus folks promote themselves as the best science toy store online. I have to agree. Their collection of toys, games, puzzles, and novelties are the best I found anywhere in cyberspace.

Shopping on the Internet and Beyond

Exclusive Deal

Copernicus

Free gift with your first order plus $5 off your first order or $50 or more.

Exclusive deal for readers of this book only!
You must mention this offer when you place your order.

Company
Copernicus (Charlottesville, VA)

Where
World Wide Web

Web Address
http://netmar.com/mall/shops/smartoys

Email
smarttoys@aol.com

Prices
From $1.50 to $60.

Shipping Fees (in the U.S.)
Based on weight—averages approximately 6 percent of the order total.

International orders are accepted.

Dad can do 0 to 60 in 7.5 seconds. But after that, I have to push him home.

The Perfect Stroller

Now here's a case where father is the necessity of invention.

Geologist John Ingalls was working in the Northwest Territories with his young daughter constantly in tow. He needed a "simple way to transport her comfortably from jets to floatplanes, in and out of skiffs, and across rocky terrain. Unable to find just the right stroller to meet his daughter's needs, John set about inventing one. He grabbed a child carrier backpack, attached two large wheels, and used an aluminum ski pole for the handle."

He perfected his invention over the following 25 years, the result of which is The Stroller Pack, so advanced in design, enginnering, and practicality that it almost seems a shame to call it a stroller—I'd like to rename it the Advanced Child Transportation Unit.

The Perfect Stroller (continued)

To a certain degree, the design is intended to solve problems parents face with their strollers every day. For example, the stroller's fabric comes off the frame and is machine washable, thus elminating the problem of carriers that "get covered with sticky stuff." Children outgrow strollers rapidly. The Stroller Pack is versatile enough to handle babies from six months old up to five years. Most stroller bars are always at a single height, which means many adults have to stoop when pushing the stroller. The Stroller Pack's handles extend to accomodate the pusher.

The Stroller Pack weighs 10 pounds and is made of aircraft-grade aluminum. It can handle a weight capacity of 100 pounds (when used as a luggage carrier or handtruck). Folding time is 60 seconds or less.

The basic Stroller Pack is "equipped with quick-release wheels, shoulder straps, and tuck-away waist belt to convert the stroller into a backpack." This unit sells for $279. You can add any of seven different accessories: a Freight Bag for schlepping gear (other than your child); a Sun Rack for protection against sun and rain; a Rain Fly, "which gives head-to-toe protection and turns the unit into a "kid's own spaceship;" a Snack Bar for feeding and drawing; an Underseat Pouch for carrying objects; an Accessory Bag with a shoulder strap for carrying groceries, diapers, etc.; and Fenders for keeping dirt off your child's elbows and his or her hands off the wheels.

Three basic Stroller Pack packages are available; each includes some combination of the accesories listed previously for an overall deal that costs less than the basic unit plus the accessories.

The Stroller Pack has won many awards, including one of the Best New Products of 1993 by Backpacker Magazine and the "Great Expectations Award" from the 1991 Juvenile Products Manufacturing Association.

The company views this stroller as the first and last you'll ever have to buy. They stand behind the product for a lifetime, ensuring you that, if it *ever* breaks, they will fix it free of charge.

Company
Stoller-Pack / Skaggs & Ingalls (Juneau, AK)

Where
World Wide Web

Web Address
`http://www.parentsplace.com/shopping/ strollpak/index.html`

Email
`strollerpack@parentsplace.com`

Prices
From $279 to $380.

Shipping Fees (in the U.S.)
$25 via 3-day Federal Express.

International orders are accepted.

For More...

For more great kid-related shopping opportunities, see the next page.

Remember!

The World Wide Web is available from all the major online servises including America Online, CompuServe, and Prodigy.

Honorable Mentions
in the category of
Kid's Stuff

Baby and Toddler Development

First-rate child-development and safety products. Over 1 million customers across the country.

Company
Right Start

Web Address
http://www.shopping2000.com/shopping2000/rightstart/

Children's Clothing

Embroidered, patchwork clothing for boys and girls, age 6 months to 4 years.

Company
Rebecca Raggs

Web Address
http://www.best.com/~ggate/rraggs.cgi

Dinosaur Silouhettes

Dinosaur skulls cut to scale. Use as mobiles, stencils, or instructional tools. Washable.

Company
Dinosaur Silouhettes

Web Address
http://www.tagsys.com/Ads/RedRock/

Email
office@tagsys.com

Discovery Channel CDs

Educational CD-ROMs for kids of all ages.

Company
Discovery Channel

Web Address
http://www.shopping2000.com/shopping2000/discovery/

Discovery Toys

Toys to "nourish the whole child in every aspect of development...mixed with plenty of fun."

Company
Discovery Toys

Web Address
`http://www.internet_cafe.com/discovery`

Disks, Games, and Toys

Private party ads, on Prodigy, for disks, games, and toys.

Prodigy
Jump *classifieds* then select *browse ads*

Gel-Free Diapers

"Tushies, the only gel-free disposable diapers with natural blend cotton for natural absorbency...no chemical absorbents, dyes, or perfumes."

Company
RMED

Web Address
`http://www.parentsplace.com/shopping/tushies/index.html`

Email
`tushies@parentsplace.com`

How-to-Play-with-Kids Videos

Videos to help parents and grandparents be better play partners with kids.

Company
PlaySkills Videos

Web Address
`http://www.mountain.net/ADZone/ads1/playskills.html`

Kid's Natural Skin and Hair Care

Shampoo, conditioner, bubble bath, and more made with tea tree oil.

Company
Tyler and Treva Nally

Web Address
`http://netmar.com/~back2nat/TTOKidsCare.html`

Email
`back2nat@netmar.com`

Musical Potty

"Musical potty sings your toddler's praises when toilet training meets with success."

Company
Hop On

Web Address
`http://www.parentsplace.com/shopping/potty/index.html`

Email
`torgersen@www.telusys.com`

Parenting Books

Books on every stage of parenting from conception to childraising. Good selection.

Company
Cody's Books

Web Address
http://www.parentsplace.com/shopping/
codys/index.cgi

Email
codys@parentsplace.com

Quality Toys for All Ages

"A fine collection of children's toys for the little ones and the not-so-little ones. Items range from wooden building blocks, musical instruments, dolls, and teddy bears to theater costumes."

Company
Grand River Toy Company

Web Address
http://www.cheetahs-gold.com/cheetah/grt/
grthome.html

Rocking Animals

Forget the rocking horse, how about a rocking brontosaurus, goose, dragon, or swan. "Truly works of art."

Company
Heirlooms of Tomorrow

Web Address
http://www.webstore.com/ht01.htm

Toys and Games

Private party ads, on America Online, for toys and games.

America Online
Keyword *classifieds*

Toys and Gifts

Stuffed animals, inflatable toys, and a Toy-Of-The-Month Club available to members of CompuServe.

Company
Tomorrow's Child

CompuServe
Go *tom*

"Value" Books

Books for kids that teach values via fantasy and enchantment stories.

Company
Torgersen

Web Address
http://www.telusys.com/Don.Torgersen/
torgersen.html

Email
torgersen@www.telusys.com

Liquor

What was once Chicago's little-known wine and spirits treasure is now the world's pleasure.

Sam's Wine Warehouse

Internet World listed Sam's Wine Warehouse as one of the Web Hot Spots, and for good reason. With a massive inventory and bargain prices, Sam's is truly the Wal-Mart of the liquor business. Their warehouse, located in Chicago, has been a family-owned operation for more than 35 years.

Don't let the name of this electronic storefront mislead you, though. Sam's offers much more than wine, including a wide range of fine liquors—from their collection of rare scotches to their variety of grappas (a dry, clear brandy made from grape pomace—fast becoming the highbrow drink for fast-track yuppies in the know).

But Sam's collection of wines from around the world does indeed set this distributor apart from other liquor distributors. They offer "thousands of labels of wine from more than 12 countries, including Argentina, Chile, France, Germany, Hungary, Italy, Mexico, Portugal, South Africa, Spain, Switzerland and the U.S."

And the prices here are as low as the selection is large: "Sam's volume purchasing, coupled with tax-free shipping to most destinations in the U.S., allows Sam's to be a low-price leader. To give just one example, Sam's has the lowest price on Dom Perignon anywhere in the U.S." (15 percent lower than the national retail price.)

When I checked the current month's specials on California Cabernet Sauvignon, I found a Clos du Bois 1991 Marlston for only $15.99 per bottle and a Sterling Reserve 1988 for just $15.99. Sam's prices for single-malt Scotches are also unrivaled among retailers. A bottle of 1976 Glenlivet sells for $39.99 and Macallan 12-year-old Scotch is just $29.99.

Except for the monthly specials and few other exceptions, Sam's doesn't list prices for its inventory. But they're certainly not trying to hide anything. As manager Brian Rosen puts it, "Sam's is no longer going to show prices with products.....In our never-ending battle to keep our inventory deep and extensive yet prices low, we are in the fortunate position to reduce prices every day. With our immense buying power, the prices of most products change daily. Often the prices on the Web pages were too high or incorrect."

For current price information on any item, you are invited to call Sam's toll-free, seven days a week. The range of prices is truly vast because Sam's offers several rare and exotic products as well as the more commonplace brands. For instance, their extremely rare Vielle #1 Age D'or 1883 Vintage Cognac sells for $5,400—spare change for the rich and famous, but don't drop that bottle!

Shopping on the Internet and Beyond

 **Exclusive Deal**

Sam's Wine Warehouse

5 percent off any order,
including repeat orders.

Exclusive deal for readers of this book only!
You must mention this offer when you place your order.

Company
Sam's Wine Warehouse (Chicago, IL)

Where
World Wide Web

Web Address
http://www.ravenna.com/sams/

Email
sams@ravenna.com

Shipping Fees (in the U.S.)
Actual charges—but tax-free purchasing in most of the U.S. will usually offset shipping charges.

International orders are accepted.

 Subscribe to Sam's free electronic newsletter, sent regularly to your email address, to keep abreast of current specials.

It may be Connecticut's superstore, but they'll deliver to just about anywhere in the world. (Of course, if you're stuck at a weather station in Antarctica, you'll have to negotiate with FedEx to get that shipment of brandy delivered.)

Wine and Liquor Warehouse

Warehouse Wines and Liquors has been serving Connecticut for more than four generations, and has recently opened up shop on the Web to serve customers around the world.

Although the company has been a local concern for most of its existence, its selection hardly reflects what you would expect from a local operation. "Our superstores currently stock over 5,500 brands of wine from over 12 countries, totaling more than 1.7 million bottles in stock. We also carry over 250 brands of beer from 32 countries, which all add up to over 200,000 bottles/cans in stock. Our spirits inventors is chock-full of single malt Scotch whiskies, bourbons, Cognacs and brandies, as well as the best in gin, vodka, rum, and tequila."

Warehouse Wines and Liquors specializes in low-volume items that are either hard to find or are little known. So if you're looking for that special Bordeaux that you discovered while traveling in Europe but can't find it locally in stores, this is the place to begin your search.

The company is a price leader, too. For example, a 1.75-liter bottle of Tanqueray vodka sells for just $19.99, Macallan 12-year-old Scotch lists for $29.99, and the excellent-but-underpriced Chilean Santa Rita Reserva Cabernet sells for just $6.99 per bottle.

Wine, Liquor Warehouse (continued)

Perhaps one of the more unique features of Warehouse Wines and Liquors is their custom wine cellar service. The company designs and builds custom, temperature-controlled wine cellars and wood racking storage systems for business and home use. If you're a wine connoisseur with an extensive collection of vintages, this service might be just what you need to protect your investment. And, at your next party, you can impress your boss by offering a tour of your wine cellar. Of course, you can probably expect a cut in pay the next day.

Company
Warehouse Wines and Liquors (Stamford, CT)

Where
World Wide Web

Web Address
http://www.netaxis.com/wine/wine.htm

Email
wine@winenliquor.com

Prices
$5 to $200 (and higher for rare products)

Shipping Fees
Actual charges.

International orders are accepted.

Hot Tip!

Consumer Reports magazine is available from all three major online services.

Shortcut
Keyword *consumer* (America Online), Go *consumer* (CompuServe), Jump *consumer reports* (Prodigy).

Join the Great American Beer Club for relief from whatever ales ya.

Beer Club

Perhaps you're old enough to remember those Leave It to Beaver days when there really was such a thing as "the milkman," who regularly brought cold milk and dairy products to your doorstep. Everything was made locally and the milk was even taken from local cows. It didn't get any fresher than that.

The Great American Beer Club doesn't bring milk to your door—perish the thought. Instead they bring the '90s version of "the milkman" to you in the form of the best microbrewed beers from around the U.S.

If you're accustomed to drinking name-brand commercially brewed beers and you've never tried microbrewed beer, The Great American Beer Club has a great taste treat in store for you. Even if you've tried microbrewed beer, chances are that you've only been able to taste brands made locally. Here's why: "Mass-produced beer—even imported—includes additives to help prolong shelf life. Microbreweries are geared toward lower production and immediate consumption, so preservatives are unnecessary," says the club's president and co-founder, Douglas Doretti. "We are able to offer these specialty beers to our members while flavor and freshness are at a peak."

Microbreweries model their production on the German Purity Law of 1516, which mandates that only barley, hops, yeast, and water can be

Beer By Mail (continued)

used in the brewing process. Consequently, true microbrewed bears are free of preservatives, fillers (such as rice and corn), and foaming agents—all of which are typical ingredients in mass-produced beers. To keep shipping costs reasonable and to ensure that members receive fresh beer, the club only ships within the U.S.

Membership in The Great American Beer Club is $15.95 per month and includes a free club T-shirt (with a minimum six-month membership) and a subscription to the club newsletter, *Expeditions*. But these perks aren't the true reasons for joining. Each month, members receive a 12-pack of three types of handcrafted beer in 12 oz. bottles (four bottles of each type). The beer is selected from more than 150 top microbreweries from around the U.S. and includes lagers, ales, stouts, pilsners, and porters, among other brews. Monthly selections are chosen by a panel of tasters. (Tough job, but somebody's gotta do it.)

Shopping on the Internet and Beyond

Exclusive Deal

The Great American Beer Club

With a 12-month membership, get one free month and a T-shirt.

Exclusive deal for readers of this book only! You must mention this offer when you place your order.

Company
The Great American Beer Club (Lakemoor, IL)

Where
The World Wide Web

Web Address
http://www.w2.com/beerclub.html

Email
tryasip@aol.com

Price
$15 per month

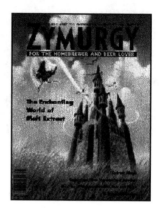

Zymurgy is the science of fermentation—as in beer brewing. It's also the name of the American Homebrewers Association's magazine, free to subscribers—er, scientists.

Brewing Your Own

Ever wanted to brew your own beer? If you've ever had homebrewed beer, you know that the taste is unique—unlike most commercial brands but similar to some microbrewery beers. Even if you have a favorite microbrew, it's still not the same as the personal touches of flavor you can create when you brew your own.

As a homebrewer, you join one of the fastest-growing hobbies in the world. In fact, homebrewing starter kits are now commonly available in retail stores. So why not also join *the* organization devoted to this fun hobby—the American Homebrewing Association (AHA)?

According to the group, "the AHA promotes public awareness and appreciation of the quality and variety of beer through education, research, and the collection and dissemination of information; we serve as a forum for the technological and cross-cultural aspects of the art of

Brewing Your Own (continued)

brewing, and we encourage the responsible use of beer as an alcohol-containing beverage."

When you join the AHA (their motto: Relax, don't worry, have a homebrew!), you'll receive five issues (per year) of *Zymurgy,* the only magazine devoted to the art and science of homebrewing. Each issue includes:

• Award-winning homebrew recipes

• Articles for homebrewers of every brewing level

• Reviews of homebrewing kits, equipment, and supplies

• Ideas from experts on ways to brew better beer and build brewing equipment

• Articles that keep you up to date on the developments and news in the world of brewing

• Information about new products for homebrewers

• Tips and techniques to help you perfect your art

"In addition to *Zymurgy,* members of the AHA receive periodic discounts on books published by Brewers Publications and free entry to the Members-Only Tasting at the Great American Beer Festival held each fall in Denver, Colorado." You'll also get access to the National Homebrewers Conference and several other AHA programs.

Company
American Homebrewers Association

Where
World Wide Web

Web Address
http://www.csn.net/aob/aha.html

Email
service@aob.org

Prices
For membership, from $28.95 (U.S.) to $43.95 (international). For books and other brewing products, from $5 to $80.

Shipping Fees (in the U.S.)
$4.00

International orders are accepted.

Whatever you need to brew your beer, you're sure to find it here.

Homebrew Supplies

Okay, so you've decided to brew your own beer. But where do you go for the best selection of starter kits, ingredients, and other equipment for your homebrewing needs?

Homebrew Supplies (continued)

It's an easy answer if you're on the Web: point your browser to S.P.S. Beer Stuff. "Here you can count on honest, friendly service. We store all hops, grains. dried malt extract, and corn sugar in oxygen-barrier bags to maintain maximum freshness. Our yeast is stored in the refrigerator and our hops in the freezer. Unlike some homebrew shops that display their products in front of the window in direct sunlight, our supplies are stored in a cool, dim environment that also equates to maximum freshness. We want to help you brew greet beer at affordable prices."

S.P.S. offers more than 100 varieties of canned malt extracts, a variety of starter kits and other equipment from around the world, grains, hops, yeast, additives, cleaners, books, videos, and even gift certificates. When you visit their Web site (the company says their orders have doubled since going online), you'll also find answers to frequently asked questions about homebrewing. S.P.S. Beer Stuff is a great resource for beginners and expert brewmasters alike.

Shopping on the Internet and Beyond

Exclusive Deal

S.P.S. Beer Stuff

15 percent off your
first order of $20 or more.

Exclusive deal for readers of this book only!
You must mention this offer when you place your order.

Company
S.P.S. Beer Stuff (Cedar Rapids, IA)

Where
World Wide Web

Web Address
http://www.netins.net/showcase/spsbeer/

Email
spsbeer@netins.net

Prices
From 35 cents to $125

Shipping Fees
UPS charges. No handling fees.

A little prevention can save you a lot of money, not to mention your life.

Pocket Breathalyzer

Have you ever left a party, fumbled for your car keys, and then wondered if you perhaps have had too much to drink? Drinking and driving is not only dangerous, it can also be extremely costly. According to the Minnesota Department of Public Safety, the average cost of a DWI offense is $15,105! That includes towing and impound charges, driver's license reinstatement fees, high risk insurance, fines, and lawyer's fees.

And did you know that the symptoms of intoxication are not generally evident to others until

Pocket Breathalyzer (continued)

the blood alcohol concentration reaches .15 percent or higher, which is 50 to 90 percent more than the legal definition of intoxication (depending on which state you live in)? A company called Innovative Marketing Ideas has come up with a way to remove the "guess factor" from alcohol impairment. It's a product called PreVent, a pocket-sized, disposable breathalyzer that can be used anytime, anywhere.

According to the company, "PreVent will give the consumer accurate results within 30 seconds of using it." After blowing into the PreVent tube, built-in crystals either appear yellow (below the legal alcohol blood-level limit) or blue (over the legal limit). Since the legal blood-level limit is .08 percent in some states and .10 in other states, the company makes both .08 percent and .10 percent versions of the PreVent tube.

Each PreVent tube is intended to be used one-time only, so they are sold in packs of eight. The life you save may be your own, not to mention the other savings to your bank account when you PreVent yourself from driving drunk.

Company
Innovative Marketing Ideas

Where
World Wide Web

Web Address
http://www.prevent.com

Email
bjn@theinternet.com

Prices
$19.95 (eight-pack)

Shipping Fees (in the U.S.)
$4.95

International orders are accepted.

For More...

For more great liquor shopping opportunities, see the next page.

Shopping on the Internet and Beyond

Exclusive Deal

Innovative Marketing Ideas

Receive two additional PreVent tubes ($5 value) on your first order of an eight-pack (10 tubes total).

Exclusive deal for readers of this book only!
You must mention this offer when you place your order.

Honorable Mentions
in the category of
Liquor

Australian Wines

Australian wines direct...but do not ship to the U.S.

Company
Nicks Wines

Web Address
http://www.sofcom.com.au/Nicks/index.html

Boutique Winery

A 6-acreVineyard located in Upstate New York which boasts classical varieties of wine.

Company
Six Mile Creek Vineyard

Web Address
http://www.spinners.com/sixmilecreek/
welcome.html

Complete Home Brewing Kits

Complete home brewing kits with *everything* you need. Good selection of kits to choose from.

Company
Dowling's Home Brewery

Web Address
http://www.primenet.com/commercial/
dowling.html

Ferment Your Own

Selection of beer and winemaking supplies

Company
BrewCrafters

Email
catalog@brewcrafters.com

Gold Medal Wines

Premium Russian River Pinot Noir wine. Their first release in 1992 won the Gold MEdal from the California State Fair. A 92 rating from *Wine And Spirits Magazine.*

Company
BearBoat Winery

Web Address
http://www.bearboat.com/

Great Wine

"A full-service retail and information source, offering wines that have limited market exposure and tend to be difficult to find."

Company
Virtual Vineyards

Web Address
http://www.virtualvin.com/

Home Brewing Equipment

"Quality home brewing equipment, ingredients and books. Good prices."

Company
East Coast Brewing Supply

Web Address
http://virtumall.com/EastCoastBrewing/ECBMain.html

Malt Scotches

A selection of over 100 single malt Scotches and "discriminating fine wines. Will ship anywhere in the world."

Company
The Wine Specialists

Web Address
http://town.hall.org/food/Wine/

Mini Home Brewery

A home brew kit in a bag that yields 40 glasses of pub style beer.

Company
Premier Mini Brewery

Web Address
http://www.human.com/mkt/ddist/

Email
ddist@human.com

Paso Robles Region Wine

A central ordering and information site for ocal wines from the Paso Robles region of California.

Company
Wine Online

Web Address
http://www.callamer.com/~mwinfo/wineon.html

Private Reserve Chadonnay

"One of the most distinguished chardonnay producers in California. Triple 90 ratings from *Wine Spectator Magazine.*" The vineyard produces only 1,000 cases a year.

Company
Forest Hill Vineyards

Web Address
http://branch.com/wine/

South African Estate Wine

Award-winning fine red and white wines from the Rhebokskloof Estate in South Africa

Company
Rhebokskloof Estate

Web Address
http://www.os2.iacess.za/rhebok/index.htm

Table Wines

Choose from a selection of Napa Valley red table wines.

Company
UVE Enterprises, Inc.

Web Address
http://mmink.cts.com/mmink/dossiers/uve/
uve.html

Wine of the Month Club

Discriminating wine of the month with plans from $32 to $100 per month. Special discount programs.

Company
Ambrosia Catalogue of Fine Wine

Web Address
http://www.shopping2000.com/shopping2000/
ambrosia/

Wines from Around the World

"Offering Austrian, French, Italian and Spanish wines (other countries to come) from $5 to $500. They have about 500 wines in stock with a total selection expected to grow to around 1,500. Transportation issues limit shipment to European countries only.

Company
World Wide Winery

Web Address
http://www.intellectics.co.at/
casadelvino/

Music, Videos, & Video Games

Grab your ocarina and let's start dancing!

Hard-To-Find Musical Instruments

It's a common problem: You're listening to some folk music and suddenly are overcome by a desire to own and play your own set of dumbeks (Middle Eastern hourglass drums). Where *do* you turn for help?

Since 1974, Mickie Zekley has been traveling the world in search of hard-to-find musical instruments. The result? His company, Lark In The Morning, now offers more than 6,000 musical items, including instruments from different cultures, antique instruments, instructional books, videos, cassettes, and CDs.

When you visit Lark's online catalog, you'll find everything from bodhrans to bagpipes to dulcimers to hurdy gurdies, and of course, the ever popular dumbeks. You'll even find finger cymbals, which will come in handy if you ever decide to go public with your belly dancing routine.

Okay, so maybe your musical needs are a bit less exotic. The company also offers several guitar lines, including Spanish classical guitars, fingerpicking guitars, and even the folksy Lowden guitars ("great for backpacking").

And after you've purchased your new instrument, where do you go to learn to play it? You might want to attend their "Lark In The Morning Music Celebration," an eight-day camp for all ages, held among the idyllic redwoods in Northern California. The camp draws traditional musicians from around the world for a festival of music and dance, and offers beginner instruction for many instruments, including guitar, flute, fiddle, and pennywhistle.

But you don't need to play an instrument to make use of Lark's online catalog. You'll find hundreds of CDs, cassettes, books, and music-related artwork. If you do play, you'll also find music stands, sheet music, instructional videos, and even tools for maintaining your instrument.

Musical Instruments (continued)

Company
Lark In The Morning

Where
World Wide Web

Web Address
`http://www.mhs.mendocino.k12.ca.us/MenComNet/`
`Business/Retail/Larknet/larkhp.html`

Reminder! This Web address is case sensitive. Make sure you enter it *exactly* as shown.

Email
`larkinam@mcn.org`

Prices
From 10 cents to $10,000 (for rare and antique instruments).

Shipping Fees
$3 minimum.

International orders are accepted.

Lark's Web site includes dozens of articles, including interviews with musicians, historical information about instruments, and maintenance tips.

If it's music CDs you want, seek and ye shall find 'em at CDnow.

Music CDs for Every Taste

CDnow stocks more than 6,000 album titles on CD, which on the surface is not all that impressive. Superstore chains like Tower Records offer a comparable selection. But there's a difference here. When you go to Tower Records or one of its competitors, you have to sift through numerous bins to find what you're looking for—if what you're looking for is even in stock. Retail stores are a great resource if you're looking for something that's popular now, but the farther back in the past you want to travel, the more difficult it becomes to find unusual items.

That's where CDnow comes in. These folks brag that "no other online site offers its customers as much as CDnow does." As a veteran online traveler, my initial reaction was, "We'll just see about *that.*"

CDnow's premier feature is a search engine that's designed to help customers locate music CDs for virtually any category of interest —from rock to classical to jazz to folk—even Klezmer (whatever *that* is).

I decided to put the search engine to the test. In the Find Music section (for everything *not* classical), you can search by category—either by artist, album title, song title, or record label. To provide myself with an introduction to the search feature, I threw the database a softball. I began with the name of the classic rock-and-roll song "Signs" by Five Man Electrical Band. The search engine thought for about three seconds and then identified the song as part of three different "70s Hits" albums, but I was also shown 30 other albums. The word "Signs" is used in more song titles than I had realized.

I then tried to throw the search engine a curve. I selected an artist search and entered the name of Jazz saxophone great Phil Woods. The search engine returned with ten album titles and even displayed all of the song titles for each album.

Music CDs (continued)

I pressed on with my fastball. I clicked on the "That's Classic" section, where you can search for classical recordings by multiple criteria—using one or more of the following categories:

- Composer
- Album Title
- Work Title
- Conductor
- Orchestra
- Performer
- Label

I entered "Beethoven" as the composer, "Karajan" as the conductor, and "Berlin Philharmonic" as the Orchestra, and left the other fields blank. The search engine mused over my challenge for about a half second and then displayed nine titles, a few of which I never knew existed. I was duly impressed. CDnow truly lives up to its billing.

You'll realize an added benefit of CDnow when you look at prices. The company discounts most titles because "we don't have to pay for floor space." They try to deliver domestic orders within three to six business days, with international orders typically received in under two weeks.

A bonus feature of CDnow is its online link to the *All-Music Guide*, a journal that provides ratings and reviews by a distinguished group of more than 150 well-known, freelance writers, each expert in a particular genre of music. You'll also find other links to reviews and informational articles about music and musicians. I'm convinced that CDnow is the one-stop shop for both amateur and seriously hardcore audiophiles, regardless of their category of interest.

Company
CDnow

Where
World Wide Web

Web Address
http://cdnow.com/

Email
manager@cdnow.com

Prices
About 10 to 15 percent less than most retail record stores; $8 to $9 average.

Shipping Fees (in the U.S.)
$2.49 for the first item. 49 cents for the next five items up to a maximum of $4.94.

International orders are accepted.

Psychedelic Jimi, for those who remember the true meaning of Acid Rock.

Artistic Vintage Rock Memorabilia

If you're yearning for art relating to your favorite rock group or rock artist, you might be in

Vintage Rock (continued)

luck, provided you're aligned with the tastes of the ArtRock Online gallery. These folks feature posters and other artwork relating to the Beatles, Jimi Hendrix, The Grateful Dead, Led Zeppelin, and more than 50 other bands and music artists worthy of iconic memorial. In most cases, you'll see a poster of the artist you've selected. You can then elect to purchase this poster for your own use.

ArtRock Online features a "high-quality collection of rock posters and related artifacts spanning the ultra-psychedelia of the Haight-Ashbury heyday, '70s supergroup bombast, the F-U pretensions of the surly punk scene, new wave neurosis, late '80s underground, up through the alternative rock of the fragmented '90s." How's that for an in-depth catalog description?

"Almost all our inventory is limited edition, first-run prints," the company says, and they also carry prints of original art by Jerry Garcia and The Cure's Robert Smith.

You can view art by selecting either the Bands or the Graphic Artists category. In either case, you'll be able to preview images so that you can evaluate whether you want to purchase them. The databases are easy to work with, so even novice Internauts can have fun here.

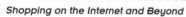

Shopping on the Internet and Beyond

Exclusive Deal

ArtRock Online

20 percent off your
first order of $30 or more.

Exclusive deal for readers of this book only!
You must mention this offer when you place your order.

Company
ArtRock Online (San Francisco, CA)

Where
World Wide Web

Web Address
http://www.artrock.com

Email
artrock@artrock.com

Prices
From $10 to $1,000.

Shipping Fees
Vary based on order quantity.

International orders are accepted.

Island Trader offers kalimbas either flat or a-gourd-ian style.

Kalimba City

It's the '90s, and guitars and drums are out. You know that. Ever see a kid in a garage band these days? Today, they're playing everything from spoons and washboards to kalimbas and mallets.

And no, Kalimba is not the cub in *The Lion King*, it's a uniquely African, finely handcrafted, musical instrument that you can purchase online from the Island Trader home page.

The Kalimba—sometimes called an imbarra, sensa, or the less romantic thumb piano—is a

Kalimba City (continued)

percussion instrument fashioned from spring steel keys and fastened tightly to a wood soundboard. Because each instrument is hand-made, the tone of each instrument is different.

Also online are a variety of mallets for kalimbas and xylophones. You won't find these items at Guitar Warehouse—these are instruments of distinct craftsmanship and unique cultural flavor. And Island Trader, located in Seattle, Washington, has been making and trading them for years. The instruments are reasonably priced, from $18.50 for the basic Flat Kalimba all the way to $235 for a well-packed Xylophone.

The company also offers a wide selection of stands for your new instrument, so you'll be ready to jam with the big boys. In fact, if your group is looking to be the next Hootie and The Blowfish, don't let your guitarist play the piano—hand him a kalimba.

Company
Island Trader (Seattle, WA)

Where
World Wide Web

Web Address
`http://www.dash.com/netro/sho/ema/isletrd/isletrd.html`

Prices
From $18 to $250.

Shipping Fees (in the U.S.)
$4 to $5

International orders are accepted.

Remember!

For periodic updates of this book and additional discounts, send email to *shop@easton.com*. See *Introduction* for more details.

Flash back to an era when ideas, ideals, and passionate debate were the three essential foodgroups for the brain.

And The Beatniks Go On

Interested in inviting Timothy Leary to dinner, but a little leery he'll start having flashbacks? Then check out Sound Photosynthesis, an "archive for the coming millennium," which sells thousands of hours of unique audio and video material documenting some of the greatest minds of our era, including Richard Feynman, Maria Gimbutas, Timothy Leary, John Lily, Terence McKenna, and many more. John Lilly and Terence McKenna may sound like characters from one of Dennis Miller's acts, but they're actually some of the brightest thinkers of our time.

One of the highlights is Leary's "Flashlight Rave," a great rap at a San Francisco Rave and available on audiocassette or videotape. The documentation includes "scenes mixed with the night's music and dancing, a continuous rhythmic experience—fun and thought-provoking."

Sound Photosynthesis boasts an enormous audio-visual library on psychedelics, shamanism, religion, and related topics. Some of the more popular selections can be viewed online, but if you want to grab the information and go, the company's catalog can be downloaded in ASCII or RTF format. Their entire inventory exceeds 2,000 entries.

The Beatniks Go On (continued)

You can be assured of quality, too. Sound Photosynthesis has been professionally documenting individuals and events via audio, video, graphic arts, and publications for more than 20 years.

Allow six to eight weeks for your order to be filled, however, you can also specify rush delivery. And while some of this material might be a little specific for the general Web user, if you know your specifics, this is *the* place for counterculture at its best and most interesting.

Company
Sound Photosynthesis (Mill Valley, CA)

Where
World Wide Web

Web Address
http://www.photosynthesis.com/home.html

Email
soundphoto@aol.com

Prices
From $10 to $200.

Shipping Fees
Based on order total and destination.

International orders are accepted.

Hard-to-Find Music Marketplace

You remember that album you used to have? The one with those guys in the makeup? And the guy with the tongue? No, the *other* guy with the tongue....

If you're looking for a hard-to-find LP, CD, or music memorabilia, try this site. It's a real GEMM.

Well, if you're still trying to find that elusive KISS album, search no more. The Global Electronic Music Marketplace (GEMM) has solved your problem—or at least made it surmountable.

Not a retailer, GEMM is a way to browse and search the inventories of many private-party sellers. There is never a charge to search the database and only a tiny fee (about 20 cents) for posting your advertisements. "GEMM is open to anyone with new or used music" or music-related merchandise.

You can do a simple search, like "Presley," or you can subscribe to one of the lists, which allow you to be automatically notified of future matches if your current search turns up nothing.

GEMM is a non-profit organization. And they are not just a record store. In addition to new and used LPs and CDs, you can find, and bid for, rare, impossible-to-find memorabilia like handwritten lyrics from David Crosby (you can actually see the rum and Coke stains), Joe Walsh, Donovan, and more. There are certified gold Beatles records for sale, checking in at around

$8,500, as well as instruments used by the Fab Four. There's even a former Elton John piano selling for $14,000, as well as objects from Streisand, Dylan, and other heavyweights. When Elvis is ready to come out of hiding, he'll probably show up at this site looking for all his musical belongings.

Company
GEMM (La Jolla, California)

Where
World Wide Web

Web Address
http://gemm.com/

Email
admin@gemm.com

Instant Information
gemm@gemm.com

Prices
From $1 to $5,000 and up.

Shipping Fees
Vary by seller.

International orders are accepted.

Did You Hear the One about the Traveling Notebook Computer?

Computers, music, and humor—it's not often you find these three topics in the same book, much less in the same sentence. Now, thanks to Vince Emery, you can find them all on the same cassette tape, too. It's *The Funniest Computer*

Fire up your PC and invite it to sing along with "HAL's Song," what HAL 9000 might have sounded like had 2001: A Space Odyssey been a musical comedy.

Songs, a collection of 12 side-splitting tunes by eight different performers.

When you order this tape, you'll get such hits as:
- Please, Mr. Compatibility
- I Built a Better Model than the One at Data General
- I'm a Mainframe, Baby
- Engineer's Rap
- Killer-Byte Blues
- Uncle Ernie's Used Computers' Babbage's Birthday Bargain Bash

Actually, you can't exactly call these "hits," but they're certainly not "misses," either. If you're into computers, you'll find plenty to laugh about on this tape. *And* you'll learn stuff. For instance, listen to "Do It Yourself (You Can Build a Mainframe from the Things You Have at Home)" to find out how you can turn your trash into a powerful computer—and clean out your attic at the same time. *The Funniest Computer Songs* makes a great gift for programmers, power users, or anybody who spends far too much time around a computer.

Hear the One About...? (continued)

You can also order the Star Trek comedy album, which includes ten songs and skits by some of America's funniest comedians, who gather here to lampoon the TV shows, the movies, and the Star Trek characters.

All orders come with a money-back guarantee—and your postage will be refunded *both ways*.

Shopping on the Internet and Beyond

Exclusive Deal

Vince Emery Productions

On your first order, buy two albums or cassettes and get the third one free.

Exclusive deal for readers of this book only! You must mention this offer when you place your order.

Company
Vince Emery Productions
(San Francisco, CA)

Where
World Wide Web

Web Address
http://www.emery.com/funny.htm

Email
comedy@emery.com

Prices
$8.95 each.

Shipping Fees
$1 per order in the U.S. and $2 per tape internationally.

International orders are accepted.

Star Trek Generations is now available on video disc.

Video Disc Emporium

If you own a video disc player, you're probably a true videophile—an aficionado of classic films and TV shows. Video discs currently provide the best way to preserve films, using digital formats that provide for impeccable playback of both audio and video.

One of the best clearinghouses for video discs is Flicks on Disc, which offers about 4,000 titles. Some of their more intriguing offerings are "Special Editions," which typically include film footage not included in the theatrical (or televised) releases. Many of these Special Editions are true collector's items, and often cost two to three times more than their "standard" versions.

Even so, Flicks on Disc provides excellent discounts for both standard and Special Edition video discs. (Discounts are based on the manufacturer's suggested retail price.) Their Web site lists discounts from 15- to 25 percent, with discounts classified by film company. Flicks on Disc buys used discs, too, so you can often get tremendous bargains on pre-owned discs that are in excellent condition. Used discs sell for about 50 percent off the list price.

Video Disc Emporium (continued)

Flicks on Disc also offers subscriptions to laser discs that are available in their series line. For instance, you can order the entire *Star Trek— The Original Series* and receive two discs per month. By taking advantage of this subscription service, you can spread the cost of your series purchase over several months or even years. (At two discs per months, it would take you about 18 months to receive the entire *Star Trek* set.)

Don't have a video disc player? For video games, you'll want to know that the company also sells Super Nintendo and Sega Genesis video game cartridges at 15 percent off the list price.

Shopping on the Internet and Beyond

Exclusive Deal

Flicks on Disc

$5 off your first order of $60 or more.

Exclusive deal for readers of this book only! You must mention this offer when you place your order.

Company
Flicks on Disc (Portland, OR)

Where
World Wide Web

Web Address
http://www.teleport.com/~gilbert/flicks/ public_html/index.html

Email
gilbert@teleport.com

Prices
From $18 to $240.

Shipping Fees
Vary depending on location and product.

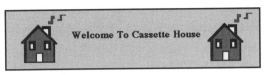
Welcome To Cassette House

Even though Cassette House is literally a mom-and-pop outfit, some of their clients are industry leaders.

Bargain Blank Cassettes and DATs

What do I have in common with Walt Disney Animation and National Public Radio? We all buy our blank audiocassettes and DATs from Cassette House—a company that sells superior-quality, name brand tapes at the lowest prices I've found anywhere.

Since I am constantly dubbing courtesy copies of my radio program for show guests and the press, it's no exaggeration when I say that a dozen eggs last longer in my house then a dozen blank tapes. Even when I bought blank cassettes in quantity from my local warehouse-type store, I was spending about $2.50 a pop for top-grade 60-minute tapes. Then a friend told me about Cassette House, which has saved me hundreds, if not thousands, of dollars—and counting.

Clear-shell, top-notch BASF chrome tapes range in price (depending on length) from as little as 41 cents for 10 minutes to $1.30 for 90 minutes. The boxes run about 14 cents each, with labels costing only 4 cents per cassette. So your total for a cassette, box, and label of this super-superior tape runs a mere $1.48 for a 90-minute cassette. A comparable cassette at a music store would cost about $4.

If your blank audiotapes needs don't require *the best* quality, consider their "Songwriter's Special" tapes—white-shell TOMEI-brand cassettes that

Blank Tapes and DATs (continued)

cost half as much as the BASF chrome tapes. For instance, 90-minute tapes cost as little as 63 cents each.

Cassette House also carries all the supplies you need to customize your cassette boxes using a laser, ink jet, or dot matrix printer. They sell J-cards (the inserts that fold into the case) six to a sheet and cassette labels twelve to a sheet. Their color selection is out of this world, with over *eleven* to choose from, including aqua, mauve, peach, purple, and green. Ditto for the labels, which match the J-cards' colors perfectly.

The same phenomenal deals apply to Cassette House's DATs, which include a generous selection of computer-grade DDS tapes in addition to DATs intended for voice and music. Cassette House carries brand names as well as a house brand, the latter of which can save you as much as 50 percent.

New DATs—Ampex, Panasonic, TDK, and Sony—range in price from $5 to $7.25 depending on length and quantity purchased. Cassette House's biggest sellers in the DAT category are their OEM tapes, which have been used only once but save you big bucks many times over. These DATs have been run once "to test a DAT data drive as it comes off the assembly line. The drive manufacturers always uses virgin tape for the test; hence, the one pass per tape." Cassette House has sold over 60,000 of these with "excellent results." They offer a money-back guarantee, so there is no risk to you.

DAT insert cards, cleaning cartridges, and storage boxes are also available.

Cassette House has been in business since 1981

and is run by a husband and wife team for whom service is everything. They use everything they sell. As songwriter/musicians, they realize "we all need to save money while waiting for the big hit in the sky!" You can't argue with 'dat.

Shopping on the Internet and Beyond

Exclusive Deal

Cassette House

$3 off your first order of $50 or more.

Exclusive deal for readers of this book only! You must mention this offer when you place your order.

Company
Cassette House
(Kingston Springs, TN)

Where
World Wide Web

Web Address
http://www.edge.net/ch/index.html

Email
artmuns@edge.ercnet.com

Prices
From 6 cents to $20.

Shipping Fees
Actual costs based on weight of the merchandise.

International orders are accepted.

Hot Tip!
Be sure to check out CompuServe's Consumers' Forum, which is chock full of fabulous freebie info and great shopping resources. Go *conforum*.

From contemporary films to cult classics, it doesn't get any better than Best Video.

25,000 Videos

"If you're into film and video, it doesn't get any better than this" claims Best Video, and they're right. Nowhere in cyberspace did I find a more outstanding selection or better prices. They even offer a video-by-mail rental service.

Best Video is renowned in and around Connecticut. Customers often drive over two hours from Boston and New York to buy their videos here—of which Best Video carries over 25,000 in 240 categories. There are sections devoted entirely to a particular director, performer, or topic such as government paranoia films and Scandinavian cinematic masterpieces. Over 125 new titles are added *every week*.

But Best Video goes well beyond film, and in fact includes videos of every genre. The Art section has concerts, profiles, complete operas, and performance of works by Mozart, Puccini, and Strauss. The Special Interests area has videos related to the Bible, business, science, and sports. And this is just a *tiny* sampling.

If you prefer to peruse a printed catalog offline, Best Video sells theirs for $3.95, which entitles you to $3.95 off your first purchase or rental or "an all expense-paid trip to Tahiti on your 130th birthday." If you don't find what you are looking for in the catalog, the company also offers a free search service. Tell them what you are looking for and their video sleuths will track it down.

The only information you won't find online are their prices. "Every day, many video tapes are reduced in price," says Best Video's owner Hank Paper, "so there is no catalog pricing that can be accurate. In general, though, film classics and many foreign titles and recent top hits are in the $14.95 to $19.95 range, with hard-to-find public-domain titles selling for $19.95 to $29.95."

If you are a diehard renter, Best Video is still your best source. They offer a rental-by-mail program in which your choices are shipped priority two-day air with a pre-paid priority return. You can order one tape or as many as you like, and the videos are yours for three nights. Best Video also has a "4 tapes for 7 nights deal"—a full week, perfect for "a Fellini retrospective or to watch all four versions of Othello."

Best Video lives up to their name in terms of selection and service. Their president's motto sums up their attitude perfectly: "There are few things in life more satisfying than a good movie, and it's been my mission to see that you find what you're looking for."

25,000 Videos (continued)

Company
Best Video (Hamden, Connecticut)

Where
World Wide Web

Web Address
http://www.bestvideo.com/

Email
bestvid@aol.com

Prices
From $10 to $150 and up.

Shipping Fees
Actual charges. $3.00 for the first tape. $1 each additional tape.

International orders are accepted.

Off The Shelf's logo indicates they're a music and video house, but what it doesn't say is their video game collection is rivaled by none.

Video Game Gear

Off The Shelf Music and Video is "the leading East Coast retailer of music, movies, and video games, with a combined inventory valued at more than $50 million." Even though they cater equally to all three categories of entertainment, their video game selection was by far the best I've found online in terms of inventory and prices.

In fact, it's a game selection to die for and far better and more extensive than what I've found during my pilgrimages to Toys 'R' Us—with prices as good and in some cases better. They carry cartridges for all brands and units such as 3DO, Jaguar, CDI, Nintendo, Sega, and more. Whatever you video game desire, Off The Shelf probably has it.

The games are rated according to quality—and since the company only stocks games they have tried and liked, it seems as though their grading curve is a little steep. In fact the lowest "grade" I could find was a "B-" given to TNN's Bass Tournament.

The company rates game systems, too. Off The Shelf describes (my beloved) Game Boy as "ever aging" and "probably on it's last leg. Good for playing Tetris on airplanes." At first I was a bit offended, but then realized that all I play on my Game Boy is Tetris.

Off The Shelf offers more than 25 games for the Game Boy—not bad, considering it is an elderly piece of technology and when you consider that the company offers only the latest titles.

With respect to the larger, more popular systems, the inventory is endless. My search of the Sega Genesis revealed an impressive five, packed pages of cartridge titles, from the Addams Family to Zool.

The company also carries a full line of accessories for every hardware unit. The prices are low (with only a few games piercing the $60 dollar level) with rocket-fast delivery within three to seven days, depending on destination. So, if they say you can order Mortal Kombat 3, you won't have to buy Stinky the Cyber Skunk just to bide your time until your back order is filled. Besides, Stinky got a B-, equivalent to an F on this scale.

Video Game Gear (continued)

Shopping on the Internet and Beyond

Exclusive Deal

Off The Shelf Music and Video

$5 off your first order of $50 or more.

Exclusive deal for readers of this book only!
You must mention this offer when you place your order.

Company
Off the Shelf Music and Video (Holyoke, MA)

Where
World Wide Web

Web Address
http://empire.na.com/ots/otshp.html

Email
ecmg@empire.na.com

Prices
From $5 to 349.

Shipping Fees
Based on destination.

International orders are accepted.

For More...

For more great music, video, and video game shopping opportunities, see the next page.

Honorable Mentions
in the category of
Music, Videos, & Video Games

20 Categories of Music

Good online catalog of CDs. Useful search mechanism.

Company
Noteworthy Music

Web Address
http://www.netmarket.com/noteworthy/bin/
main

Audio Ads

Private party ads on the Internet for audio equipment.

Usenet Newsgroup
rec.audio.marketplace

Reminder

Internet Usenet Groups are available on all major online services. On AOL, keyword *usenet*. On CompuServe, go *usenet*. On Prodigy, jump *usenet*.

Audio and Video Equipment

Private party ads on America Online for TVs, stereos, and VCRs.

America Online
Keyword *classifieds* then select *general merchandise boards*

Audio and Visual Items

Private party ads on Prodigy

Prodigy
Jump *classifieds* then select *browse ads*

Blues Guitar Sheet Music

Online catalog of blues guitar tablature music books.

Company
Custom Enterprises

Web Address
http://www.msen.com/~ce/

Buy and Trade

There are two music-related internet groups in which music lovers can barter, buy, and trade.

Usenet Newsgroups
```
rec.music.makers.marketplace
rec.music.marketpace
```

CDs, Records and Audiotapes

Private party ads on America Online for CDs, records, and cassettes.

America Online
Keyword *classifieds* then select *general merchandise boards*

Classical & Jazz Audio & Video

Shop for titles from the Verve, Deutsche Grammophon, London, and Philips Classics. Over 5,000 CDs, cassette, videos, and laser discs.

Company
The Music Place

CompuServe
Go *theplace*

Compact Disc Club

Get 10 free CDs when you join this ubiquitious club.

Company
Columbia House Music

CompuServe
Go *freecd*

Prodigy
Jump *columbia music*

Consumer Electronics

Private party ads on America Online for Consumer Electronics.

America Online
Keyword *classifieds* then select *general merchandise boards*

Custom CDs

Have CDs "pressed" from your music or any audio. Custom cover, box, and label.

Company
Van Riper Editions

Web Address
```
http://branch.com:1080/vanriper/
vanriper.html
```

Email
```
vanriper@branch.com
```

Disks, Games, and Toys

Private party ads on Prodigy.

Prodigy
Jump *classifieds* then select *browse ads*

Electronics

Private party ads on CompuServe for electronics, TVs, and VCRs.

CompuServe
Go *classifeds* then select *tv/misc/hobbies/collecting/cooking*

First Rate Rock Apparel

Music t-shirts from the company that does major concert tours.

Company
Winterland Plugged In

Web Address
`http://www.mca.com/winterland/index.html`

Game Board

Diverse selection of games sold on the Internet.

Usenet Newsgroups
```
rec.games.board.marketplace
rec.games.frp.mareketplace
rec.games.video.marketplace
```

High-Level Computing Videos

The spot for video lectures by leading technologists on topics like compilers, artifical intelligence, virtual reality, graphics architecture, databases, and a whole lot more.

Company
University Video Communications

Web Address
`http://www.uvc.com/index.html`

Home Theater Systems

All the components you need to create your own Bijou. Good prices.

Company
Authorized Electronics

Web Address
`http://www.shopping2000.com/shopping2000/
authorized/authorized.html`

Innovative Electric Guitars

Guitars made of solid aluminum—best sound, sustain, tones, and harmonic qualities.

Company
Abel Axe

Web Address
`http://www.tcd.net/~abel`

Email
`abel@tcd.net`

Koa Ukeleles

Choose from soprano or standard. Made exclusively of Hawaiian woods by a master Ukelele open-air shop on the island of Maui.

Company
Exotic Woods

Web Address
`http://hookomo.aloha.net/~jimad/
ukulele.html`

Laser Discs

Searchable, online laser disc catalog.

Company
Video Disc International

Web Address
`http://www.thesphere.com/VDI/`

Laser Discs and Equipment

Large inventory of laser discs and laser disc equipment.

Company
Laser's Edge

CompuServe
Go *le*

Movies

Private party ads on America Online for videos rated G, PG, and R.

America Online
Keyword *classifieds* then select *general merchandise boards*

Movies and Music

Discount CDs and videos in all categories at competitive prices.

Company
Entertainment Works

CompuServe
Go *ewk*

Musical

Private party ads on CompuServe for music and musical instruments.

CompuServe
Go *classifieds* then select *tv/misc/hobbies/collecting/cooking*

Wearable Jazz & Blues Greats

Fabulous photographs of jazz and blues legends on high-quality sweats and tees.

Company
Mason Editions

Web Address
http://www.w2.com/masoneditions.html

Musical Equipment

Private party ads on America Online for studio and musical equipment.

America Online
Keyword *classifieds* then select *general merchandise boards*

Narada Records

This instrumental music is "finely crafted with an evocative, heartfelt nature and timeless character."

Company
Narada Productions

CompuServe
Go *np*

New Age Music

AOL catalog from the record company considered responsible for the new age music craze.

Company
Windham Hill Records

America Online
Keyword *2market*

"No Strings" CD Club

Get 10 CDs for the price of one. Cancel anytime.

Company
BMG Direct Marketing, Inc.

CompuServe
Go *cd*

Online Music Ads

Private party ads on CompuServe for records, CDs, and tapes.

CompuServe
Go *classifieds* then select *tv/misc/hobbies/collecting/cooking*

Online Music Ads

Private party ads on America Online for music CDs, records, and cassettes.

America Online
Keyword *classifieds* then select *general merchandise boards*

Records and CDs

Excellent selection of CDs. Vinyl Lovers section too.

Company
Sound Wire!

Web Address
http://www.soundwire.com/whatis.html

Email
feedback@soundwire.com

Science Videos

Professional and education videos for "visualizing complex sets of scientific data."

Company
Science Television

Web Address
http://www.service.com/stv/home.html

Sega Store

Sega hardware, software, accessories, apparel, and electronic toys direct from the manufacturer.

Company
Sega Mall Store

CompuServe
Go *sgm*

Tower Records Online

Offers every music category; features box sets. Excellent direct order prices.

Company
Tower Records

Web Address
`http://www.shopping2000.com/shopping2000/`
`tower/`

Unusual Music

Singular selection of underground, new dance, and "4th world" music.

Company.
City of Tribes Communications

Web Address
`http://www.organic.com/Music/`
`City.o.tribes/`

Video Bargains

All categories of videos, some for as little as $9.95. Low price guarantee. Will price match.

Company
Time Warner Viewer's Edge

CompuServe
Go *vid*

Tower Records and Tapes

Tower Records on America Online.

America Online
Keyword *tower*

Video Catalog

Over 2,000 titles from classics to blockbusters. Ships within 48 hours. Easy returns.

Company
Critics' Choice Video

CompuServe
Go *ccv*

Video Club

Alluring incentives, such as videos for a penny, when you join this sibling club of Columbia House.

Company
Columbia Video

Prodigy
Jump *columbia video*

Video Equipment

Private party ads on CompuServe for video games and equipment.

CompuServe
Go *classifieds* then select *tv/misc/hobbies/collecting/cooking*

Video Games

Private party ads on America Online for Nintendo, Sega, Game Boy and related items.

America Online
Keyword *classifieds* then select *general merchandise boards*

Video Games

Prodigy members select from a wide range of players and cartridges. Look for their "Specials" section.

Company
Sears

Prodigy
Jump *sears*

Videotapes and Videodiscs

Private party ads on America Online for video tapes and discs.

America Online
Keyword *classifieds* then select *general merchandise boards*

Special Occasions

CreataCard— for those special occasions that you forget to remember.

GREETING CARDS

Okay, its three days before your mother's birthday, and as usual, you've spent so much time slumming around the Web that you'll never get a card off on time. So what are your options? A mad dash into a greeting card store trying to match card, emotion, and envelope—which can be about as easy as orienting the same-color sides on a Rubik's cube? Yikes. Besides, you don't really want to leave your computer, do you?

Well, welcome to CreataCard Online—the card shop that allows you to select and personalize your card and then have your sentiment mailed for you. And you can do all this *from your computer.*

Your occasion options include Birthday, Romantic, and Thinking of You cards. For holiday cards, you can schedule these far enough in advance that

you'll probably forget you even sent the cards by the time your intended receives them.

For example, on Father's day, the company sends cards 10 days ahead of time, giving the postal service ample time to open it, look for a check, reseal it, and get it to Dad before the eventful day.

All cards come complete with cover illustration, some witty little verse, and a place to customize the card with the recipient's name, a personal message, and a closing. Room for the personal message is only 60 spaces long, so make it lovingly brief.

CreataCard currently sends cards only within the U.S. and Canada, so if your loved on is on a business trip to India for a month, you'll just have to do it the old fashioned way.

Company
American Greetings

Where
World Wide Web

Web Address
http://www.pcgifts.ibm.com/vendor02/aghome.htm

Email
webmaster@greetingcard.com

Prices
$3.99 per card, including personalization.

Shipping Fees
Included in price.

When you're striving for that "Best Costume" award, be sure to check out Tombstone Productions.

Costumes for Every Event

Okay. It's October 31 and you threatened yourself (back on New Year's Day) that you'd work out all year, and to date you've blown it off. Sure, your fingers are buff from all that pointing and clicking, but you don't have the pecs to go out dressed as Batman. Well, fear not, fellow crimestopper. Help is on the way! Tombstone Productions, a one-stop Halloween and costume shop, has everything you need, including a full Batman chest piece with abs of steel. Holy Hulk Hogan!

Actually, Tombstone accurately boasts that they're the Internet's biggest retailer of horror products, Halloween costumes, masks, special-effects supplies, props, even concession equipment.

With everything from rippling-muscled Batman and Robin costumes down to $25 Ghost Robes, Tombstone's menu of costume selections is pretty darn vast. You can even get the complete RoboCop costume made for you, directly from movie molds. Yes, for only $3,000, you can walk around in a suit that prompts bystanders to shout "Hey! I just saw you on HBO!"

Tombstone's theme seems to be movie related— be it costumes of movie characters, film props (in-

cluding those elusive "gory guts," "cut-out brains," and the ever popular "beating heart"), or the concession equipment used to feed moviegoers. Been dying to own one of those big, scary looking, rotating weenie ovens now showing at a theater or a 7-11 near you? Look no further.

There is also an impressive supply of special-effect devices, including flashpots, lasers, foggers, and more. However, they won't sell any of their fire-emitting products to minors, so youngsters will need to have Mom or Dad log on with them for the flashy stuff. When you're ready to plan your next Halloween party (or if you'd just like to scare the bejeebees out of your nosy neighbors), make sure you check out Tombstone Productions.

Company
Tombstone Productions (Holyoke, MA)

Where
World Wide Web

Web Address
http://empire.na.com/tomb/costumhp.html

Email
ecmg@empire.na.com

Prices
From $4 to $20,000.

Shipping Fees
Based on the amount of your order.

Who would have guessed? Santa's now sledding through cyberspace.

Cyber Christmas Cottage

Chestnuts roasting on an open Pentium? Jack frost nipping at your Mac? Just what the heck is going on here?

Well, unofficially, it's Santa's favorite Web site. Officially, it's the Cape Fear Christmas House, "the year 'round Christmas store," a company so dedicated to the spirit of St. Nick that they've figured out a way to keep the 24-hour holiday alive, worldwide, 365 days a year.

So avoid the rush and do your Christmas decoration shopping at home. No screaming crowds. No large men dressed like Santa who, three hours later, undress into unemployed construction workers. It's a real shop, using the technology of computers present to reminisce you back to Christmases past.

The shop is divided into several theme "rooms," including Papa's Study, Nannie's Parlor, O Holy Night, Little Nell's Room, Little Will's Room, the Toy Maker's Shop and Gift Emporium. Each of these areas has enough ornaments and St. Nick knacks to fill a Fingerhut catalog three times over.

They also have one-of-a-kind items, such as their six-foot-tall soldier nutcracker—a won-derful conversation piece on any miniature golf course.

This company is so dedicated to Christmas that they have the distinction of owning the domain "noel.com," which probably makes them more devoted to Christmas than Norelco.

Since Christmas is a holiday celebrated world-wide, the Web has really opened this company up to the entire planet, with orders from Guam, New Guinea, and even further-flung locations. And with their low prices, there's something here for everyone.

Cape Fear is a family-owned business located on the historic riverfront of Wilmington, North Carolina. These folks have been spreading Christmas cheer since 1991, and shall remain the champs until somebody places "It's A Wonderful Life" online with real-time graphics and audio.

Company
Cape Fear Christmas House (Wilmington, NC)

Where
World Wide Web

Web Address
http://www.noel.com/xmas/

Email
info@noel.com

Prices
From $3.95 to $2,700.

Shipping Fees
Based on order total and method.

International orders are accepted.

For More...

For more special occasion shopping opportunities, see the next page.

Honorable Mentions

in the category of

Special Occasions

Christmas Gnomes

From the Cairn Studio, choose from Mr. Claus, Clarence with Wings and others.

Company
Tom Clark's Gnomes

Web Address
http://www.wilmington.net/cfch/
gnomes.html

Christmas Software

"Eliminate the hassles of exchanging and tracking holiday cards and gifts." Software to track your holiday card and gift giving.

Company
M. Masters

Web Address
http://www.mmasters.com/mmasters/sox/
index.html

Email
davek@mmasters.com

Hallmark Greetings

Greeting cards, on CompuServe and America Online, for all occasions, including sending service.

Company
Hallmark Cards

America Online
Keyword *hallmark*

CompuServe
Go *hal*

Holiday Items and Sales

Private party ads, on CompuServe, for holiday specials.

CompuServe
Go *classifieds* then select *miscellaneous info/merchandise*

Holiday Specials

Private party ads, on CompuServe, for holiday specials.

CompuServe
Go *classifieds* then select *miscellaneous info/merchandise*

Holiday Cards

Quick selection of out-of-the-ordinary Christmas and New Year's cards.

Company
Cathay Creations

Web Address
http://www2.forum.net/cathay/

Email
cathay@forum.net

Luminaries

Featuring sixteen-foot hanging light sets in the shape of chili peppers. Your choice of red or green.

Company
Casa Noel

Web Address
http://www.olworld.com/olworld/mall/
mall_us/c_gifts/m_casa/index.html

Email
casanoel@rt66.com

Occasion Card Service

Select a card for virtually any occassion or thought. Select a greeting card, and your own words, and they mail it.

Company
 Greetings Expressed

Web Address
http://gei.na.com/

Occasion Card Service

Innovative cards with custom inscriptions. "Mail for you" option available. Free reminder service.

Company
Greet Street

America Online
Keyword *2market* then select *collections*

Email
greetst@aol.com

Seasonal Stationery

Note cards and letterhead with seasonal themes. Inventory rotated to coincide with major holidays.

Company
Arthur Thompson

Web Address
http://www.shopping2000.com/shopping2000/
arthur_tho/

Silk Wreaths

Quality silk wreaths. Choice of colors. Lighted and unlighted.

Company
Bonnie's Bouquets

Web Address
http://www.webstore.com/bb01.htm

Sports

When you can't go outside to skate, you can stay and condition inside with Skates Away's slideboards.

Skating on Thin Blades

When I was growing up, street skates were heavy, clunky four-wheel affairs that you could attach and tighten to your shoes via a grossly misnamed device called a skate key. My, how times have changed. I'm not sure who first realized that the design of hockey skates (one thin blade) could work for street skates, too, if you just make the blade roll. But he or she was definitely onto something big.

Today, inline skating is no longer a fad embraced mostly by the Venice Beach crowd. It's a worldwide sports phenomenon because it can be either recreational or competitive, it's relatively safe (it's up to *you* to put on that helmet), and it's suitable for both sexes and for all ages.

Whether you call it rollerblading or inline skating, the Skates Away Web site can get you skating in style. (By the way, technically speaking, the generic term for the sport is inline skating, while Rollerblade is a brand name.) The company features the full line of Bauer and Rollerblade skates at discount prices—from $99 for the Bauer F-3 recreational skate to $299 for the top-of-the line Rollerblade Aeroblade ABT. Rollerblade also offers children's models starting at $69. So, it doesn't matter whether you're a beginner or an expert, you'll find what you need here—and you'll get some real bargains.

If you're into customizing your skates, you'll want to browse through Skates Away's numerous line of parts, including Hyper wheels "at down and dirty prices" and Team Labeda wheels for professional racing. The company also offers bearings, axle kits, and maintenance kits.

And if you already own boots that fit perfectly but you want to upgrade your skate frame package, Skates Away will be more than happy to mount a new frame for you. Their fee for mounting is $20. Just send them your boots.

Skates Away's strong suit might be inline skates, but they're also a great site for any time of skating equipment, including a complete line of Bauer hockey skates, snow skates (yes, there really is such a thing), and slideboards for conditioning and practicing your skating technique indoors.

When you're ready to skate on by, be sure to stop by Skates Away.

Skates Away (continued)

Company
Skates Away

Where
World Wide Web

Web Address
http://www.dnai.com/~gui/
skatesproductinfo.html

Email
gui@dnai.com

Prices
From $4.50 to $300

Shipping Fees
Based on weight. $5 to $32 in the U.S. $6.75 to $45 in Canada. $47 to $160 internationally.

International orders are accepted.

In the Mountains

If you love the mountains, you'll love the Mountain Gear Web site. For just about any sport or recreational activity that you can do in the mountains, this company can get you set up right, and at discount prices.

"Mountain Gear started selling quality backpacks back in 1979 and has since become the place to come for high quality outdoor equipment. Specializing in a broad range of climbing, mountaineering, telemarketing, cross-country skiing, kayaking, canoeing, and backpacking equipment, we pride ourselves on assisting our customers in making the best equipment decisions regarding their personal objectives and goals."

The online catalog lists items and prices for climbing harnesses and caribiners, skis, boots and

The "Sorceress" may look like a medieval torture device, but it's actually the latest in comfort harness gear for serious rock climbers.

climbing shoes, tents, backpacks, and outdoor clothing for hiking, skiing, and rock climbing. The items listed are heavily discounted from the retail price, often 20 percent or more off.

The company manages these great prices by offering overstocked items and the previous year's merchandise (closeouts), along with some products that have cosmetic flaws. But you can return any item if you're not pleased.

In fact, one of the company's main goals is to provide excellent, personal service. "Our staff consists of avid climbers, skiers, boaters, and backpackers who use and understand the products that we sell. This enables us to answer your questions from a personal point of view, not a textbook. As we strive to meet the growing needs of our customers, it is our goal to continue to offer the best products and give you the best service in the business."

Since the online catalog only lists "hot," heavily discounted items, you might want to request a catalog for the company's full line of products.

In the Mountains (continued)

Company
Mountain Gear (Spokane, WA)

Where
World Wide Web

Web Address
http://www.eznet.com/mgear.html

Email
mgear@eznet.com

Prices
From 25 cents to $2,000.

International orders are accepted.

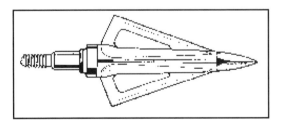

These arrow blades look sharp because they are sharp, and they're available at great prices, too.

Discount Archery Products

Before you invite your son to shoot that apple off the top of your head, check out this Web site for the best and most accurate archery equipment available, at some of the lowest prices you'll find anywhere.

Actually, only about 5 percent of FS Discount Archery's products are for target shooting; the other 95 percent is devoted to bowhunting, so maybe you *don't* want your son shopping here. For the serious bowhunter, FS Discount Archery offers a tremendous selection at prices you won't find in retail stores. Since the company serves as a distributor for more than 120 manufacturers of archery equipment, you're basically getting the goods at the same cost that retailers pay.

For those in the arrow know, here are a few examples: Carbon Specter arrows sell for $39.95 per dozen, and raw shafts are only $29.95 per dozen. Easton's all new pure carbon shafts (no relation) sell for $37.95 per dozen.

The company sells virtually everything archery related, except for bows. You can order the Arrow Shop cutoff saw for cutting tubular arrow shaft materials, for $66.95 (which includes blade). You'll also find a full line of broadhead blades, wrist releases, and target sights.

The Web site also includes some great links to other archery-related Web pages, so if you're an archery enthusiast or interested in becoming one, you'll find plenty of information here, even if you're not ready to make a purchase.

Company
FS Discount Archery

Where
World Wide Web

Web Address
http://www.vpm.com/fsarrows/

The X-zylo looks a little like a marching band brass drum, but it's a lot smaller and you can throw it a heck of a lot farther.

Frisbee Fest

Actually, they're not called Frisbees anymore—at least not by the true enthusiast. They're *discs*. Of course, you already know that if you're among the initiated. What you might not realize is that the discs themselves have been elevated to what is practically an art form.

Some discs are specially designed for extreme aerodynamic capabilities, while other discs have unique, artistic designs at their center. If you're a true disc thrower, you probably wouldn't be caught dead with a generic Frisbee. So let the Internet Disc Shoppe (IDS) be your online alternative for finding that ultimate disc creation.

The IDS isn't a distributor or retailer. In fact, they don't sell products directly. Instead, they're a clearinghouse maintained by enthusiast Christopher Gronbeck for individuals and companies who have unique disc products to sell.

If you've been away from the sport for awhile, this site might very well bring back your zest for disc tossing. A recent visit to the Web site provided a glimpse into some intriguing offerings. For instance, the Princeton Clockwork Orange Disc incorporates scenes and quotations from the film *A Clockwork Orange* on the disc surface.

Then, there's the Stanford University Men's Ultimate Moving Pictures Disc, which, when you spin the disc clockwise with your finger, you can watch a player lay out, get up, and throw.

And if you want to show your online allegiance, you might be interested in the CREST Aztec Sun Calendar Design. In addition to its interesting Aztec imprint, it includes World Wide Web, Gopher, and FTP addresses. The site includes a life-size picture of the disc, which sells for $6 plus $3 shipping and handling.

One of the most intriguing products I found was the X-zylo Flying Gyroscopic Cylinder, which weighs less than an ounce and can soar up to 600 feet. According to its maker, this one "baffles NASA experts...The X-zylo is an amazing flying cylinder that relies on gyroscopic forces combined with aerodynamic phenomena that enable X-zylo to fly with spectacular soaring characteristics."

So go toss the X-zylo into the air and tell your dog to go fetch. That'll confuse him.

Company
The Internet Disc Shoppe (Bowie, MD)

Where
World Wide Web

Web Address
http://www.digimark.net/disc/

Email
ceg@digimark

Prices
Typically $9 to $10 dollars, including postage

Shipping Fees (in the U.S.)
Included in most prices.

International orders are accepted.

You'll find a boatload of marine goodies at BOATNET.

Boats and Boating Supplies

If your license plate reads, "My other car is a boat," then I've got a site for you. BOATNET is a great place to shop for power boats, sailboats, and even commercial vessels. You'll also find lots of boating-supply merchandise and even information about cruises.

The BOATNET Web page is a clearinghouse for companies and individuals selling boats, boating services, and boating supplies. The site is currently divided into seven sections, or links:

- *Boat Show* features the newest models of sail and power boats offered by boat builders around the world. Here, you can explore the latest features and layouts of a multitude of boats.
- *Charter World* takes you on a tour of various charter fleets located in the world's great cruising areas. Explore the boats, meet the captains and crews, and check out the cruising grounds before making your reservations.
- *Yacht Lease* provides information regarding lease options for boat owners or those who would like to have access to a boat for a frac-

tion of the cost of ownership. You can lease a yacht or own a yacht and have it earn its keep.
- *Marine Marketplace* lets you browse through marine-related products and services offered by retailers around the world.
- *Maritime Art Gallery* is for the true boating enthusiast, and features beautiful images from maritime artists across the globe.
- *BOATNET Newsstand* offers several marine-related publications.
- *BOATNET Internet Explorer Page.* This area provides links to a multitude of other marine-related sites. You can visit maritime museums, boating newsgroups, weather stations, and many other interesting sites-on-the-water.

The Boats For Sale section is organized by location (for sale in the Pacific Northwest, California, the Gulf Coast, Florida, and so on) so that you can expediently look for boat sales that are accessible from your area. This section also lists boats for sale in the United Kingdom, Australia, and the Mediterranean.

If you only want to purchase something that you find on BOATNET or just browse the information here, you can do so without becoming a member. However, if you want to sell your boating wares here, you'll need to open an account. In any case, if you're at home on the water, you'll definitely be at home on this page.

Boats and Supplies (continued)

Company
BOATNET (Bellingham, WA)

Where
World Wide Web

Web Address
http://www.boatnet.com/boatnet/

Email
boatnet@boatnet.com

Prices
From $7 to $400,000

International orders are accepted.

Souvenirs! Hey, getcher red hot baseball caps!

Minor Leagues, Major Buys

I don't know about you, but the 1994 baseball strike left a bad tasete in my mouth for professional baseball. But let me stress *professional* baseball. The strike didn't do any serious damage to the sport itself, and in fact I suspect it caused a renewed interest in little league and minor league activity.

That's one of the reasons I feel so strongly about the proprietors of the Minor Leagues, Major Dreams Web site. These folks are true fans of many minor league sports—not just baseball (although that's their focus). They also sell merchandise related to arena football, minor league hockey, college baseball, and Indy 500 Brickyard 400 racing.

Want to show allegiance for your Albuquerque Dukes (the L.A. Dodgers AAA farm team)? This company sells wool baseball caps with the team logo embroidered, for $16. You can order caps for any minor league team in the U.S.—from class A to AAA.

You can also order their "fotoball baseballs," which are top-quality synthetic leather baseballs with your team's logo embroidered into the skin. At this writing, the sale price for one of these balls was $8, and the company had a full set of balls for every team from the Arkansas Travelers to the Winston-Salem Warthogs.

The company also sells jerseys, T-shirts, and jackets, so you can deck yourself out in full fan clothing fare. You can even order merchandise for the Colorado Silver Bullets, the first women's pro baseball league, currently sponsored by Coors.

So if you'd like to tell the major-league boys of summer to take a hike, march on over to this site to show your appreciation for the semi-pro athletes who work hard for little pay, solely because they love the sport—just like you do.

Shopping on the Internet and Beyond

 Exclusive Deal

Minor Leagues, Major Dreams
10 percent off
your first order of $50 or more.

Exclusive deal for readers of this book only!
You must mention this offer when you place your order.

Company
Minor Leagues, Major Dreams (Anaheim, CA)

Where
World Wide Web

Web Address
www.minorleagues.com/minorleagues

Email
mlmd@minorleagues.com

Prices
From $4 to 95.

Shipping Fees (in the U.S.)
$4 (all orders)

International orders are accepted.

Leave those paddle boats in the dust...er...mud, with the newest form of boating—called seacycling.

Seacycling in Style

The Seacycle company boasts that they'll "change your perception of pedal-powered boats." They've certainly changed my perception. Until I visited this site, I had no clue that an alternative was available for traditional pedal-powered boats.

You've probably tried that traditional variety—paddle boats. They're a great "together" activity for couples on their first, second, or third date, but beyond that, they're what? Booooring.

Enter the Seacycle. This is a streamlined catamaran that can cruise at 5 mph and sprint at over 10 mph. It's light, portable, and loads easily on a cartop carrier. It will ride well even on choppy water, and comes in one- or two-person configurations.

You can watch the Seacycle in action by downloading any or all of the three videos that are available on this Web site. You'll also find com-

plete specifications for the product online to help you decide whether to buy.

According to the company's president, "The Seacycle's racing appearance, speed, and ease of use makes it an ideal watercraft for touring, exercise, sightseeing, and also fishing. It has already proven to be an excellent rental product. Its good looks attract the rider and its quickness, and performance does the rest. The twin hull catamaran configuration offers stability and ease of transport as the whole boat can be assembled/disassembled without tools. Four hulls can be transported on top of a single car roof rack."

When you actually see what the Seacycle looks like, you'll immediately notice that it's much cooler looking than any paddle boat that you might have test drive around the local pond. The Seacycle catamaran is sleek, durable, fast, and exciting.

If you're looking for a romantic Seacycle built for two, this company's got the right product for you.

Shopping on the Internet and Beyond

Exclusive Deal

Recreation Industries

$25 off a seacycling accessory.

Exclusive deal for readers of this book only!
You must mention this offer when you place your order.

Company
Recreation Industries (Victoria, BC)

Where
World Wide Web

Web Address
www.islandnet.com/~seacycle/seacycle.html

Email
seacycle@islandnet.com

Prices
$1800

Shipping Fees (In the U.S.)
Approximately $150.

International orders are accepted.

The Softhead Doornob comes in a variety of colors and some pretty interesting names, including the Raging Squid, Mean Joe, Pink Mau Mau, and Old Blue.

Capt'n Mike's Tackle Towne

If you're into fishing, these guys will really lure you in with a selection of tackle and fishing gear that you won't find in any sporting goods store. Even the larger chains like REI and Popular Outdoor don't offer the range of fishing gear you'll find here.

For instance, Tackle Towne offers hooks within six different categories:

- Owner Hooks. The world's only line of hooks with a triple-edged cutting point.
- Area Rule Engineering. This world-famous line of engineered lures for big game fish is considered a must for any serious sports fisher.

- Burns Bombs. The latest from the Southern California Long Range innovators. Very effective for elusive wahoo.
- Collector Lures. Endorsed by many respected big game captains, these lures are included in trolling patterns for blue or striped marlin.
- PILI Lures. A line of innovative and proven lures for trolling or casting from Pacific Island Lures, Inc.

There are also plenty of pictures of most of the lures in a full range of available colors, so you'll be able to see exactly you're ordering.

Tackle Towne also sells a complete line of fishing accessories from top-of-the line monofilament fishing line to ergonomically correct handles for big game reels. You can also order Hobie sunglasses, fishing sportswear, gaffs, reel side-pates, and reel and rod covers, lure bags, rigging cases, and tackle boxes.

Tackle Towne even sells more than 40 fishing videos to help you become expert at catching the ones that usually get away.

Company
Capt'n Mike's Tackle Towne (Carlsbad, CA)

Where
World Wide Web

Web Address
http://www.awa.com/cm

Email
catmikes@awa.com

Prices
From $2 to $2,000

Shipping Fees
Vary based on order size.

International orders are accepted.

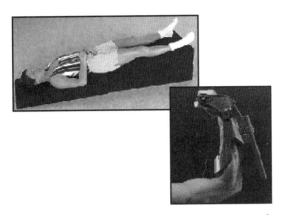

Nordic track sells a lot more than its famous cross-country ski systems—everything from swing weights to the Bodyslant Gravity Pillow.

NordicTrack

Ever since 1975, when NordicTrack debuted their cross-country ski machine, people from around the world have been shedding pounds and inches on the "best aerobic exerciser ever developed."

It has earned this reputation because the NordicTrack aerobic trainer "spreads the workload over all your major muscle groups to easily elevate your heart rate to fitness-building level. If you want to lose weight and keep body fat under control, nothing measures up to NordicTrack because you work both upper and lower body to burn the maximum amount of calories—up to 1,100 an hour." That's equivalent to 7.3 Twinkies or 24.4 Chicken McNuggets.

While NordicTrack is best known for their cross-country ski systems, the company's World Wide Web site highlights some of their lesser known products, as well as some accouterments for NordicTrack owners (of which there are over 4 million).

To accessorize your skier, consider one of the NordicTrack bookholders, ski grips, ski tunes (CDs and tapes with a good beat) and my favorite, NordicVision—videos that "let you ski the world as you exercise," with video vistas of Seefeld, St. Moritz, and Aspen. It's not exactly virtual reality, but it does look like a fun way to interrupt the monotony of your daily workout routine.

Non-cross country exercise devices include a Power Ab Board, Casio Blood Pressure Watches, swing weights, and a Bodyslant Gravity Pillow—a foam-padded wedge that places your legs higher than your heart to neutralize the pull of gravity and increase blood circulation.

Considering that NordicTrack's ski machines outsell actual pairs of cross-country skis, they must be doing something right. If you're trying to get your exercise routine on track, I highly suggest you point your Web browser to NordicTrack.

Company
NordicTrack (Chaska, MN)

Where
World Wide Web

Web Address
http://www.shopping2000.com/shopping2000/nordic_track/

Prices
From $9.95 to $2,300.

Shipping Fees
Extremely varied based on your purchase.

International orders are accepted.

Remember!
If you have full Internet access, you also have access to the World Wide Web. All you need is a Web browser, such as Mosaic or Netscape.

When Jake's done working over you and your body, he'll peel you off the floor witrh the Turbo-powered Bissell vacuum.

Famous Name Workout Equipment

At the time of this writing, The USA Direct Web site carried three item categories: workout machines from Body by Jake, toning equipment from Denise Austin, and a turbo-powered Bissell vacuum. Now I can't substantiate my claim, but I do wonder if there is a subliminal message here: If you can't work it off, you can suck it out by retrofitting the Bissell and turning it into a home-made liposuction device.

Anyway, if you're determined to do some spot toning work as a part of a fitness regime, you'll find plenty of help with The Body by Jake lineup, which includes the Hip and Thigh Machine and the Ab and Back Plus. The Hip and Thigh apparatus has a special Internet price tag that's $50 cheaper than what you'd pay if you bought it from one of Jake's infomercials for the exact same product. There's no extra discount on the Ab and Back Plus, though, which is priced similarly as the infomercial offer, but online shopping is known for out-of-the-blue incentives, so keep your eye out for a sudden price reduction.

The Dennis Austin line takes up a lot less space in your house than Jake's inventory, with three "simple workout tools for women's problem areas." There's a Super Tummy Trimmer for all forms of ab and stomach exercises, an Ultra-Arms device, and a Bun Firmer—a product name for which you can supply your own joke. The Austin line is sold as a set and costs a lot less than Jake's—at a total cost of $49.98.

Of course I can't leave this site without a brief mention of the vacuum. It's the Bissell Plus upright Vac with a detachable portable in one unit. (Portable, huh? My liposuction theory gains credibility) with "best-in-its-class bare floor cleaning." (Notice their use of the word "bare.") It has a "powerful 9.5 amp motor and a hard case body" (hard case body?) complete with "extension wands and crevice tools." I rest my case.

Company
USA Direct

Where
World Wide Web

Web Address
`http://www.shopping2000.com/shopping2000/`
`usa_direct/usa_direct.html`

Prices
From $49.98 to $249.50.

Shipping Fees
On the high side. Vary by product.

Remember!

For periodic updates of this book, send email to *shop@easton.com*. See *Introduction* for more details.

Lace up your Web walkers and browse on over to California Best for the best in fitness gear, at discount prices.

High Performance Fitness Apparel

In 1979, Cal Best began with a single store location. Now they have over 150,000 square feet of retail space and a catalog business that's so successful the company ranks as one of the country's top 50 nationwide sporting goods specialty retailers.

Their success formula is revealed in their mission statement: "Provide every customer with the highest quality brand merchandise, the largest selection, and an expertly trained sales staff. With this philosophy, Cal Best has established a reputation of professionalism and service that few competitors can match."

The breadth of their inventory supports their assertions. You can find running gear for men and women, cycling clothing, and running shoes on their Web site, and every item sports a brand name. The prices are very good, too. You get a capsule product description along with two prices: "Elsewhere" and "Ours."

A random sampling showed the Timex 100 Lap Ironman Indiglo watch with a price difference of over $5.00 ($49.99 versus $55 "Elsewhere") and a $13 savings on their Reebok Relaxed Fit Tights ($34.99 versus $48.00).

And the savings continue.

During my visit, California Best was offering $10 off a first order of $30 or more (*not* a "Shopping on the Internet" Exclusive Deal) as well as a buck-saving Sportsclub. For $25, you get "5 percent off every order, a 5 percent credit towards your account, two-day shipping upgrade on selected orders," as well as travel discounts and a quarterly sports newsletter.

California Best's online catalog doesn't include everything in their 350-item inventory, but it's a good selection of basic fitness gear. Their prices are excellent and it seems apparent that they've done much of the shopping legwork for you by offering what they consider the best gear available.

Company
California Best (Chula Vista, CA)

Where
World Wide Web

Web Address
http://www.shopping2000.com/shopping2000/cal_best/

Prices
$40.00 and up.

Shipping Fees
$3.99 to $4.99 per item destination.

International orders are accepted.

For More...

For more great sports shopping opportunities, see the next page.

Honorable Mentions
in the category of
Sports

Abdominal Trainer

"A simple, but effective device for complete abdominal training."

Company
Modern Body Design

Web Address
http://www.ipworld.com/MARKET/FITNESS/
MODBODY/HOMEPAGE.HTM

Authentic Sports Caps

Don the caps the pros wear. Genuine issues of the NFL, NBA, NHL, and all baseball leagues.

Company
Village League Sports

Web Address
http://branch.com:1080/sportcap/
village.html

Autos, Books, and Cycles

Private party ads on Prodigy.

Prodigy
Jump *classifieds* then select *browse ads*

Bicycles and Accessories

Private party ads on CompuServe.

CompuServe
Go *classifieds* then select *cars/boats/planes/rvs/cycles*

Bicycles and Parts

Supplies on sale on the Internet.

Usenet Newsgroup
rec.bicycle.marketplace

Hot Tip!

Internet Usenet Groups are available on all the major services. On America Online, keyword *usenet*. On CompuServe, go *usenet*. On Prodigy, jump *usenet*.

Boats and Accessories

Private party ads on CompuServe.

CompuServe

Go *classifieds* then select *cars/boats/planes/rvs/cycles*

Boats

Boats for sale on the Internet.

Usenet Newsgroup

`rec.boats.marketplace`

Collectors

Private party ads on AOL for collecting non-antiques and sports acessories.

America Online

Keyword *classifieds* then select *general merchandise boards*

Discount Ski Lift Tickets

"Value-priced lift tickets to over 100 resorts in the U.S. and Canada." Their page also includes resort information, condition reports, ski news, even skiing humor.

Company

Ski America

Web Address

`http://www.ultranet.com/`

Discount Sports Gear

Find reduced prices on top of their lines of sports gear and athletic shoes from name brand manufacturers.

Company

Holabird

Prodigy

Jump *holabird*

Fitness and Weight Control

Private party ads on CompuServe offering equiment and information.

CompuServe

Go *classifieds* then select *miscellaneous/info/merchandise*

Golf Equipment and Accessories

Clubs, accessories, and men's and women's apparel from this prominent company.

Company

Austad's

CompuServe

Go *au*

Prodigy

Jump *austads golf*

Golf League Tracker

Prints customized score cards—including handicap adjustments for the course. Free trial program online for downloading.

Company
Option Software

Web Address
http://www.smartpages.com/golf.html

Golf Software, Socks and Ties

Simulated golf game software plus golf neckties and socks.

Company
DMS Marketing

Web Address
http://www.webcom.com/~dms/golf.html

Golf Stuff

Full line of clothing, clubs, balls, bags, and other golfing accessories.

Company
Fore Play Golf

Web Address
http://www.4play.com/

Email
shop@4play.com

Golf Tee Setter

Set your tee in hard or soft turf. For beginner through pro. Easy to use.

Company
Tee-Setter

Web Address
http://hps.com/Products/TeeSetter/

Email
RandyDean1@aol.com

Golf Tours

The best courses in the Western United States, with golf outings organized and serviced by the company whose credo is "Golf is our business."

Company
Preferred Golf Tours

Web Address
http://mmink.cts.com/mmink/dossiers/
prefgolf.html

Gym in a Bag

"Simple and easy-to-use exercise system for a great workout anytime."

Company
Exer-Genie

Web Address
http://www.olworld.com/oldworld/mall/
mall_us/c_sports/m_gymina/

Health and Fitness

Private party ads on Prodigy.

Prodigy
Jump *classifieds* then select *browse ads*

Kite Pins

More than 200 kite pins in stock, plus event and club pins from throughout the U.S. and around the world.

Company
Cascade Kites

Web Address
http://www.teleport.com/~crowell/

Email
dgomberg@ednet1.osl.or.gov

Kites

More than 200 kites in stock, from radical new sport kites to traditional lazy-day-in-the-meadows varieties. Stunt kites too.

Company
Into The Wind Kite Catalog

Web Address
http://www.dash.com:80/netro/sho/ema/
intowind/intowind.html

Email
intowind@aol.com

Online Surf Shop

Specializing in surf gear with an emphasis on "style, comfort, quality, innnovation, and practicality." Custom surfboards are available.

Company
Blue Planet

Web Address
http://hawaii-shopping.com/spiderweb/
blueplanet

Email
74742.411@compuserve.com

Outdoor and Camping Equipment

Browse selections from Campmor's 8,000 item catalog—a leading mail-order retailer since 1978.

Company
Campmor

CompuServe
Go *cam*

Hot Tip!

If you're a CompuServe user, be sure to check out the Consumers Forum, which is chock full of fabulous freebie information and great shopping resources. Go *conforum*.

Planes, Boats and Bikes

Private party ads on America Online.

America Online

Keyword *classifieds* then select *general merchandise boards*

Sailing Gear for Women

Small boats, wetsuits, clothing, gloves, training aids, and books all tailored for women.

Company
She Sails Catalog

Web Address
http://www.aztec.com/pub/aztec/shesails/

Email
shesails@clark.net

Skydiving Gear

New and used gear—including rigger supplies. Product catalog online.

Company
Action Air Parachutes

Web Address
http://www.webcom.com/~skydance

Soccer Gear

More than 120 styles of shoes, videos, and bags.

Company
TSI Soccer

Web Address
http://www.tsisoccer.com/tsi/

Email
tsi@cybernetx.net

Sporting Goods

Private party ads on America Online for sporting and athletic goods.

America Online

Keyword *classifieds* then select *general merchandise boards*

Sports Insignia Bed and Bath Products

Bed and bath products with all NFL, NBA, and most collegiate sports teams represented. Comforters, towels, shower curtains, and bedding.

Company
Downey Company

Web Address
http://www.sibylline.com/webboard/flyers/downey/downey.html

Sports Insignia Clothing

Top-quality sportswear with college and pro teams logo. Christmas ornaments too!

Company
TransAmerica Sports Experts

Web Address
http://www.ceainc.com.TransAm/index.html

Email
transamerica@ceainc.com

Sports Supplements

Vitamin supplements and energizers formulated for maximum atheletic performance and endurance.

Company
S&K Labs

Web Address
http://www.stw.com/skl/skl.htm

Tennis Paraphernalia

Rackets, shoes, tennis clothing, strings, and accessories.

Company
Rays Tennis Shop

Web Address
http://www.cts.com/~tennisal/

Email
tenisal@cts.com

Thoroughbred Racing Memorabilia

Seats, footsools, jackets, calendars, car mats, ties, triple crown plates, and videos.

Company
Thoroughbred Racing

Web Address
http://www.shopping2000.com/shopping2000/
thoroughbred/

Email
race777@aol.com

Three Stooges Pro Golf Shop

Golf umbrellas, posters, t-shirts, scratch pads, coffee mugs, and more imprinted with a photo of the Three Stooges dressed in golf garb.

Company
Planet Companies

Web Address
http://www.planetsurf.com/golf.html

Windsurfing Vacation Spots

Online brochure featuring "Warmth and wind...around the world. From Aruba to Maui to Margarita, wind awaits."

Company
Windsurfing World Travel Ltd.

Web Address
http://www.rscomm.com/adsports/wsw/
travel.html

Wood Duck Kayaks

Rare, handcrafted wood kayaks customized to your specs.

Company
Wood Duck Kayaks

Web Address
http://www.olworld.com/olworld/mall/
mall_us/c_sports/m_wooduk/index.html

Email
olworld@olworld.com

Regional Usenet Private Party Ads

Shopping on the Internet and other online services is a smart and convenient way to buy new products at bargain prices. But what if you're in the market to buy or sell used items? Do you have to rely on the classified ads in your local paper?

Not at all. Many Usenet groups (or newsgroups) on the Internet have been set up for precisely this purpose. But there's one major problem with newsgroups whose subscribers post merchandise ads: Location, location, location.

Think about it. You might be willing to spend Saturday afternoon at a garage sale in your neighborhood hoping to snap up a bargain. But you certainly wouldn't consider driving a hundred miles up the road just to browse through somebody's used goods.

The same situation holds true on the Internet. Suppose you're shopping for a pre-owned car. Hundreds of Usenet newsgroups will have ads for vehicles that you might very well drool to own. The problem is that, because the Internet is a global affair, most of the advertisers will be located hundreds or even thousands of miles from you. If you live in, say, San Francisco, there's no point in traveling to Montreal just to test drive a car—no matter how great the vehicle seems to be.

For this reason, Internet users have set up Usenet newsgroups that cater to advertisers in a particular state or region. Whether you're in search of an automobile, an ottoman, or an Audubon painting, both the shopping and shipping (if any) will be easier to arrange if both the buyer and seller are in the same general "neighborhood."

With these factors in mind, I've put together the following list to help you identify private-party buyers and sellers who are in "your neck of the woods." Of course, I've included Usenet newsgroups throughout the world.

Location	Region	Usenet Newsgroup
Alabama	Huntsville	hsv.forsale
Australia	Entire Country	aus.ads.forsale
		aus.ads.wanted
		aus.ads.forsale.computers
		aus.ads.commercial
California	Entire State	ca.forsale
	Los Angeles	la.forsale
	San Diego	sdnet.forsale
	Santa Cruz	sco.forsale
Canada	Atlantic Side	can.atlantic.forsale
	Edmonton	edm.forsale
	Ontario	kw.forsale
		ont.forsale
	Ottawa	ott.forsale
	Toronto	tor.forsale
Florida	Entire State	fl.forsale
Georgia	Entire State	ga.forsale
Indiana	Purdue University	purdue.forsale
Japan	Country	fj.forsale.autos
		fj.forsale
		fj.forsale.books
		fj.forsale.tickets
		fj.forsale.comp
Maryland	University of Maryland	um.forsale
Minnesota	University of Minnesota	umn.general.forsale
Nevada	Entire State	nv.forsale
New England	Entire Region	ne.forsale
New Jersey	Entire State	nj.forsale
New Mexico	Entire State	nm.forsale
New York	Entire State	ny.forsale
	Long Island	li.forsale
Ohio	Entire State	oh.forsale

Location	Region	Usenet Group
Oregon	Portland	pdaxs.ads.appliances
		pdaxs.ads.lostrfound
		pdaxs.ads.cars.service
		pdaxs.ads.homes.ne
		pdaxs.ads.boats
		pdaxs.ads.audio_video
		or.forsale
		pdaxs.ads.antiques
		pdaxs.ads.cars.rv
		pdaxs.ads.homes.n
		pdaxs.ads.computers
		pdaxs.ads.fencing
		pdaxs.ads.food
		pdaxs.ads.furniture
		pdaxs.ads.homes.sw
		pdaxs.ads.homes.nw
		pdaxs.ads.homes.se
		pdaxs.ads.jewelry
		pdaxs.ads.clothing
		pdaxs.ads.hotels
		pdaxs.ads.movies
		pdaxs.ads.music
		pdaxs.ads.notices
		pdaxs.ads.real_estate
		pdaxs.ads.printing
		pdaxs.ads.cars.misc
		pdaxs.ads.office
		pdaxs.ads.personals
		pdaxs.ads.wanted
		pdaxs.ads.misc
		pdx.forsale
		pdaxs.ads.cars
		pdaxs.ads.books
		pdaxs.ads.cars.audio
		pdaxs.ads.sports
		pdaxs.ads.restaurants
		pdaxs.ads.sales
		pdaxs.ads.tools
		pdaxs.ads.tickets
		pdaxs.ads.apartments

Location	Region	Usenet Group
Pacific Northwest Region	Entire Region	pnw.forsale
Pennsylvania	Entire State	pa.forsale
	Philadelphia	phl.forsale
	Pittsburgh	pgh.forsale
South Africa	Entire Country	za.ads.lifts
		za.ads.jobs
		za.ads.misc
South Carolina	Florence	us.sc.florence.forsale
	Lancaster	us.sc.lancaster.forsale
	Rockhill	us.sc.rockhill.forsale
	Charleston	us.sc.charleston.forsale
	Chester	us.sc.chester.forsale
	Columbia	us.sc.columbia.forsale
Texas	Houston	houston.forsale
	Texas A&M University	tamu.forsale
	University of Texas	utexas.forsale
United Kingdom	Country	uk.forsale
Utah	Entire State	utah.forsale
Washington	Seattle	seattle.forsale
Wisconsin	University of Wisconsin	uwisc.forsale
	Entire State	wi.forsale

Index

B

G

R

S